Third Edition

THE BASICS OF BIOETHICS

Robert M. Veatch

Kennedy Institute of Ethics
Georgetown University

Routledge
Taylor & Francis Group

LONDON AND NEW YORK

First published 2012, 2003, 2000 by Pearson Education, Inc.

Published 2016 by Routledge
2 Park Square, Milton Park, Abingdon, Oxon OX14 4RN
711 Third Avenue, New York, NY, 10017, USA

First issued in hardback 2017

Routledge is an imprint of the Taylor & Francis Group, an informa business

ISBN 13: 978-1-138-42501-9 (hbk)
ISBN 13: 978-0-205-76562-1 (pbk)

Cover Designer: Bruce Kenselaar

Library of Congress Cataloging-in-Publication Data
Veatch, Robert M.
  The basics of bioethics / Robert M. Veatch. – 3rd ed.
    p. cm.
  Includes bibliographical references.
  ISBN-13: 978-0-205-76562-1 (alk. paper)
  1. Medical ethics.   2. Bioethics.   I. Title.
  R724.V39 2012
  174.2–dc23

                                    2011030636

BRIEF CONTENTS

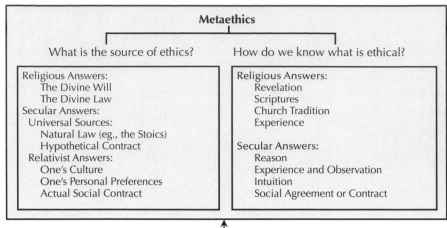

Metaethics

What is the source of ethics?

Religious Answers:
  The Divine Will
  The Divine Law
Secular Answers:
  Universal Sources:
    Natural Law (eg., the Stoics)
    Hypothetical Contract
  Relativist Answers:
    One's Culture
    One's Personal Preferences
    Actual Social Contract

How do we know what is ethical?

Religious Answers:
  Revelation
  Scriptures
  Church Tradition
  Experience

Secular Answers:
  Reason
  Experience and Observation
  Intuition
  Social Agreement or Contract

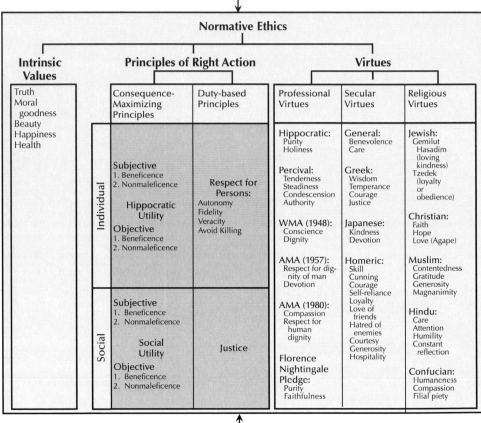

Normative Ethics

Intrinsic Values

Truth
Moral goodness
Beauty
Happiness
Health

Principles of Right Action

	Consequence-Maximizing Principles	Duty-based Principles
Individual	**Subjective** 1. Beneficence 2. Nonmaleficence **Hippocratic Utility** **Objective** 1. Beneficence 2. Nonmaleficence	**Respect for Persons:** Autonomy Fidelity Veracity Avoid Killing
Social	**Subjective** 1. Beneficence 2. Nonmaleficence **Social Utility** **Objective** 1. Beneficence 2. Nonmaleficence	**Justice**

Virtues

Professional Virtues	Secular Virtues	Religious Virtues
Hippocratic: Purity Holiness **Percival:** Tenderness Steadiness Condescension Authority **WMA (1948):** Conscience Dignity **AMA (1957):** Respect for dignity of man Devotion **AMA (1980):** Compassion Respect for human dignity **Florence Nightingale Pledge:** Purity Faithfulness	**General:** Benevolence Care **Greek:** Wisdom Temperance Courage Justice **Japanese:** Kindness Devotion **Homeric:** Skill Cunning Courage Self-reliance Loyalty Love of friends Hatred of enemies Courtesy Generosity Hospitality	**Jewish:** Gemilut Hasadim (loving kindness) Tzedek (loyalty or obedience) **Christian:** Faith Hope Love (Agape) **Muslim:** Contentedness Gratitude Generosity Magnanimity **Hindu:** Care Attention Humility Constant reflection **Confucian:** Humaneness Compassion Filial piety

Rules and Rights (Codes of Ethics)
(How Rigidly Do Rules Apply)

Antinomianism   Rules of Thumb (Guidelines, Situationism)   Rules of Practice   Legalism

No Rules Apply ← ——————————————————————— → Rules Apply Rigidly

Cases (Casuistry)

CONTENTS

LIST OF FIGURES

LIST OF CASES

PREFACE

A great deal has happened in the fast-moving world of bioethics since the previous edition of this book appeared in 2003. The U.S. government has passed a health care bill designed to provide basic health insurance to many more Americans. Stem cell research has progressed to the point that the first experiments using stem cells in humans have been launched renewing the moral controversy over procurement of these cells from human embryos. Human hearts have been procured and transplanted from critically ill newborns who were allowed to die by their parents and physicians stimulating major controversy over whether the infants were actually dead when their hearts were removed. The tragic case of a permanently unconscious woman named Terri Schiavo created a public furor when state and federal politicians intervened to attempt to stop the removal of her feeding tube. UNESCO has adopted the Universal Declaration on Bioethics and Human Rights, the first global code of ethics adopted not by a professional physician organization but by a public international agency representing virtually all the citizens of the world. It is becoming increasingly commonplace for kidneys obtained from living donors to be exchanged among pairs and even large groups of recipients creating new possibilities for safer and more efficient transplant, but leaving certain needy people essentially at the end of the line for organs.

At the same time, the world of the academic and professional study of bioethics has become increasingly complex and sophisticated. New general theories of the ethics of health care have emerged; new scholarship makes clearer the disputes that lead to major options for public policy and clinical decisions. New bold claims have been made about a "common morality" that can be the source of national and international ethical stances in bioethics.

All of these developments are addressed in the third edition of *The Basics of Bioethics*. This volume had its origins in the courses I have taught over the years, first at Columbia University's College of Physicians and Surgeons, Vassar College, and Brown University, but for the past decades at Georgetown University as well as regular visiting professorships at the St. George's University School of Medicine in Grenada and Union University in New York. These chapters started out as the lectures I have given to upwards of 12,000 medical school and philosophy students throughout my career. The analysis and the cases have been tried on countless students and colleagues for whom I am forever grateful.

When the first edition of *The Basics of Bioethics* appeared in the final weeks of the twentieth century, no current, brief survey existed that was a suitable introduction to the field. Textbooks, anthologies, casebooks, and single-authored perspectives were available to provide perspective on the issues of bioethics, but no introduction to the field of bioethics under several hundred pages in length. The first edition served that purpose. It was intended for health professionals and lay people who wanted an introduction to the issues in a relatively small edition suitable for use in short courses in schools of medicine, nursing, and the other health professions; continuing professional education; undergraduate courses in philosophy, religion, and the social sciences; and in adult education.

This new edition continues to be committed to that purpose. It provides a relatively brief introduction to bioethics intended for those who are not specialists in the field. My goal is to present an understandable, fair, and balanced survey of the major issues embedded in a systematic framework based on the ethical principles and other theoretical tools increasingly available to bioethics.

Major changes in Basics of Bioethics, third edition:

- *In Chapter 2, a discussion of the moral status of embryonic stem cells and a new case study of infant heart transplant and whether an infant whose heart survives transplant can be considered dead by cardiac criteria are added.*
- *Chapter 5 now includes a discussion of the new UNESCO Universal Declaration of Bioethics and Human Rights.*
- *Coverage of the case of withdrawing nutrition from Terri Schiavo is added to Chapter 7.*
- *Chapter 8 is updated with a discussion of Obama's "Affordable Health Care Plan" as well as a discussion of living donor organ procurement. A discussion of the new liver transplant policy and the controversy over whether livers should be allocated locally or over a broader area is also included.*
- *A new case of the first attempt in humans to use stem cells to regenerate spinal cord nerve cells to try to treat a paralyzed spinal cord injury patient can be found in Chapter 9.*
- *Updated references and examples appear throughout the entire third edition.*

This edition retains the chapter structure of the second edition including new chapters added at that time. It adds to each chapter new material on developments since the appearance of the second edition. The approach is systematic. Rather than discussing issue by issue every topic in the current bioethics literature, we begin with an introduction to ethical theory and a brief history of biomedical ethics. The first chapter is designed for the reader who has not been exposed to formal ethical theory. It provides a "map" of the ethical terrain, a schema outlining four levels of moral discourse or ethical analysis. This scheme is summarized in the diagram that appears at the front and back of this volume. On this diagram virtually every dispute in bioethics can be mapped.

Some disagreements exist at one of the levels. For example, much of bioethics in the late decades of the twentieth century involved controversies over which ethical principles prevailed. This can be seen in the central shaded boxes at the level of "Normative Ethics" in the figure. Other disputes involve questions of whether to resolve moral controversies by working at this normative level or at some other level (by applying a code of ethics or by focusing on an individual case, for instance). Portions of this central diagram of the "Four Levels of Moral Discourse" are reproduced in various chapters when the ethical controversies of bioethics are presented in greater detail. I hope this diagram will make more clear, especially to the reader not trained in ethical analysis, exactly what the basis is for moral disagreements in the field of biomedical ethics.

Law has in a sense taken over the practice of medicine. In a way that is too bad. Law is obviously important, but it's not all there is to medicine. Medicine is a profession, and, traditionally, one of the chief characteristics of a profession is that it has its own ethic. At least until recently self-regulation was the definitive sign that medicine was a profession; it didn't engender much controversy. In this volume, we look at the controversies over self-regulation in medicine and some of the ethical problems that emerge. This edition is able to incorporate a major development in this movement to a more public bioethics—the adopting by UNESCO of its Universal Declaration on Bioethics and Human Rights which places bioethics norms for the first time in the hands of the global public—patients and the public as well as health professionals.

We ask in the first two chapters why the old Hippocratic Oath is in trouble, and what the alternatives are. In Chapter 3 we discuss what may first seem like a disparate collection of topics: abortion, stem cells, the definition of death, and the welfare of non-human animals. We shall see that they all raise the question of who has moral standing and why. Next, in Chapter 4, we discuss the ethics of benefiting patients. That may sound like a platitude. It seems like it is obvious that the health professional's goal must be to benefit his or her patient. However, we shall see that benefiting patients is increasingly controversial morally. There are in fact many situations in which physicians decide not to provide benefit, at least if they follow more contemporary ethical thinking, rather than the traditional Hippocratic Oath.

Next, in Chapter 5, we deal with the major challenge to the Hippocratic perspective, what is often referred to as *the ethics of respect for persons* or *the ethics of liberal political philosophy*. This includes an alternative set of ethical principles that is now being used in place of the Hippocratic Oath. We will be talking about rights of patients and rights of physicians, particularly in terms of fidelity, autonomy, and veracity, and why these principles are causing big problems for health professionals.

Chapters 6 and 7 deal with one of the hottest issues in medical ethics, the care of the terminally ill. Traditional medical ethics of the past hundred years was committed to preserving life, sometimes preserving it at all costs. Life, at least human life, was deemed sacred or ultimately valuable. We shall see that this notion is enormously complex. Euthanasia has variously been taken as referring to active killing for mercy, the forgoing of medical treatment even though the result is likely to be death, and sometimes simply any good death. In Chapter 6 we will begin to examine these issues by dealing with competent patients. Then in Chapter 7 we will grapple with what the real complications are today—dealing with incompetent patients who are terminally ill and consider if these patients would be better off if they were not treated so aggressively. It is here that this edition incorporates the now-infamous case of Terri Schiavo.

We then turn, in Chapter 8, to *the* issue of medical ethics for the twenty-first century, the social ethics of health care including the morality of allocating scarce medical resources as well as other conflicts such as medical research pitting the individual against the interests of society. In this edition we include a discussion of the major ethical issues raised by the Affordable Health Care Act, the new federal health insurance law. We shall examine the role physicians have to play as society's agent, or gatekeeper, allocating a pie that is too small to give everyone all the health care he or she needs.

Next, in Chapter 9 we step back a bit from the principles of normative medical ethics to ask about an underlying basic value commitment that shapes positions taken on just about every issue in medical ethics: whether humans are going too far in attempting to remake their own basic nature. Here we will focus on genetics, stem cell research, and birth technologies—genetic screening and engineering as well as in vitro fertilization and surrogate motherhood—as the area of medicine that poses this question of fundamental value orientation most dramatically.

Chapter 10 provides the opportunity to examine what should happen when these ethical principles and value orientations conflict as well as how we should move up and down the ladder of the levels of moral discourse from principles down to codes of ethics and to the individual case or—if one is more clinically oriented—from case up to the level of principles and other questions of normative ethics.

The final chapter turns to the "The Virtues in Bioethics." Discussion of the virtues of the physician is as old as the profession of medicine itself. The Hippocratic Oath touted the virtues of "purity" and "holiness"; the ancient Confucian medical ethical texts advocated "compassion," "humaneness," and something mysteriously called "filial piety." Perhaps because these virtues sounded so platitudinous, they more or less disappeared from bioethics in the early years of its renaissance at least in the last decades of the twentieth century. However, stimulated in part by new developments in feminist bioethics and nursing ethics, a new interest in the virtues of the health professional has emerged. And the virtues have become more controversial. It is now of real substantive importance whether a physician or nurse should give primary attention to being "caring" or "benevolent." Older virtues have, at least in some bioethical approaches, become more debatable, sometimes, as in the case of Percival's virtue of "condescension," even offensive. The chapter contrasts the historical virtues in health professional codes with the sometimes very different virtues put forward in various religious and secular ethical systems.

These eleven brief chapters will give the reader a general framework by which the full range of ethical issues in health care can be addressed. It is not that every topic in contemporary medical ethics will have been examined explicitly; that would be impossible in a volume of this size. Rather the goal is to understand the basics of how different approaches to ethics come into play in the biomedical world and why the historical framework of the Hippocratic Oath is increasingly seen as outdated and wrong morally. We will end with a set of principles that are alternatives to that tradition that will address the major themes of health care ethics of today: confidentiality, informed consent, honesty in communication between patient and provider, the care of the terminally ill, health insurance, and the allocation of scarce resources. We will have some sense of who has moral standing and why that question is crucial not only for the abortion debate, the use of human embryonic stem cells, and deciding when an individual is dead, but also how animals are treated in research, education, and other spheres of life. We will have some understanding of whether the human's role is that of co-creator of a new genetic and reproductive future or is better seen as one of proceeding more humbly with fear and trembling out of fear that we may be playing with Promethean fire when we attempt to play like one of the gods. We will see how various people have resolved conflicts among ethical principles and among different theoretical approaches to bioethics.

A large number of people have played a role in developing the three editions of this book. I have tried out many of the ideas and chapters on the Scholars of the Kennedy Institute of Ethics, students and faculty at St. George's University and Union University, and other colleagues in the field of biomedical ethics. I continue to acknowledge the help of many people in the production of the first and second editions.

I am grateful for the continuing, unfailing dedication of the professional staff of the Kennedy Institute's Bioethics Research Library and for administrative assistance from Moheba Hanif and Sally Schofield. Matt Westbrook, Patrick Gordon, and Samantha Thompson provided research assistance during the writing of this revision. Most of all I am grateful to the thousands of students who have pursued these issues with me by demanding clarity and enjoying the debate. Many have told me that these are the real issues that will make the health care professions rewarding for them even if they will also make life very difficult. Just as important, others have conveyed that, while they are not planning careers in the health professions, exploring these issues will make them better patients, surrogate decision makers, and participants in the public policy discussion. If so, that is good. I have long held that lay people are always necessarily the primary medical decision makers in our society and that they must be not only partners in the health care enterprise, but primary in that partnership.

RMV, Washington, D.C.

1

A Map of the Terrain of Ethics

CASE 1

The Boy Who Ate the Pickle

A 9-year-old youngster named Yusef Camp who lived in inner-city Washington ate a pickle that he had bought from a street vendor. Soon after eating it he went into convulsions and collapsed on the sidewalk. A rescue squad took him to the nearest emergency room where his stomach was pumped. Tests revealed that the pickle contained traces of marijuana and PCP. The boy suffered severe respiratory depression and was left unconscious, unable to breathe for an unknown period.

The emergency room personnel restored respiration by putting him on a ventilator, but they were unable to restore him to consciousness or get him breathing adequately on his own.

The physicians concluded that his brain function was irreversibly destroyed and that there was no possibility of recovery. They might have simply pronounced him dead and then stopped the ventilator, but the situation soon became more complicated. Two of the attending neurologists were convinced that the patient's brain was totally dead, but one believed that he had minor brain function still in place. So they were incapable of pronouncing the patient dead based on loss of brain function. Now the question became, What should they do? Their patient was still living but permanently unconscious, breathing only because he was on a ventilator.

The physicians pointed out that there was nothing more they could do except keep the ventilator running, perhaps indefinitely and maintain the boy in a persistent or permanent vegetative state. (The longest case on record of maintaining a patient in what is called a permanent vegetative state is over thirty-seven years.)

The parents were Muslims, members of the Nation of Islam, who firmly believed in the power of Allah. They believed that Allah would intervene if it was his will, and that it was the physicians' job to give Allah that opportunity. How should the physicians respond?

The physicians, the parents, and everyone else involved in this case face some difficult and controversial ethical choices. They need to determine the proper definition of death, the role of parents and other surrogates in deciding about medical care for a minor, the proper ethics of terminal care, the morality of using scarce medical resources, and the role that minority religious perspectives ought to play in modern, secular medical care. In order to sort out these disparate and complex ethical issues we need a map of the ethical terrain: an overview of the kinds of ethical issues at stake and the terminology for labeling the disputes. This chapter will provide a basic map of that terrain. Once that overview is in place, we can begin sorting out the issues facing Yusef Camp's parents and physicians.

THE LEVELS OF MORAL DISCOURSE

The Level of the Case

Often in biomedical ethic, the discussion begins with a case problem. Someone faces a concrete moral dilemma or two people disagree about what in a specific situation is the morally appropriate behavior. Some people may mistakenly think that ethical choices do not occur all that often in medicine. They think that an "ethics case" is an unusual, special event. In fact, ethical and other value choices occur constantly, but, fortunately, in almost all situations the ethically correct course is obvious. The decision can be made with little or no conscious thought. Ethical choices have still been made—even if the decision maker does not even realize it. He or she can rely on well-ingrained moral beliefs and get by quite adequately. Occasionally, however, the choice does not come as easily. As in the case of Yusef Camp, the choice requires more careful, conscious thought. The physician faced with a choice may turn to colleagues or to a hospital ethics committee for advice. A lay person may turn to friends or to a trusted religious or secular group for guidance.

One kind of advice may come in the form of mentioning other cases that seem similar, cases that have been resolved in the past. They may be in the form of a Biblical story or a legal case about which the culture has reached agreement. These agreed-upon cases are sometimes referred to as "paradigm cases." Most people can agree that, in matters of ethics, similar cases should be treated similarly. In fact, one of the identifying characteristics of an ethical judgment (as opposed to a matter of mere taste or preference) is this awareness that if the relevant features are similar, then cases should be treated alike. As long as people can agree on what should be done in the paradigm case and can agree that the new case is similar in all relevant respects, they will be able to resolve their problem. This approach relying on paradigm cases is sometimes called **casuistry**. As seen in Figure 1, this is the lowest or most specific level of what can be

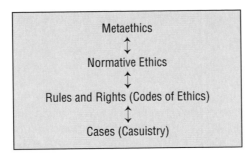

FIGURE 1   The Four Levels of Moral Discourse

considered the four major levels of moral discourse. This figure is a simplified version of the more elaborate map of the ethical terrain that appears on the front and back inside covers of this book.

Rules and Rights (Codes of Ethics)

But what if the basic ethics we learned as children does not settle the problem? What if we cannot agree on a paradigm case or cannot agree that our present problem is like the paradigm case in all relevant respects? We may, at that point, move to a second level of moral discourse, the level of **moral rules** and **rights**. Sometimes rules and rights tell us what is legal, but they may also describe what is ethical. Since not everything that is legal is also ethical (and not everything that is illegal is necessarily unethical), it will be important to note the difference. If a rule or a right is considered *ethical*, it will be seen as grounded in a moral system, an ultimate system of beliefs and norms about the rightness or wrongness of human conduct and character. Groups of rules or rights claims are sometimes called *codes of ethics*.

Yusef Camp's physicians may consult the Code of Ethics of the American Medical Association to see whether that group considers it ethical to stop treatment in such cases. His parents might consult an Islamic code. Some of the parties in the dispute may bring out the Hippocratic Oath or a "patients' bill of rights."

Sometimes the parties to an ethical dispute may cite a rule-like maxim. "Always get consent before surgery" or "a patient's medical information must be kept confidential" are examples of such maxims. These rule-like statements are usually quite specific. A large number of them would be needed to cover all medical ethical situations. If there is agreement on the rule that applies, then the case problem might be resolved at this second level.

Sometimes these maxims are stated not as rules but as *rights* claims. The statement, "a patient has a right to consent before surgery" would be an example. So would the statement "a patient has a right to have his or her medical information kept confidential." Rules are expressed from the perspective of the one who has a duty to act; rights claims from the vantage point of the one acted upon. Often rules and rights express the same moral duty from two different perspectives. "Always get consent before surgery" expresses from the health provider's point of view the same moral notion that is expressed from the patient's vantage point as "a patient has a right to consent before surgery." They are then said to be "reciprocal." If one person has a duty to act in a certain way toward another, that other person usually can be said to have a right to be acted upon in that way.

Medical professional, religious, cultural, and political organizations sometimes gather together collections of rules or rights claims. When they do, they "codify" them or produce a *code of ethics*. They can also take the form of *oaths* as in the Hippocratic Oath or *directives* as in the "Ethical and Religious Directives for Catholic Health Facilities." When the statements are made up of rights claims, they are often called *bills of rights* as in the American Hospital Association's "Patient's Bill of Rights" or *declarations* as in the new "Universal Declaration on Bioethics and Human Rights." Chapter 2 looks at various oaths, codes, and declarations, and sees what their implications are for cases like Yusef Camp's. We will discover how controversial these codifications are. Proponents of such codes not only have to determine what rules and rights are appropriate, but also which humans (and non-humans) have the moral standing to have claims based on these rules and rights. Chapter 3 takes up this question of who has this moral standing. Here we address the question of whether Yusef Camp has the moral standing of a living human being or is already dead—according to a brain-oriented definition of death. We will also see the implications for the moral status of fetuses and non-human animals. We will at this point also confront the new controversy over the use of stem cells.

These rules and rights claims may provide enough moral guidance that the problem being disputed can be resolved. They rest, however, on the authority of the groups creating the codes (or on the inherent wisdom of the maxims themselves).

One of the controversies in ethics is how seriously these rules and rights must be taken. At one extreme, an ethical theory could include the view that there are no exceptions to the rules or rights. This view, which almost no one actually holds, is sometimes called **legalism**. At the other extreme, someone might hold that every case is so unique that no rules or rights can ever be relevant in deciding what one ought to do in a specific situation. This view, which is as implausible as legalism, is called **antinomianism**. Two intermediate positions are more plausible. **Situationalism** holds that moral rules are merely "guidelines" or "rules of thumb" that must be evaluated in each situation. The **rules of practice** view holds that rules specify practices that are morally obligatory. In this view the rules are stringently binding on conduct. Exceptions are made only in very extraordinary circumstances—much less easily than in the situationalist position. The continuum is represented in Figure 2 and in the more complete map of the ethical terrain inside the front and back covers.

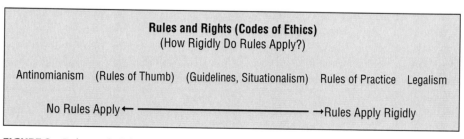

Rules and Rights (Codes of Ethics)
(How Rigidly Do Rules Apply?)

Antinomianism   (Rules of Thumb)   (Guidelines, Situationalism)   Rules of Practice   Legalism

No Rules Apply ← ——————————————— →Rules Apply Rigidly

FIGURE 2   Rules and Rights

Normative Ethics

People in an ethics dispute may not be able to determine which rule or rights claim applies or how it should be applied. If the citing of various rules or rights claims cannot resolve the matter at controversy, a more complete ethical analysis may be called for. The parties may have to move to a third level of moral discourse, what can be called the level of **normative ethics**. It is at this level that the broad, basic norms of behavior and character are discussed. It is in these basic norms that rules and rights claims will be derived and defended. It is also at this level that the norms of good moral character are articulated. The key feature of these norms is that they are general: They apply to a wide range of conduct and character. If "always get consent before surgery" is a moral rule, it might be associated with some broader ethical norm, such as respect for autonomy. Since these norms (like autonomy) are very broad, only a few norms will be expected or needed in a "normative ethical theory."

ACTION THEORY   As illustrated in Figure 3, normative ethics involves at least three kinds of questions. An ethical theory at the normative level, therefore, must address three separate issues. Much of recent biomedical ethics has dealt with the principles of morally right action. The focus is on the action itself; not on the character or motives of the actor. The central normative ethical question has been "what principles make actions morally right?" The answer involves some list of **moral principles** such as beneficence, nonmaleficence, respect for autonomy, or justice. These are proposals for characteristics of actions that make them morally right. Someone might claim, for example, that doing good (beneficence) or respecting autonomy will tend to make an action (or perhaps a set of actions) morally right. The principles of right action were almost the entire focus of bioethics in the 1970s and '80s and remain a dominant part of the discussion. They will be considered in more detail in Chapter 4, when we take up the principles that concentrate on producing the best possible consequences, and in Chapters 5–8, when we consider some additional principles that do not deal with maximizing good outcomes. The figures in these chapters (and the inside covers of this book) expand the map of the terrain of ethics by providing charts of possible consequence-maximizing principles and of ones that attempt to identify certain moral duties that are independent of producing good consequences.

If a bioethic includes more than one ethical principle, the **action theory** portion of normative ethics will have to address the question of how to resolve the conflicts that arise among them. There are several different possibilities for resolving these conflicts. They will be explored in Chapter 9.

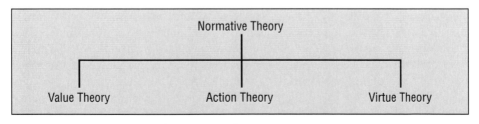

FIGURE 3   Three Questions of Normative Ethics

VALUE THEORY   Since beneficence (or producing good consequences) is one possible principle of right action and nonmaleficence (or avoiding producing bad consequences) is another, a second question that has to be addressed in a full normative theory is, "What kinds of consequences are good or valuable?" This branch of normative theory is therefore called **value theory**. Some of the questions of value theory are taken up in Chapter 4, where the principles of beneficence and nonmaleficence are discussed. The map of the options for this part of normative theory is expanded in that chapter in Figure 9. Just as there are disputes about what the proper list of principles is, so there are disputes about what kinds of things are valuable. Some kinds of things, like money, seem to be valuable, but only instrumentally—because it will buy something intrinsically valuable. The real question here is, What kinds of things are intrinsically valuable? Among the standard answers are happiness, beauty, knowledge, and—importantly for biomedical ethics—health. Some people also consider morally good character to be among those things that are intrinsically valuable.

VIRTUE THEORY   That brings us to the third question of normative ethics: "What kinds of character traits are morally praiseworthy?" A morally praiseworthy character trait—such as compassion or benevolence or faithfulness—is called a *virtue* and, hence, this part of normative ethics is referred to as **virtue theory**. For a fuller list of the virtues and a discussion of their role in bioethics, see Figure 1 in Chapter 11 and the discussion of virtue theory in that chapter.

The virtues refer not to the character of actions, but to the character of the people who engage in the actions. *Benevolence* and *beneficence* should be contrasted. *Benevolence* is a virtue, the virtue of willing to do good. *Beneficence* is a principle of actions, the principle of actually acting in such a way that good consequences result. One can of course will the good (show the virtue of benevolence) but end up not doing the good (being beneficent). One can also be malevolent, but nevertheless beneficent. (This person would not be of good will, but would nevertheless act in such a way that good results are produced, perhaps because the malevolent one has calculated that it is in his or her self-interest to produce the good consequences.)

This means that normative ethics involves questions of ethical principle (action theory), intrinsic goods (value theory), and good character (virtue theory). Depending on the question asked and the situation, one may be more interested in one of these questions than another. In the 1970s and '80s, for example, most biomedical ethics concentrated on the principles of right action. Theorists of the time wanted to get straight on whether an action by a physician was morally right if it was designed to produce good consequences, but simultaneously violated respect for autonomy or involved telling a lie. The bioethicists of that time did not really care very much about the character of the physician; the issue was what made his or her external conduct morally right, not whether the physician had a virtuous disposition. Ethicists who attacked the mainstream medical paternalism of the day in the name of the principle of autonomy were concerned that the benevolently paternalistic physician was *acting* immorally by violating the principle of autonomy even if his heart was in the right place. Only in the late 1980s did biomedical ethics return to the more traditional interest in the virtuous character of the health provider. Since then, there has been more of a balance between ethics concerned about actions and ethics concerned about the character of the actors. Since action theory and virtue theory ask different questions, it is normally a mistake to think of the two as being in conflict. They are simply different aspects of the general considerations of morality.

Metaethics

Sometimes if people can get clear on which principles or virtues or intrinsic goods are at stake, they can then resolve lower-level moral disputes. They might agree on the principle of autonomy (or beneficence) being dominant, for example, and then be able to settle disputes about which moral rules or rights are legitimate. In the more interesting and complicated cases, however, the disagreement may remain intractable. The parties to a dispute may not be able to determine which principles should prevail. One person, for example, might give priority to the principle of beneficence while another might believe that autonomy should take precedence (even if respecting autonomy will lead to less good consequences, that is, being less beneficent). Or they may not agree on whether right action or virtuous character is more important. When disputes of this sort linger, the discourse must move to a fourth and final level, the level of **metaethics**.

Metaethics deals with the most basic questions of ethics: the meaning and justification of ethical terms, how people know which principles or virtues are the correct ones, and the ultimate grounding of ethics. Here we are no longer interested in the substantive questions of which actions are morally right or which traits of character are morally praiseworthy. Rather we are dealing with even more basic issues of where to look to get answers to these questions and how we can know when we have the right answer.

Religious ethics has, by now, fairly standard answers to these metaethical questions. To the religious person, claiming an action is right *means* it would be approved by the deity or is in accord with laws created by the deity. For them, to say that a character trait is virtuous is to say that it would be approved morally by God. Religious people also have well-worked-out notions of how humans can know something is ethical: by revelation and reason, by reading the scriptures, and by religious authorities such as the pope, church councils, Islamic *fatwas*, or Talmudic law. More mystical religious people may rely more on direct spiritual revelation.

Secular people are not satisfied with these positions, but have analogous answers of their own. The grounding of ethics may be in natural law or in some **contract** (actual or hypothetical) among people. Traditional secular ethics have shared with monotheistic religions the notion that ethics is **universal**; that is, for a specific moral case at a specific time and place, all people *ought* to reach the same ethical judgment about whether the behavior involved is morally right or wrong. Of course, universalists recognize that not all people actually will agree on such judgments, but they believe that there is some universal standard (such as the divine will or reason or natural law) against which people's judgments can be tested. If two people disagree, say, about whether a particular abortion in a particular set of circumstances is immoral, then at least one of them must be mistaken.

Other secular theories share with polytheistic religion the notion that there is more than one standard of reference for moral matters. These metaethical positions are called **relativist** because they hold that moral judgments are relative to the multiple standards or authorities that exist. For example, for believers in polytheistic religion,

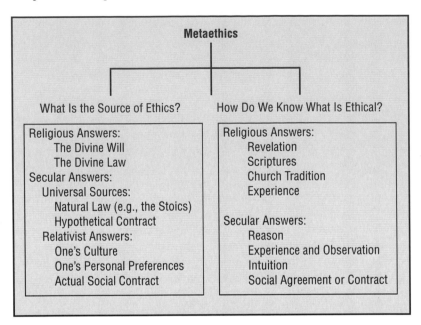

FIGURE 4   Metaethics: The Meaning and Justification of Ethical Judgments

different cultures may have different deities. One culture's god might approve of a merciful killing of a suffering patient while another culture's, while considering exactly the same case, might disapprove. Likewise, a secular ethic might be relativist if it holds that the ultimate standard of reference for moral judgments was the norms agreed upon in a particular culture. These alternative answers to the question of the source of ethical judgments are summarized in Figure 4 and in the chart on the inside covers of the book.

Metaethics also deals with a related question of how we can know the content of these moral norms. While for religious ethics the divine will or divine law is known through revelation or reason, scripture, or church tradition, in secular ethical systems it is known through reason or through empirical experience. The German philosopher Immanuel Kant based knowledge of ethics in reason; the British empiricist David Hume in the experience of sympathy. These religious and secular answers to the question of how we can know what is ethical are also included in Figure 4 and in the inside covers.

These metaethical questions take us well beyond what bioethics normally addresses. Fortunately, many have found that even if there is serious disagreement at this most abstract level, those who cannot agree on matters of religion and secular philosophy can nevertheless reach some converging consensus at the lower three levels of moral discourse. They can agree on normative ethical matters of **moral principles**, **virtue theory**, and intrinsic goods (**value theory**). They can agree on many **moral rules** and **rights**. Therefore, they can sometimes agree on what is morally right in a particular case, even if they have no agreement in metaethical matters. This is sometimes referred to as a *common morality*, an agreement on many, indeed most, ethical matters across cultures, religions, politics, and time periods.

A FULL THEORY OF BIOETHICS

Even though we need not spend much time in bioethics going all the way up the "ladder" of the levels of moral discourse, a full theory would need to climb all the way to this top level. In fact, some people would claim that traveling up this ladder from the case through rules and rights to normative theory and finally to matters of metaethics is traveling the wrong way. They hold that, in matters of ethics, one must start at the top and work one's way down. One would then first get clear on the meaning and justification of ethical claims—on metaethics—and then identify principles of right action, traits of good character, and intrinsic goods at the normative level, which would, in turn, lead to identifying lists of rules and rights, which would finally tell us how to act and what character traits one should have in particular cases. They claim one should reason from top to bottom rather than from case to the more abstract levels.

While the theorists defending the top-down approach fought bitterly with the bottom-up clinicians for the last decades of the twentieth century, there is now something of a rapprochement. More and more there is agreement that what is critical is that, for a full and consistent approach to bioethics, eventually all four of these levels must be brought into "equilibrium." It seems less and less important where one starts. If one begins with a case intuition and discovers that that intuition cannot be brought in line with firmly held beliefs about moral rules and principles, then something must give. Either one adjusts the case intuition or, if the case judgment is firm and unrelenting, then maybe the commitments at the higher levels will have to be adjusted. One will move up and down the ladder of the levels of moral discourse. Hence, in Figure 1, the arrows moving from one level of discourse to another are shown pointing in both directions. If one wants a full and consistent set of positions in bioethics, eventually a stable equilibrium is needed. The result is now often called a *reflective equilibrium.* Chapter 9 illustrates how questions at all four levels of moral discourse can be brought together to develop a set of judgments that rests in an equilibrium. In that chapter we examine the current controversies over genetic engineering and new birth technologies: in vitro fertilization, surrogate motherhood, cloning, and stem cell technologies. In these debates we are witnessing the tensions during the process of the emergence of a stable or equilibrium state in the moral debate.

In the case of Yusef Camp, the boy who ate the pickle, it appears that the physicians and the parents are not yet in such a stable state. If they were to start going up the ladder of the levels of moral discourse, they might turn to various codifications of moral rules and rights. Some of their options are presented in Chapter 2.

Key Concepts

Action Theory   The branch of normative ethics pertaining to the principles of morally right behavior (as opposed to virtuous character, cf. Virtue Theory, Value Theory).

Antinomianism   The position that ethical action is determined independent of law or rules; cf. Situationalism, Rules of Practice, Legalism.

Casuistry   The approach to ethics that addresses case problems by applying paradigm or settled cases attempting to identify morally relevant similar and dissimilar features.

Contract Theory   A type of metaethics that maintains that the source of moral rightness or the way of knowing what is moral stems from actual or hypothetical social agreement.

Legalism   The position that ethical action consists in strict conformity to law or rules; cf. Antinomianism, Rules of Practice, Situationalism.

Metaethics   The branch of ethics having to do with the meaning and justification of ethical terms and norms; cf. Normative ethics.

Moral Principles   General and abstract characteristics of morally right action. The main elements of part of normative ethics called action theory; cf. Action Theory, Moral Rules.

Moral Rules   Concrete statements specifying patterns of morally right conduct, sometimes believed to be derived from more abstract moral principles or, alternatively, created as summaries of patterns of individual case judgments.

Normative Ethics   The branch of ethics having to do with standards of right or wrong; cf. Metaethics.

Relativism   In metaethics, the position that there are multiple sources or groundings of moral judgments such as the approval of various cultures to which any correct moral judgment must conform; cf. Universalism, Situationalism.

Rights   Justified moral or legal claims to entitlements or liberties often seen as taking precedence over ("trumping") considerations of consequences. Rights normally stand in a reciprocal relation with moral or legal rules; that is, if someone has a rights claim against some other party, that other party is duty-bound by a rule requiring that the right be respected.

Rules of Practice   The position that rules govern practices such that actions are normally judged by rules; cf. Antinomianism, Situationalism, Legalism.

Situationalism   The position that ethical action must be judged in each situation guided by, but not directly determined by, rules; cf. Antinomianism, Rules of Practice, Legalism.

Universalism   The position in metaethics that there is a single source or grounding of moral judgments such as the divine will or reason to which any correct moral judgment must conform; cf. Relativism.

Value Theory   The portion of normative ethics having to do with rational conceptions of the desirable. Value theory addresses the question of which outcomes are considered good consequences of actions.

Virtue Theory   The portion of normative ethics having to do with virtues, that is, persistent dispositions or traits of good character in persons.

Bibliography

WORKS ON BASIC ETHICS

Beauchamp, Tom L. *Philosophical Ethics: An Introduction to Moral Philosophy*, 3rd ed. New York: McGraw-Hill, 2000.

Copp, David. *The Oxford Handbook of Ethical Theory*. New York: Oxford University Press, 2007.

Frankena, William. *Ethics*, 2nd ed. Englewood Cliffs, NJ: Prentice-Hall, 1973.

Gert, Bernard. *Morality: Its Nature and Justification.* New York: Oxford University Press, 2005.

Rachels, James, and Stuart Rachels. *The Elements of Moral Philosophy.* New York: McGraw-Hill, 2006.

Shafer-Landau, Russ, ed. *Ethical Theory: An Anthology.* Malden, MA: Blackwell, 2007.

Thiroux, Jacques P., and Keith W. Krasemann. *Ethics: Theory and Practice,* 10th ed. Upper Saddle River, NJ: Prentice Hall, 2009.

WORKS ON BIOMEDICAL ETHICS

Baker, Robert B., and Laurence B. McCullough. *The Cambridge World History of Medical Ethics.* Cambridge, England: Cambridge University Press, 2009.

Beauchamp, Tom L., and James F. Childress. *Principles of Biomedical Ethics,* 6th ed. New York: Oxford University Press, 2009.

Beauchamp, Tom L., LeRoy Walters, Jeffrey P. Kahn, and Anna C. Mastroianni. *Contemporary Issues in Bioethics,* 7th ed. Belmont, CA: Thompson Wadsworth, 2008.

Garrett, Thomas M., Harold W. Baillie, and Rosellen M. Garrett. *Health Care Ethics: Principles and Problems,* 5th ed. Upper Saddle River, NJ: Prentice-Hall, Inc., 2009.

Glannon, Walter. *Biomedical Ethics.* New York: Oxford University Press, 2005.

Gert, Bernard, Charles M. Culver, and K. Danner Clouser. *Bioethics: A Systematic Approach.* New York: Oxford University Press, 2006.

Jonsen, Albert R. *The Birth of Bioethics.* New York: Oxford University Press, 1998.

Park, Jennifer A., and Victoria S. Wike. *Bioethics in a Changing World.* Upper Saddle River, NJ: Pearson Education, Inc., 2010.

Pence, Gregory E. *Classic Cases in Medical Ethics: Accounts of the Cases That Have Shaped and Define Medical Ethics.* New York: McGraw-Hill Higher Education, 2008.

Pence, Gregory E. *The Elements of Bioethics.* Boston, MA: McGraw-Hill, 2007.

Steinbock, Bonnie, John D. Arras, and Alex John London, eds. *Ethical Issues in Modern Medicine: Contemporary Readings in Bioethics,* 7th ed. New York: McGraw-Hill Higher Education, 2009.

Veatch, Robert M., Amy M. Haddad, and Dan C. English. *Case Studies in Biomedical Ethics.* New York: Oxford University Press, 2010.

Veatch, Robert M. *A Theory of Medical Ethics.* New York: Basic Books, 1981.

Veatch, Robert M., ed. *Medical Ethics,* 2nd ed. Boston, MA: Jones and Bartlett, 1997.

2 The Hippocratic Oath and Its Challengers: A Brief History

In Case 1 in Chapter 1 the health care providers and the parents disagreed about how a permanently unconscious young boy should be treated. While the physicians felt it was appropriate to discontinue life support, the parents wanted it to continue. In fact, they could not even agree on whether the boy was dead or alive. Where might a physician, a parent, or a social observer of this scene turn for moral advice about how to handle a case like this? One possibility is to look at a code of ethics. These codes have been prepared by many different cultural, religious, and professional groups. They are lists or codifications of rules of the sort we identified in Chapter 1 as the second level of moral discourse, the next level of generality to which one might move if intuitions about specific cases resist resolution. Codes are meant to present moral rules (or perhaps rights) from the perspective of the group doing the writing. Sometimes they are limited to a specific domain such as medicine; in other codes the scope is more general.

THE HIPPOCRATIC TRADITION

The Hippocratic Oath

For many years, some physicians have used the **Hippocratic Oath** as that summary of moral/medical wisdom. It is not, however, a timeless document used throughout history in all parts of the world. It is part of a collection of writings known as the *Hippocratic Corpus*. We really don't know who wrote the oath. The fifth-century B.C.E. physician known as Hippocrates (one of the original leaders of medicine on the island of Cos in ancient Greece) was almost certainly not the author (Edelstein, 1967). The oath is generally believed to have been written about one hundred years later. It is one of several ethical writings along with other, more scientific ones.

Most people have not thought extensively about where the oath came from and, more importantly, about the belief system on which it was based. A provocative observation on the island of Cos should arouse curiosity. On the island are the ruins of a Greek healing temple. According to local folklore the school of Hippocrates was associated with this temple.[1] When local residents are asked what happened to the building, they say the destruction happened during the Christianization of Greece. Apparently, at some point in history, the Hippocratic and Christian schools of thought were sufficiently at odds that they battled to the point that the temple was destroyed. At some point in history Greek ethics and medicine were very different from ancient Christian ethics and medicine (Veatch and Mason, 1987). This raises questions that should concern moderns who see themselves standing in the Christian tradition, but also affirming the oath.

The most famous twentieth-century scholar of this period, Ludwig Edelstein (1967), thinks that the Hippocratic tradition arose from the Pythagorean cult (named for the same Pythagoras who gave us the Pythagorean theorem), a cult that was interested in science, philosophy, and religion, and, if Edelstein is correct, produced a school of medicine in ancient Greece known as the Hippocratic school. More recent scholars have questioned this conclusion (Miles, 2004), but some acknowledge that the oath has many elements that suggest it came from a school of thought similar to that of the Pythagoreans (Carrick, 1985, p. 163; cf. von Staden, 1996, p. 409). The critical fact is that these scholars recognize the oath as coming out of a specific context of Greek thought of the day it was written.

If all this is true, why should a group of modern, secular Western physicians caring for a Muslim patient in Washington, D.C., turn to a 2500-year-old Pythagorean cultic ritual oath for moral guidance? One will begin to see that however helpful it was for an ancient medical group, for those practicing medicine today it is controversial.

THE OATH OF INITIATION SECTION   The oath is divided into two parts, an oath of initiation followed by a code of conduct. The oath of initiation contains a pledge of loyalty to the teacher. If the teacher should ever become short of funds, it is the student's moral duty to come to the rescue. There is also a rather strange oath of secrecy. This does not refer to a pledge of confidentiality. Rather, one taking the oath pledges not to reveal the knowledge of healing to lay people. Knowledge taught to physicians was believed to be very powerful. That power in the hands of the untrained could cause great harm. Pythagoreans also believed that knowledge should not be revealed to anyone outside the cult. We still see this attitude in modern medicine, particularly in some older physicians who are uncomfortable about sharing medical information with patients.[2] This traditional practice is at odds with our current belief that the physician has a duty to educate patients about their medical conditions and a duty to obtain consent to treat that requires that the patient be informed.

The oath section also contains a pledge to the Greek gods and goddesses Apollo, Aesclepius, Hygeia, and Panacea. Modern physicians have felt it necessary to modify that sentence. They might substitute authorities within their own religious tradition or even secular authorities.

By contrast, other religious traditions, such as Judaism and Christianity, base their ethics on a covenant relationship between Yahweh and his people. They do not include a vow of secrecy. The Judeo-Christian belief, especially in Protestantism, is that all are capable of using knowledge responsibly.

Education is also important in secular *liberal political philosophy.* Liberal political philosophy has its origins in the philosophy of Locke, Hobbes, and Rousseau and reaches its best-known political expression in the documents of the American founding fathers. It stresses the importance of the individual and commands respect for individual liberty even if other people believe they know what is best. It also incorporates a belief in the equality of moral worth of all persons, providing a basis for various concerns about social justice. Its proponents believe that people have a right to know; the development of an informed consent doctrine illustrates the pervasiveness of this conviction. None of this discussion of patients' rights appears in any of the Hippocratic writings. We begin to see that the Judeo-Christian attitude and that of secular liberalism, as well as other traditions, have medical ethical doctrines that differ from this old cultic Hippocratic tradition.

THE CODE SECTION OF THE OATH   The second half of the oath contains the code of ethics itself. It is divided into three parts, dealing with dietetics, pharmacology, and surgery.[3] The third section contains an odd prohibition that requires physicians to swear that they will never practice surgery. Translations differ a bit, but the best translation prohibits operating "even on sufferers from stone," which presumably refers to bladder stone surgery. Because that was relatively simple surgery even in ancient times, this statement seems to emphasize that the prohibition is categorical and not merely reflecting an awareness that surgery in ancient times was too dangerous.

Why would a medical ethical oath forbid its physicians to practice surgery? One explanation is that the original meaning was that the Hippocratic physician should not practice surgery because surgery involves contamination, that is, touching blood and waste products, which is religiously defiling. Pythagoreans worried about such ritual contaminations. The oath does not say that surgery is inherently dangerous, but rather that Hippocratic physicians should leave surgery to persons who practiced that particular branch of medicine. In short, there is a moral division of labor like that seen in some traditional cultures, in which those in priestly roles were kept "pure." This interpretation is supported by the fact that the oath holds out "purity and holiness" as the two key Hippocratic virtues.

The oath also contains other prohibitions. The Hippocratic physician will not give deadly drugs. Euthanasia is proscribed, as are abortifacients.[4] Most important, the oath contains what can be called its core principle, namely, that the physician should *benefit the patient according to his ability and judgment.*[5] Decisions are made as to what should benefit the patient, based on the *physician's* ability and judgment, not the patient's. Hence, the Hippocratic ethic is often considered *paternalistic*; that is, it approves of actions intended to benefit another person even if that person does not want the benefit. Often in medicine this paternalism arises because the health professional is focusing exclusively on medical benefits of treatments while the patient may be willing to sacrifice these medical benefits in order to obtain nonmedical benefits considered more important or desirable. (Smoking, consuming unhealthy foods, and failing to exercise are all possible examples.)[6] Such actions pose a potential conflict with the principle of autonomy (see Chapter 5).

By contrast, other ethics are of a different style. Some interpretations of Judeo-Christianity, for example, see it as less paternalistic and different from the Hippocratic Oath in other significant ways. The other major religious and secular traditions of the world—Hinduism, Buddhism, various Chinese traditions, Marxist thought, and, for our purposes probably the most significant, to liberal political philosophy of the modern West—all have something that can be considered an ethic for medicine. All of these will be seen as contrasting to the Hippocratic tradition. Hence, if physicians or parents or anyone else seeking moral guidance for a case such as that of Yusef Camp, they will need to determine on which of the many ethical systems that are available they wish to rely.

Modern Codes in the Hippocratic Tradition

PERCIVAL'S CODE OF 1803   Several modern professional ethical codes stand in the Hippocratic tradition, at least in the sense that they stress the duty of the physician to benefit the patient. By far the most important for the English-speaking world is the code of Thomas Percival, published in 1803 (Percival, 1985 [1803]). The need for a written ethical code for medicine arose from a typhoid and typhus epidemic in Manchester, England, that occurred in the 1790s. As a result the Manchester infirmary staff members were overworked. Medicine in the eighteenth century in Britain was divided very much the way it was in the Hippocratic tradition. There were physicians who specialized in dietetics, surgeons, and apothecaries, who worked with drugs. With the pressure of this epidemic, it was more than they could handle. They began to fight among themselves about who should be doing what.

A physician named Thomas Percival had quit practicing medicine around this time because of a physical disability. He was well educated, and everybody thought well of him. The physicians embroiled in the dispute asked him to mediate the dispute. The result was a volume of ethical guidance. Thus, the purpose of the code was originally to mediate quarrels among physicians, not to deal with relationships with patients. Percival's code was published in revised form in 1803. While it is largely compatible with the Hippocratic Oath, Percival was more influenced by the philosophy of the Scottish enlightenment, which also based morality on producing good consequences. In fact, Percival had little to say about the actual Hippocratic Oath. Nevertheless, he focused on benefit to the patient rather than the rights of patients in matters such as informed consent or open disclosure.[7]

This duty to benefit the patient combined with the absence of any recognition of the rights of patients is the hallmark of the Hippocratic tradition. It is one of the major differences between medical ethics that is Hippocratic and many of the other religious and secular ethics we shall be considering. The focus on benefit to the patient has become the foundation not only of British, but American professionally sponsored medical ethics as well.

THE AMERICAN MEDICAL ASSOCIATION CODE OF 1847   In the United States at the beginning of the nineteenth century, a number of schools of medical thought existed side by side, just as in ancient Greece. Members of these schools began to fight among themselves, each wanting to establish theirs as the dominant school. In 1847, one group, representing what we now call allopathic (or orthodox and scientific) medicine, founded the American Medical Association (AMA) to accomplish this end and to combat what they thought of as quackery.

They recognized that if theirs was going to be a profession, as opposed to a mere business, they had to have a code of ethics. (Sociologists of the professions note that writing a code of ethics is often a distinguishing mark of a profession.) In writing one, they turned to Percival's code, taking whole sections of it and incorporating them into their original 1847 Code of Ethics of the AMA (AMA, 1848). So both Britain and the United States had codes of ethics that are essentially Hippocratic in their content, focusing on benefit to the patient. However, they both also discussed the duties of physicians to benefit society, something the Hippocratic ethic never mentioned.

THE WORLD MEDICAL ASSOCIATION DECLARATION OF GENEVA, 1948   Just after World War II, the World Medical Association, a conglomeration of national medical societies, needed a code to respond to the medical experiments in the Nazi concentration camps. In 1948 this group developed the Declaration of Geneva (World Medical Association, 1956). Its contents are remarkably similar to the Hippocratic Oath. Deleting from the old oath the references to Hygeia and Panacea and all the old gods and goddesses and the prohibition on surgery and abortifacients, it still includes the key sentence that is a slightly modified version of the **Hippocratic Principle**. It now reads, "the health of my patient will be my first consideration." Essentially, then, a Hippocratic Oath in modern language governs this organization of world medical associations. The World Medical Association is no more cognizant than the Hippocratic Oath of the problem that arises when the patient does not want her health maximized, that is, when she has something else on her agenda other than health, or when she disagrees with the physician about what would count as improving her health.

OTHER CONTEMPORARY OATHS OR CODES IN THE HIPPOCRATIC TRADITION
Just under half the medical schools in the United States and Canada (47 percent) still administer some version of the Hippocratic Oath to their graduates, but only one school (State University of New York at Syracuse) was reported in a 1997 article still to use the original version (Orr et al., 1997). Even that school now has abandoned the verbatim oath attributed to Hippocrates. Similar patterns appear in other countries with some schools using the Hippocratic form, usually modified, and others using an oath of entirely different origin.

In post-Soviet Russia, physicians have constructed an oath for the Russian physician ("Solemn Oath of a Physician of Russia," 1993). Wanting to replace the Soviet oath with its significant Marxist influences, Russian physicians took the old Hippocratic Oath and translated it into Russian, cleaning it up in a manner similar to that of the World Medical Association. Another example is the Academic Oath of St. George's University School of Medicine in Grenada. It also uses a rewrite of the Hippocratic Oath. Its version, however, requires the graduating medical student to work for the benefit of the patient rather than merely the patient's health. The key sentence reads, "The regimen I prescribe will be for the good of my patients, according to my ability and judgment." We shall see in Chapter 4 that there can be a difference between working for the patient's total welfare and focusing more narrowly only on the patient's health.

There are other rewritings, such as the Florence Nightingale Pledge for nurses. It wasn't written by Florence Nightingale any more than the Hippocratic Oath was written by Hippocrates, but it is a thinly modified rewriting of Hippocrates' oath (Editorial Comment, 1911).

Until the later decades of the twentieth century, then, physicians and other health professionals often used some adaptation of the Hippocratic Oath as their ethical code (and some continue to do so to this day). The definitive feature is a commitment to benefiting the patient without any acknowledgment of patients' **rights**, such as the right to be told the truth or to give consent before being treated. The more purely Hippocratic codes also pay no attention to the welfare of society or other individuals (although we have seen that both Percival and the AMA depart from the standard Hippocratic formula by mentioning some secondary concern for social benefits).

But beginning about 1970, the Hippocratic tradition started to collapse. Observing this collapse is in a way quite exciting; it must be like being with Galileo during the revolution in astronomy or with Albert Einstein when atomic physics was emerging. A new medical ethics emerged on the horizon, particularly for Western culture, which has its roots in ancient Judeo-Christianity, but more explicitly in secular liberal political philosophy.

THE COLLAPSE OF THE HIPPOCRATIC TRADITION

The Hippocratic Oath is being challenged in three ways. One preliminary challenge deals with the way in which benefits are assessed. The oath makes an enormous presumption when it says that a physician should judge what is best for his or her patient according to the physician's ability and judgment. In some cases, the physician's colleagues who are competent in their field may not concur. Even if they do, the patient may prefer some other course. In this sense the oath's assessment of benefit is subjective and the physician's subjective judgment is what counts. In Chapter 4 we shall discuss further the problems with the subjective notion that it is the physician's standard of benefit that is decisive.

A second challenge involves problems that arise when benefits conflict with other kinds of moral duties, particularly those related to rights of patients and obligations owed to them. Many ethical theories hold that there is more to ethics than merely producing good consequences. They affirm moral obligations and rights that are relevant to deciding what is ethically right conduct regardless of the consequences. In Chapter 5 we shall talk about conflicts between benefiting the patient and respecting certain rights of the patient, including the right to the truth, the right to have one's autonomy respected, and the right to have promises kept. Then in Chapters 6 and 7 we shall talk about the rights of the dying.

The third challenge to the Hippocratic tradition arises when there is a conflict between the interests of the patient and those of others. The oath, at least in its original form, focuses exclusively on the individual patient. In Chapter 8 we will look at the way in which this focus on the individual conflicts with the health professional's duty to others in the society in the areas of research medicine, public health, organ transplant, or cost containment.

Codes and Oaths Breaking with the Hippocratic Tradition

THE NUREMBERG CODE, 1946   Several kinds of medical codes or oaths break with this Hippocratic tradition. The first and most dramatic challenge in modern times came shortly after World War II with the Nuremberg trials. People began to question Nazi physicians about the painful, sometimes lethal, studies they had been doing on unwilling concentration camp prisoners. It became obvious that research on humans could be ethically controversial. The agenda being pursued in these studies was set by the Nazi state. The experiments were not for the benefit of prisoners in concentration camps. It is the very nature of medical research (as opposed to innovative therapy) that the goal is to produce knowledge, not to benefit the subject. On the other hand, the Hippocratic ethic requires that physicians act solely for the individual patient's benefit. Logically, all medical research would be unethical.

The Nazi physicians had abandoned the traditional ethical commitment of the physician to the individual patient's welfare. To respond to this problem, one option would be to go back to the Hippocratic formula, requiring that physicians focus only on individual patient welfare. That would mean, however, that they could never do any more research for the purpose of promoting the good of society. While the Hippocratic ethic would have prohibited the Nazi experiments, it would also have foreclosed even the most benign and defensible research.

Instead of returning to a Hippocratic model, spokespersons for Western society acknowledged that research was necessary for the benefit of humankind, but they also realized that some protection was needed for the individual research subject. This protection came in the form of requiring consent from subjects so they could look out for their own interests. The resulting Nuremberg Code (Nuremberg Code, 1946) was the first medical ethical document in the 2500 years after Hippocrates that mentioned the concept of informed consent, that is, the notion that the patient or subject has the right to be informed of the relevant facts of what is being proposed and to approve or disapprove before the physician proceeds.

A second important difference exists between the Nuremberg Code and the codes in the Hippocratic form. The Nuremberg Code is a public document of international law, not one written by the medical profession and bestowed on the public. We are beginning to see the clash of two different perspectives that represent two radically different ethical traditions. The result was an explosion beginning in about 1970, and it was dramatic. One strand, represented by the Nuremberg Code, is grounded in liberal political philosophy. The other, from the Hippocratic tradition, shows no such influence. This Hippocratic tradition is older, is more paternalistic, and, as we are beginning to discover, is incompatible with the liberalism on which the Nuremberg Code is based, at least in certain areas like research medicine.

THE AMERICAN HOSPITAL ASSOCIATION PATIENT BILL OF RIGHTS, 1973   Another document breaking with the Hippocratic view came from the American Hospital Association (AHA) in 1973, right at the beginning of the full-blown clash between the Hippocratic and liberal traditions. The Patient Bill of Rights was revised in 1992 and then replaced with a less formal statement entitled *The Patient Care Partnership: Understanding Expectations, Rights and Responsibilities* (American Hospital Association, 2003).

The AHA documents go a long way toward focusing on the rights of patients. It includes informed consent and a right to information. Nothing like that ever appeared in the Hippocratic tradition. This affirmation of patient rights is coming not from the Medical Association but the Hospital Association. It says nothing about the more social dimensions of medical ethics such as how scarce resources should be allocated and whether those without health insurance have a right of access to medical or hospital care.

AMERICAN MEDICAL ASSOCIATION PRINCIPLES OF 1980   It was not until 1980 that the AMA changed its code in a dramatic, significant way. The new version, adopted that year and published in 1981, finally begins speaking of the rights of patients. (Modest changes were made in 2001.) The use of the word *rights* is a signal that something new is going on. A right is a claim to a moral or legal entitlement. Those rights cannot be defeated merely by appeals to good consequences that would result from failing to honor them. The Hippocratic Oath never mentions anyone's rights. The language of rights is, after all, a modern notion grounded in the liberal political philosophy.

OTHER NATIONAL MEDICAL ASSOCIATIONS   Many other national medical associations have by now abandoned their more traditional Hippocratic codes in favor of revised documents that more explicitly affirm consent, confidentiality, and other rights of patients. For example, the Federal Council of Medicine of Brazil adopted a new code in 1988. The New Zealand Medical Association did so the following year.

Sources from Outside Professional Medicine

We also begin to see the emergence of medical ethical documents from other sources to which physicians, parents, or others confronting difficult decisions such as that involving Yusef Camp might turn.

JUDAISM, CATHOLICISM, AND PROTESTANTISM   Just as international law has provided a source for a code coming from outside the medical profession, religious traditions also have medical ethics. They are seen in Talmudic Judaism (Rosner and Bleich, 1979) and Catholic moral theology (National Conference of Catholic Bishops, 2001). Protestant ethics has positions on many medical ethical issues including abortion, euthanasia, and the right of access to medical care that come from moral sources fundamentally different from those of professional medical groups.

HINDUISM   Outside of the West, many ancient religious traditions have developed medical ethical positions as well. The Hindu Vedic scriptures, for instance, contain a medical ethic. The Vedic texts are classical religious writings. One group of those writings, the Ayur Veda, contains medical material including a code of ethics called the Caraka Samhita ("Oath of Initiation [Caraka Samhita]," 1978). This code required that the physician not injure or abandon the patient and not cause his death. One of the provisions in that document that makes very little sense to Westerners, but is understood within the Vedic tradition, is a pledge of the physician that he will not treat those who are haters of the king. There is nothing like this provision in Western medical ethics, but it is perhaps more comprehensible against the backdrop of the religious traditions of ancient India including the notion of *karma* with its suggestion of a kind of fatalism and just reward.

BUDDHISM   The classical Buddhist ethic involves an eight-fold path that incorporates five precepts. These precepts include prohibitions on killing, lying, and drinking intoxicants, revealing that the Buddhist tradition has definite implications for the practice of medicine.

ANCIENT CHINESE THOUGHT   Ancient China developed a complex, rich culture that included the thought of Confucianism as well as strands of Buddhist and Taoist thinking. By the seventh century C.E., Chinese writing began to focus explicitly on medicine. Sun Simiao included a famous treatise "On the Absolute Sincerity of Great Physicians" in his work *The Important Prescriptions Worth a Thousand Pieces of Gold*. Widely believed to reflect Buddhist and Taoist influences, it affirms special moral duties for professional physicians.

ISLAM   There are a number of Muslim oaths or codes for physicians. The Islamic Code of Medical Ethics was prepared in Kuwait in an international meeting of Islamic scholars in 1981 (International Organization of Islamic Medicine, 1981). Islamic medicine has a strong prohibition on killing, including mercy killing and abortion. There is an affirmation of Allah's will, the notion that we saw in the case of Yusef Camp.

JAPAN   Japanese ethics also has rich traditions relevant to medical ethics. Consider the following case:

CASE 2
Physician Assistance in a Merciful Homicide

A young woman had just given birth, in Tokyo. She was unmarried, had no close relatives who could help her raise this child, and had a malignancy of the breast. In fact, it had now metastasized. The oncologist told her she probably only had a few more months to live. The woman said to the oncologist, "I want you to help me to do the most loving thing that I can do for my child. I would like you to tell me how I can mercifully kill my child so that when I die, the child will not be condemned to the life of an orphan."

The physician pointed out that there were other possibilities. For instance, someone could adopt the child. The mother understood all this. She said, "My child is a girl. My child has a deformed hip. That close bond between mother and child is destroyed forever with my death. So my child will never be able to do well."

There is a concept in Japanese culture called *amae*, which is roughly translated as dependency, a close bond between a mother and child that would be irretrievably destroyed with the mother's death (Doi, 1981). There is also in Japanese culture a concept called *joshi*. *Joshi* can be translated as "love killing," or mercy killing. It is sometimes carried out by the head of a household who is disgraced in business. He might, as a merciful act, kill not only himself, but also mercifully take the lives of his wife and children so they would not be disgraced. Though illegal today, this practice, which comes out of the more traditional *edo* period in Japan, still occurs. This woman's request reflected these old beliefs. Japanese people today understand the concept, and it doesn't surprise them that a mother could ask for help from her physician not only to kill herself, but to kill her infant child. The striking thing about this story is that the physician understood. Most physicians, even in Japan, would not have cooperated, but they well might understand. It is impossible to understand that story without knowing a great deal about traditional Shinto doctrine and beliefs. It is the exception rather than the rule, but it does happen.

THE OATH OF THE SOVIET PHYSICIAN   All of these traditions in medical ethics leave us with the realization that those facing a choice in Yusef Camp's case and in similar situations cannot assume that the Hippocratic ethic and the professional consensus about what is ethical are automatically correct. There are many different traditions specifying what is ethical in medicine. These are not limited to the religious traditions. In secular philosophy a number of schools of thought have implications for medical ethics that differ from the Hippocratic tradition. One example is the Soviet Oath from 1971 (Oath of Soviet Physicians, 1971). It contains, among other things, a pledge of loyalty to the Communist society. Other political philosophies have implications for medicine as well.

LIBERAL POLITICAL PHILOSOPHY   One of these is seen in the most important intellectual movement in modern Western culture, the tradition of **liberal political philosophy.** It is the dominant philosophical orientation of secular society in the United States and most other nations of the West. Liberalism emerged as the major challenger of the more paternalistic Hippocratic tradition in the last quarter of the twentieth century. Patients' bills of rights are emerging that reflect liberal political philosophy such as the Council of Europe Convention on Human Rights and Biomedicine (1997) and United States Consumers' Bill of Rights of the President's Advisory Commission on Consumer Protection and Quality in the Health Care Industry (1997).

THE UNESCO UNIVERSAL DECLARATION ON BIOETHICS AND HUMAN RIGHTS
A new and potentially very significant development in the history of codes of medical ethics emerged in 2005 when the General Conference of the United Nations Economic, Scientific, and Cultural Organization (UNESCO) adopted a Universal Declaration on Bioethics and Human Rights,[8] seen as a bioethics-oriented follow-up of the 1948 Universal Declaration of Human Rights. This document represents a new stage in biomedical ethics codifications. It is a document that plausibly can be seen as speaking for all countries of the world and it is from a public agency,

Hippocratic Codes or Oaths

Closely reflecting the Hippocratic Tradition:

> The Hippocratic Oath
>
> The Hippocratic Oath Insofar as a Christian May Swear It
>
> The Florence Nightingale Pledge
>
> The Declaration of Geneva
>
> State University of New York at Syracuse
>
> The St. George's University Academic Oath
>
> The Oath of the Russian Physician

Qualified Hippocratic Content:

> Percival's Code of 1803
>
> The AMA Principles of 1847

Non- Hippocratic Codes and Oaths

Professionally Generated Codes Significantly Departing from the Hippocratic Tradition:

> The AMA Principles of Medical Ethics 1980, 2001
>
> American Nurses Association. Code for Nurses with Interpretive Statements, 1985, 2001
>
> The Chilean Medical Association (1983)
>
> The American Nurses Association Code of Nurses (1985)
>
> The Federal Council of Medicine, Brazil (1988)

Medical Ethical System Based on Nonprofessional Ethical Traditions

> Ten Maxims for Physicians and Ten Maxims for Patients, China
>
> The Ethical and Religious Directives for Catholic Health Facilities
>
> The Caraka Samhita of the Hindu Ayur Veda
>
> The Seventeen Rules of Enjuin, Japan, Seventeenth Century
>
> The Islamic Code of Medical Ethics
>
> The Oath of Maimonides (Jewish)
>
> The Oath of Soviet Physicians (1971)
>
> The AHA Patient's Bill of Rights
>
> Council of Europe Convention on Human Rights and Biomedicin (1997)
>
> The Consumers' Bill of Rights of the President's Advisory Commission on Consumer Protection and Quality in the Health Care Industry (1997)
>
> UNESCO Universal Declaration on Bioethics and Human Rights (2005)

FIGURE 5   Types of Codifications of Medical Ethics

UNESCO, rather than the product of a professional association. Thus, it is not surprising that it announces a set of principles that go beyond the Hippocratic idea of benefiting the individual patient and protecting the patient from harm. It also includes concern for the welfare of social solidarity and responsibility as well as incorporating concerns about autonomy, consent, privacy, and justice as well as human rights, all features absent from traditional Hippocratic ethics.

For a summary of the types of codifications see Figure 5.

After exploring the question of who it is who has full moral standing in the next chapter, in Chapter 4 we will begin an analysis of the Hippocratic approach to medical ethics. We will ask what moral problems arise if we assume that the goal of medicine is to produce benefits for the patient and to protect the patient from harm.

Key Concepts

Hippocratic Oath   The code of physician ethics attributed to the Greek physician, but more likely written by his followers in the fourth century B.C.E. Often believed to be related to a Pythagorean cultic belief system.

Hippocratic Principle   The core principle of the Hippocratic Oath, holding that the physician pledges to benefit his patient according to his ability and judgment and protect the patient from harm; cf. Social Beneficence, Deontological Principles.

Liberal Political Philosophy   The dominant commitment of secular society in the United States and most other nations of the West that has its origins in the philosophy of Locke, Hobbes, and Rousseau and reaches its most well-known political expression in the documents of the founding fathers of the American political system. It stresses the place of the individual and commands respect for the liberty of the individual. It also incorporates a belief in the equality of moral worth of all persons, providing a basis for various concerns about social justice.

Rights   Justified moral or legal claims to entitlements or liberties often seen as taking precedence over ("trumping") considerations of consequences. Rights normally stand in a reciprocal relation with moral or legal rules; that is, if someone has a rights claim against some other party, that other party is duty-bound by a rule requiring that the right be respected.

Bibliography

American Hospital Association. *A Patient's Bill of Rights.* Chicago, IL: American Hospital Association, 1992.

American Hospital Association. *The Patient Care Partnership: Understanding Expectations, Rights and Responsibilities.* [Chicago, IL]: American Hospital Association, 2003.

American Medical Association. *Code of Medical Ethics: Adopted by the American Medical Association at Philadelphia, May, 1847, and by the New York Academy of Medicine in October, 1847.* New York: H. Ludwig and Company, 1848.

American Medical Association. *Current Opinions of the Judicial Council of the American Medical Association.* Chicago, IL: American Medical Association, 1981.

American Medical Association, Council on Ethical and Judicial Affairs. *Code of Medical Ethics: Current Opinions with Annotations, 2002–2003 Edition.* Chicago, IL: American Medical Association, 2002.

Baker, Robert. *Introduction to the Codification of Medical Morality: Historical and Philosophical Studies of the Formalization of Western Medical Morality in the Eighteenth and Nineteenth Centuries. Vol. 2: Anglo-American Medical Ethics and Medical Jurisprudence in the Nineteenth Century.* Robert Baker, ed. Dordrecht, The Netherlands: Kluwer Academic Publishers, 1995, pp. 1–22.

Baker, Robert, Dorothy Parker, and Roy Porter, eds. *The Codification of Medical Morality: Historical and Philosophical Studies of the Formalization of Western Medical Morality in the Eighteenth and Nineteenth Centuries. Vol. 1: Medical Ethics and Etiquette in the Eighteenth Century.* Dordrecht, The Netherlands: Kluwer Academic Publishers, 1993.

Berlant, Jeffrey L. *Profession and Monopoly: A Study of Medicine in the United States and Great Britain.* Berkeley, CA: University of California Press, 1975.

Carrick, Paul. *Medical Ethics in Antiquity: Philosophical Perspectives on Abortion and Euthanasia.* Dordrecht, Holland: D. Reidel Publishing Company, 1985.

Doi, Takeo. *The Anatomy of Dependence.* Tokyo: Kodansha International Ltd., 1981.

Edelstein, Ludwig. "The Hippocratic Oath: Text, Translation and Interpretation." In *Ancient Medicine: Selected Papers of Ludwig Edelstein*, ed. Owsei Temkin and C. Lilian Temkin. Baltimore, MD: The Johns Hopkins Press, 1967, pp. 3–64.

"Editorial Comment." *The American Journal of Nursing* 11 (May 1911): 596.

International Organization of Islamic Medicine. *Islamic Code of Medical Ethics.* [Kuwait]: International Organization of Islamic Medicine, 1981.

Miles, Steven H. *The Hippocratic Oath and the Ethics of Medicine.* Oxford/New York: Oxford University Press, 2004.

National Conference of Catholic Bishops. *Ethical and Religious Directives for Catholic Health Care Services.* Washington, DC: United States Catholic Conference, 2001.

"Nuremberg Code, 1946." In *Encyclopedia of Bioethics*, Vol. 4. Ed. Warren T. Reich. New York: The Free Press, 1978, pp. 1764–1765.

Nutton, Vivian. *Ancient Medicine.* London/New York: Routledge, 2004.

"Oath of Initiation (Caraka Samhita)." In *Encyclopedia of Bioethics*, Vol. 4. Ed. Warren T. Reich. New York: The Free Press, 1978, pp. 1732–1733.

"Oath of Soviet Physicians (1971)." In *Encyclopedia of Bioethics*, Vol. 4. Ed. Warren T. Reich. New York: The Free Press, 1978, pp. 1754–1755.

Orr, Robert D., Norman Pang, Edmund D. Pellegrino, and Mark Siegler. "Use of the Hippocratic Oath: A Review of Twentieth Century Practice and a Content Analysis of Oath Administered in Medical Schools in the U.S. and Canada in 1993." *Journal of Clinical Ethics* 8 (1997): 377–388.

Percival, Thomas. *Medical Ethics; or, a Code of Institutes and Precepts,* Adapted to the Professional Conduct of Physicians and Surgeons by Thomas Percival, M. D. Together with an Introduction by Edmund D. Pellegrino, M. D. Birmingham, AL: The Classics of Medicine Library, 1985.

Rosner, Fred, and J. David Bleich, ed. *Jewish Bioethics.* New York: Sanhedrin Press, 1979.

"Solemn Oath of a Physician of Russia." *Kennedy Institute of Ethics Journal* 3, No. 4 (1993): 419.

Temkin, Owsei. *Hippocrates in a World of Pagans and Christians.* Baltimore, MD: Johns Hopkins University Press, 1991.

Veatch, Robert M. *Patient, Heal Thyself: How the New Medicine Puts the Patient in Charge.* New York: Oxford University Press, 2009.

Veatch, Robert M., and Carol G. Mason. "Hippocratic vs. Judeo-Christian Medical Ethics: Principles in Conflict." *The Journal of Religious Ethics* 15 (Spring 1987): 86–105.

von Staden, Heinrich. " 'In a Pure and Holy Way': Personal and Professional Conduct in the Hippocratic Oath?" *Journal of the History of Medicine* 51 (October 1996): 404–437.

World Medical Association. "Declaration of Geneva." *World Medical Journal* 3, supplement (1956): 10–12.

Notes

1. In fact, there is reason to believe that Hippocrates was not a part of this temple, but rather a challenger to the earlier religious healing system.
2. Likewise, until recently, pharmacists were taught that a pharmacist was not to put the name of the prescription medication on the label and should not tell the patient the name of the drug, because somehow that was information that could harm patients. They might hear that that drug was used for other diseases and become distressed with the thought that they might have such a condition. Or they might read about side effects and become unnecessarily alarmed about them.
3. One of the reasons we are convinced that the oath is Pythagorean in origin is because that is exactly the way the Pythagoreans divided the world of medicine, even though most other Greek schools of thought did not.
4. Some people say that the Hippocratic prohibition on abortion dovetails with Christian objections to abortion (Carrick, 1985, p. 159; Edelstein, 1967, pp. 62–63; Temkin, 1991, p. 182), and that is why the two traditions came together. But if one looks at the ancient tradition of Christianity, one will see that in all the documents that exist from the first eight centuries of Christianity only eleven references are made to the Hippocratic writings (Veatch and Mason, 1987). Nine of those eleven had nothing to do with the oath. They praise the quality of the writings holding it as a model of classical Greek writing style. Only two references mention the Hippocratic Oath in eight centuries of the Christian era. Both were rather hostile to Hippocratic concepts, reflecting a difference between the Christian and Hippocratic traditions.
5. In Hippocratic medicine, physicians were always male.
6. For a longer discussion of how Hippocratic paternalism poses problems related to the fact that physicians often have a hard time knowing what will benefit the patient, see my volume *Patient, Heal Thyself* (Veatch, 2009). In that volume I argue that in the normal case physicians cannot appropriately "prescribe" treatments for patients because they do not have an adequate perspective on what will benefit the patient. Even if they know the patient's illness and the range of available treatments, they cannot know the patient's goals and values. If they do not know what the patient is trying to accomplish in life and what effects the patient will value, they cannot know which combination of risks and benefits and which expenses are worth it for the patient.
7. Classifying Percival's work as in the Hippocratic tradition is now the standard reading of his ethics. That is the position taken by Leake (Berlant, 1975; Percival, 1927; Waddlington, 1975, 1984). More recent scholarship is now questioning this reading of Percival. At least, while the Hippocratic Oath focuses on the individual, isolated patient–physician relation, Percival differs by including extensive discussion of social relations including the duty of the physician to society. It is also now becoming clear that Percival was much more conversant with the contemporary philosophical literature of the time and not just repeating Hippocratic formulas (Baker, 1995).
8. General Conference of UNESCO at its thirty-third session in 2005. The full text is available on the UNESCO website: http://portal.unesco.org/en/ev.php-URL_ID=31058& URL_DO=DO_TOPIC&URL_SECTION=201.html, accessed September 3, 2009.

Defining Death, Abortion, Stem Cells, and Animal Welfare: The Basis of Moral Standing

In the previous chapter we saw that different cultures and social groups have different medical ethical codes or oaths. One way or another they provide compilations of ethical principles, virtues, rules, or rights that specify the norms of morally right conduct and character. In addition to the question of which set of norms should be used, they must also address another major issue. To whom do these norms apply? That might seem to be a question with an obvious answer—they apply to human beings. The question is, however, far more complex. At least four problems arise.

First, some codes are written as if they apply only to members of certain professional groups. They delineate norms of conduct for physicians, nurses, or other health professionals. But even these raise troublesome questions. Are the writers claiming that they apply to all members of the relevant profession or only to those who are members of the organization that adopted the code? For example, the American Medical Association's (AMA) code prohibits active mercy killing. Does that prohibition apply to all physicians, even those who are not members of the AMA? Certainly, it does not make sense for it to apply to physicians who are not American. Also, some codes written by professional groups specify behavior that is morally required for patients and other lay people. Can these professional organizations claim authority to specify what is morally right conduct for those who are not even in the profession and cannot be members of these organizations? Can these norms be imposed on lay people who have no voice in creating them?

A second problem is that professional groups are not the only ones who write codes purporting to state norms of professional conduct. Religious groups and governmental agencies write them as well. One can imagine a religious group claiming authority to articulate norms for its physician members. It might even claim to know what the norms of conduct are for those who are not members of the religious body. Secular philosophies might make similar claims. Ethical norms are usually thought to be universal; that is, a single system of ethics applies to all. But there are many different groups claiming to know what those norms are. For example, since both religious and professional groups claim to be able to articulate the norms of conduct for physicians and other health professionals, a physician may feel he or she is subject to the norms articulated not only by the professional group, but also by his or her religion—and the two may not approve of or permit the same conduct.

Third, ethical duties in the biomedical world may extend beyond living human beings. In the era of organ transplantation, people may be seen as having moral duties regarding bodies of the newly dead. In the era of genetic manipulation, **stem cells**, and test tube babies, the same can be said for human gametes and embryos. There seem to be moral limits on how these are treated, even if they are not considered living human beings. Whether an embryo—or for that matter a fetus—has the same moral standing as (other) living human beings is a matter of enormous controversy. Whether the moral principles—such as the principle of beneficence or avoidance of killing—should apply (or could apply) to these entities with a human genetic endowment will require much more philosophical work. Also, some non-human animals appear to most people to have some kinds of moral claims on us. Those claims may not be as weighty, but they exist nonetheless. We need to understand to whom the principles apply—to which humans (if not to all) and to which beings that are not human (if any).

Finally, the very language of morality and moral standing is complex. We speak in casual conversation of humans, persons, individuals, and human beings, sometimes interchangeably and sometimes with important moral differences presumed or implied. We need to understand how these terms should be to be used in more careful ethical discourse. In this chapter we first look at these linguistic questions. Then we examine four major areas of biomedical ethics that play key roles in deciding to whom the moral principles apply and to what extent. We examine the debate about the definition of death to see when we believe we should quit treating a human as having the full moral standing that is attributed to normal humans. Following that, we look at the other end of life to the even more controversial area of abortion to see when we should begin treating humans as having full moral standing. The link between the two will quickly become clear. Third, since the writing of the second edition of this book, the new and controversial area of the use of stem cells has emerged. We will take up the aspects of the stem cell controversy related to moral standing. Finally, we look at the controversy over animals to see whether any non-human animals have moral standing and, if so, how much.

PERSONS, HUMANS, AND INDIVIDUALS: THE LANGUAGE OF MORAL STANDING

The Concept of Moral Standing

We need to identify those to whom the moral norms apply, that is, those who are owed duties of beneficence, nonmaleficence, and the other moral principles. One way of speaking is to refer to any being to whom we owe some kind of duty as having **moral standing**. We usually believe that humans (at least normal humans) have moral standing, but other animals may as well. Extremely abnormal humans also pose some difficult questions—the permanently unconscious and the severely retarded, for example. Nevertheless, most people believe these humans have moral claims as well. It is also widely believed that non-human animals are owed at least something. Almost everyone believes we should not cause them pain, certainly not without good reason. Whether we have a duty not to kill them is more controversial. Some people even believe that we have duties toward plants and inanimate objects.

Assuming we do have such duties toward non-human animals, plants, and inanimate objects, the reason we have them is the cause of further controversy. It may be because they are the possessions of another, in which case the moral claims may be indirect. Both religious and secular people often speak as if we have duties toward trees, ecological systems, or natural landscapes. For religious people, it may be because they believe that these are God's creation or God's possessions. For secular ecologists, the reasons why we have such duties are harder to articulate. It may be because other human beings have claims to enjoy the rest of nature, but often ecologists speak as if the duties toward the environment were more direct, that there is something intrinsically wrong with destroying a gene sequence even if humans have no interest in it and get no benefit from it. This may be because we believe that, even if these genes are not useful now, we may find that genetic material useful to humans in the future. Or it may be because it is intrinsically valuable and simply deserves protection.

Whenever we speak this way we can say that any animals, plants, and inanimate objects to which we owe some kind of duties have *moral standing*. Clearly, not all the moral principles can apply in each case, however. It is hard to imagine what it would mean, for example, to speak of a duty to respect the autonomy of trees or to tell the truth to them, although we can imagine what it might mean to have a duty to avoid killing them.

It is common to speak as if humans have a special moral standing. Some say that they each have maximum or "full" moral standing. Moreover, if each human has maximum standing, the standing of each is equal. Whatever duties we owe to them, we owe to them equally. Those who hold such a view would say that these humans have *full and equal moral standing*.

It is not that those outside this group have no standing at all. For example, it seems we owe lower animal such as rabbits something. At least we should not inflict pain on them without good reason. It appears that we can divide the world into those who have full standing and those to whom we owe some lesser duties. Most people, rightly or wrongly, tend to treat lower animals as having a lesser status. They would be quite willing to sacrifice a rabbit for the welfare of a human child, but unwilling to sacrifice a child for the welfare of rabbits, even if the amount of good we could do to the rabbits of the world was enormous. Likewise, if a human child and a bobcat were both starving and we have enough food only for one, certainly most people would favor giving the food to the child. (In fact, many would support killing the bobcat to feed to the child, but no one would favor killing the child to feed to the bobcat.) We can say of such special moral status that we give the child that he or she has full moral standing.

One of the critical questions in biomedical ethics is who has full moral standing. When we divide living beings into those with full standing and those with some lesser standing, there is a burden of justification when the time comes to draw the dividing line. It is that problem that is addressed in this chapter.

Moral and Descriptive Uses of the Term *Person*

The English language has done us a disservice by giving us so many ways of referring to humans while at the same time often lacking precision in how these terms
are used. We speak of human beings, persons, and individuals, as well as using
more technical terms such as "moral agents." In the field of ethics, sometimes these
terms do important moral work, signifying our commitment that the being
referred to either has or does not have some kind of moral standing. The language
may signal that we have duties toward it as called for by the various ethical principles or that it has a particular type of moral standing. In other cases, however,
these words can be used in a way conveying no moral implication at all. To make
matters particularly confusing, sometimes the same word can be used both
morally and nonmorally, even by the same speaker and in the same paragraph or
sentence (see Figure 6).

PERSON DEFINED AS "THOSE WHO POSSESS CERTAIN PROPERTIES"   The word
person is particularly confusing in this regard. Some times the word is used in ways that
do not necessarily convey any moral status. Thus, a **person** can be *defined* as any
self-aware or rational being. (Other physical or mental characteristics that do not
necessarily imply a moral status are also sometimes used such as possessing an oppos-
ing thumb, a human genetic code, or self-awareness.) It should be clear that, if *person*
is defined descriptively—that is, by citing one or more crucial properties such as
self-awareness—nothing follows about whether such persons have moral status. One
always needs some moral assumption to justify a conclusion about moral status.
Likewise, those who lack the critical characteristic(s) could still have full moral
standing. Thus, it could be a correct use of the language to say, "Even though a baby is
not a person in the sense of possessing self-awareness, nevertheless, babies have full
moral standing." Such a statement would simply convey that the speaker based moral
standing on something other than that on which he or she bases personhood. Using
the language in this way, we can say that there could be human living nonpersons with
full moral standing. Likewise, although it would today be an unusual moral view, it
would not be a linguistic contradiction to say that some individuals are persons in the
sense that they possess self-awareness and yet they lack full moral standing. (Certain
racists might hold such a view, for example.) Those who use the word *person* in this
way are also using it in a nonmoral sense.

Person (nonmoral definition):

Humans (and other beings) who possess one or more critical physical or
mental capacities such as self-awareness or rationality

Person (moral definition):

Humans (and other beings) who possess full or maximal moral standing

---

FIGURE 6   Two Definitions of Person

PERSONS DEFINED AS "THOSE WITH FULL MORAL STANDING"   Making matters more confusing, others use the word *person* in a way that attributes moral standing to its referents *by definition*. According to this view, we must first determine who has full moral standing (and who does not) and then call all in the first group *persons*. Hence, one might say, "I believe that embryos have full moral standing and therefore are persons even though they obviously lack self-awareness." Or someone might say, "Even though small children possess self-awareness, they are nevertheless not *persons* because they do not have full moral standing." While this would be an unusual view about the moral status of children, if being a person means nothing more than having moral standing, it is a linguistically comprehensible statement. On the other hand, such a statement would be self-contradictory if the speaker defined *person* as meaning "one who possesses self-awareness."

The bottom line is that some use the term *person* to identify those with certain physical or mental characteristics, while others use the term to identify those who, by definition, have moral standing regardless of whether they possess any particular mental or physical characteristics.

CONFUSION RESULTING FROM SHIFTING FROM A NONMORAL TO A MORAL USE OF THE TERM *PERSON*   The problem arises when someone tries to say something like the following:

> Late term fetuses are not persons because they lack self-awareness (or self-consciousness or ability to reason). But, since lacking personhood means one lacks full moral standing, fetuses can be aborted.

Whether it is ethical to abort fetuses is controversial. One cannot validly get to the conclusion that it is ethical by using the reasoning just presented. Using the nonmoral definition, the speaker first claims that fetuses are not persons. He or she wants us to accept as obvious that fetuses do not possess some key nonmoral characteristic such as self-awareness. Then the speaker shifts to the moral meaning of the term *person*, claiming that only persons have moral standing. Notice that, as long as one defines *person* without any reference to moral standing, one has not established that only persons have moral standing. This linguistic sleight of hand seems to suggest a proof that fetuses lack full moral standing, but it is merely a linguistic shift from a nonmoral to a moral definition of persons. What is not established in the two-sentence statement is that only those with self-awareness possess full moral standing and that, after all, is what the whole abortion debate is all about.

This confusion between the position that persons have moral standing by definition and the position that personhood can be defined based on certain nonmoral characteristics leads to enormous confusion in medical ethics debates. The easiest way to eliminate this confusion is simply to exclude the use of personhood language, requiring those arguing for one or another position about moral standing to make their claim in a straightforward way. Hence, if one wants to hold that fetuses lack moral standing, it won't do to claim that they are not persons and that only persons have standing. Or if one wants to hold that they possess moral standing, it won't do to claim that they are persons and therefore they must have moral standing. Either persons have moral standing by definition, in which case little is established, or persons possess some nonmoral physical or mental characteristics, in which case claiming someone is a person tells us nothing about their moral status without going on to show that these characteristics imply moral standing.

Proving that some nonmoral characteristic such as self-awareness or a unique genetic code is what it takes to establish full moral standing is extremely difficult to do. If such a link could be proved, someone would have done so by now and the abortion, definition of death, and animal rights debates would be over. Apparently, there are no definitive secular proofs of what characteristics establish full moral standing. Instead, we rely on firmly held beliefs—either secular or religious—that cannot be proved to others who do not share those beliefs. Nevertheless, virtually everybody accepts the idea that some beings have full moral standing while others do not. The inability to prove what characteristic establishes full moral standing is the reason why we continue to have controversy over the definition of death (when full moral standing ceases), abortion (when full moral standing begins), and the moral standing of non-human animals.

Moral and Nonmoral Uses of the Word *Human*

A similar problem arises with the use of the word *human*. Sometimes those who adopt liberal views on abortion will say that human life does not begin until quickening or the third trimester of gestation or even birth. Similarly, those who are skeptical about the moral standing of anencephalic infants or the persistently vegetative may claim that such beings are not "human." Clearly, they are not challenging the genetic makeup of such beings; they are merely making claims about their lack of full moral standing.

On the other hand, conservatives may respond by pointing out that these beings clearly are "human" since they possess the genetic code of the human species. (They are not cats or dogs.) In making these claims they are relying on our consensus that the anencephalics or fetuses or persistently vegetative adults in question possess some nonmoral characteristic that makes them a part of the human species. They trade on the consensus on the characteristics of humans defined nonmorally to attempt to establish that all those with these characteristics are also humans defined as having full moral standing. Once again, it seems that one can only add confusion by sliding from a nonmoral definition to one that establishes moral status by definition. Clearly, to be a human in a nonmoral sense establishes nothing one way or another about whether that being also has full moral standing. Doing so requires a belief that all who are humans in the nonmoral sense also possess full moral standing. Or, to point out the liberal's problem, establishing that one lacks some nonmoral characteristic of human-ness, such as self-consciousness, does not prove one lacks moral standing.

The issue in this chapter is how people have attributed moral standing to individuals and, further, how they have attributed what we call *full moral standing*.

DEFINING DEATH

It is probably best to start by examining what it means to lose full moral standing. A good case could be made that when there is a quantum change so that full moral standing is lost we say that the individual has died. That means that certain moral and legal rights that once applied to this individual no longer do. We, for instance, can no longer be guilty of killing such an individual. At least for humans, the fight over the definition of death is really a fight over when we should no longer treat someone the way we normally treat living humans. Once an individual is said to have died, our moral (and legal) duties toward that individual are not the same. One cannot "kill" a corpse. Other rights claims are also terminated. To say that someone has *died* therefore means, among other things, that we no longer attribute full moral standing to the individual. To be sure, even a corpse is thought to retain some attenuated moral standing. There are things we could do even to a corpse that would be considered immoral.

In Chapter 6 we will encounter the principle of avoiding killing. A critical problem with the principle of avoiding killing—the idea that it is wrong to kill people—is that we need to figure out what it means to be dead since, once we consider someone dead, killing is no longer relevant. Up until recently, we all knew who was dead and who was alive; it was straightforward. But in the last half century it has become increasingly difficult to decide whether someone is really dead or alive.

Remember Yusef Camp, the boy we encountered in Chapter 1 who ate the pickle and was left possibly brain dead in a hospital bed. If we cannot agree on whether he is dead or alive, we are going to have a real problem figuring out how to handle such a case. We need to determine whether the clinicians who favor cessation of treatment can stop on the grounds that their patient is deceased. Alternatively, they might have to claim that it is acceptable to stop treatment even though the patient is still alive.

There are three general positions regarding what it means to be dead (Capron, 2004; Controversies in the Determination of Death: A White Paper by the President's Council on Bioethics, 2008; Lamb, 1985; Law Reform Commission of Canada, 1979; President's Commission for the Study of Ethical Problems in Medicine and Biomedical and Behavioral Research, 1981). These are defined in Figure 7.

A Somatic Definition of Death

The first, the traditional definition, can be called the *somatic definition of death* (Jonas, 1974; Shewmon, 2001). According to this view, an individual dies when there is irreversible loss of the body's capacity to carry on integrated functioning. Usually the

---

Cardiac-Oriented

  Irreversible loss of cardiac and respiratory function

Whole-Brain-Oriented

  Irreversible loss of all function of the entire brain

Higher-Brain-Oriented

  Irreversible loss of higher-brain functions (those responsible for consciousness of other functions consider crucial)

FIGURE 7   Three Definitions of Death

focus is on cessation of circulatory and respiratory function, but the body also carries on other complex, integrated functions having to do with such complex processes as digestion, elimination, reproduction, and maintaining homeostasis. What holders of this view consider essential is that a body is alive as long as it can carry out complex, integrated maintenance of the body as a whole. Thus, we can refer to this view as the somatic integration view. Sometimes (recognizing that heart function is one crucial element in bodily integration) this is simply referred to as a **cardiac-oriented definition**, keeping in mind that we are referring not just to the functioning of the heart, but also to the functioning of the circulatory and respiratory systems as well as other bodily systems. A minority of the U.S. President's Council on Bioethics (2008, p. 90) support this definition of death based on irreversible loss of somatic integration. One can infer from a study published in 2004 that about 14 percent of Ohio citizens held this minority view (Siminoff, Burant, and Youngner, 2004).

It is clearly possible for someone to be alive with a dead heart—even under this definition of death. As the following case shows, those who favor this definition can recognize that an individual can be alive even if his heart is totally removed and discarded.

CASE 3

The Man Living Without a Heart

Some year ago, a dentist named Barney Clarke was a heart patient at the University of Utah, where clinicians were experimenting with artificial hearts. Since he was at death's door and awaiting a heart transplant, the physicians removed his heart and connected his aorta and veins back up to a Jarvik-7 artificial heart pump. Barney Clarke lived for four months on that artificial heart. At times he was doing quite well with this machine running next to him, pumping like a heart would pump blood. At times he would sit up in bed, even get out of bed and go for a stroll, pulling this machine along with him on a cart. If he is carrying on a conversation, smiling, and discussing things with those at his side, would anyone, even believers in a cardiac definition of death, consider him dead?

This is an unusual case, but it seems clear that Barney Clarke was not dead during this period. What we mean by a somatic- or cardiac-oriented death is that an individual has irreversibly lost the key bodily integrative capacities and that these include cardiac and respiratory functions that normally are controlled by the heart. The fact that these functions are being maintained by some artificial device does not make one dead.

THE PROBLEM OF IRREVERSIBILITY   For an individual to be dead by this definition, the stoppage of bodily integrative function such as circulatory and respiratory function must be *irreversible*. It is very common but very wrong for clinicians and others to refer to someone who has suffered a cardiac arrest and been successfully resuscitated as having been "clinically dead." Being dead means *irreversible* loss of cardiac function. If one suffers a cardiac arrest and then is brought back, that individual was never dead. His or her tissues continued to live. Potentially, we can save that individual. Such individuals have suffered a cardiac arrest and would have died, had we not intervened with CPR (cardiopulmonary resuscitation), but it is incorrect to say that they were ever dead. Consider the recent controversy regarding the procuring of infant hearts for transplantation (Boucek et al., 2008).

CASE 4
Infant Heart Transplant

Although most organ transplants occur after those from whom the organs are taken are pronounced dead based on brain criteria, some organs are taken after patients are pronounced dead using the traditional cardiac-based criteria. Once the heart stops, the patient is pronounced dead and kidneys and other organs are removed. Historically, hearts are not procured in these cases. The reason is that if a heart can be transplanted and restarted, the one from whom the heart was taken cannot have been dead because the heart has not stopped irreversibly.

In 2008 physicians in Denver published an account of their procurement and successful transplant of hearts from three infants who were terminally ill and whose parents had chosen to forgo further life support. In each case, the heart of the infant stopped after life support was withdrawn; death was pronounced based on loss of heart function; hearts were procured and transplanted. No measurements were made that would suggest loss of brain function. In each case the infants receiving these hearts survived with the transplanted hearts functioning appropriately.

Controversy erupted in part because it was question whether the infants from whom the hearts were taken were actually dead. They were not pronounced dead based on loss of brain function. The deaths were based on heart function loss. The controversy centered on whether that function was lost irreversibly. Part of the debate centered on whether the physicians had waited long enough to establish that the hearts would not restart themselves in the chests of the original patients. Part of the controversy was over whether one could claim that the hearts had stopped irreversibly when it, in fact, was successfully restarted (in the chest of the infants receiving the transplants). The issue is of considerable substance since if the infants from whom the hearts were taken were not yet dead (because their hearts had not stopped irreversibly), then the physicians who removed them must have caused the deaths. Homicides must have been committed.

If we understand being dead as signaling a critical change in moral status, it is easy to see why it is important that people must really be dead before their organs are removed. We must follow what is called the "dead donor rule." Life-prolonging organs cannot be removed before death. This helps understand why it is important that we insist that people do not die temporarily only to be brought back to life. If they are dead, many behaviors become appropriate that are totally inappropriate for living people, even unconscious people who are not breathing and temporarily have no heartbeat. We can do things like read the person's will and transfer assets, and, with appropriate permission, remove organs for transplant. The person's spouse becomes a widow. None of that happens with a temporary cardiac arrest. For those who do not believe in reincarnation, we only get one death per individual, at least in this world.

If death is pronounced in such a case and then the patient's cardiac and respiratory function returns, we must say we made a mistake. Death was erroneously pronounced—at least in the eyes of those who hold a somatic- or cardiac-oriented definition of death.

PROBLEMS WITH A SOMATIC DEFINITION OF DEATH   There are some serious problems with a somatic definition of death. For one, there are bad consequences in continuing to use the somatic definition. Thousands and thousands of people around the world are awaiting organs for transplant. In the United States alone there are over 111,000 people on the waiting list for organs as of June 2011. If we wait until somatic integrative functions cease, for the most part those organs are no longer usable in transplants.

It would be nice to be able to get these organs to be used for life-saving transplants. Nevertheless, it is clear we cannot change the definition of death just in order to get wanted organs. In fact, if we wanted to get more organs, we might as well, for example, define all medical students as dead. Then we would get young, healthy organs, rather than waiting for people to have automobile accidents or strokes. It is obvious that we cannot just pick a definition out of thin air simply because it would be useful in saving lives. On the other hand, if there are independent reasons why the somatic-oriented definition seems wrong, then we should begin the task of determining when we believe people lose their full moral status and die.

Many people believe that the somatic- or cardiac-oriented definition of death is no longer appropriate. To claim that people die when their fluids stop flowing is to elevate blood flow to too lofty a place. Likewise, considering people alive simply because they can digest food or excrete bodily wastes seems demeaning. There is more to human life than mere bodily integration. Instead there is another, more complicated explanation of what it means to die.

A Whole-Brain-Oriented Definition of Death

That brings us up to about 1970, when we began talking about what is today sometimes called the **whole-brain-oriented definition of death**. An individual dies, according to this view, when there is irreversible cessation of all functions of the entire brain, including the brain stem (Harvard Medical School, 1968; Task Force on Death and Dying, Institute of Society, Ethics and the Life, 1972; see also The President's Commission for the Study of Ethical Problems in Medicine and Biomedical and Behavioral Research, 1981). The majority of both the 1981 President's Commission and the 2008 report of the President's Council on Bioethics held this view. This is a belief that has traditionally been based on the claim that the essence of humans is their ability to integrate bodily functions, and insofar as we believe that the brain is responsible for that integration, one is dead when and only when the brain irreversibly stops function. The 2008 report of the President's Council emphasized the brain's capacity to make possible human interaction with the surrounding environment. Of course, according to this view one can lose individual functions and still be alive. It is the integrating capacity or interaction with the environment that counts.

Whole-brain death is the current law in most jurisdictions of the world. The exceptions include some Asian countries. Japan only in 1997 adopted a brain-oriented definition of death, limiting it to cases in which organs will be procured for transplant. The resistance of brain-oriented death pronouncement in Asia can be traced mainly to the fact that it does not square well with traditional Buddhist and Shinto beliefs. Also, the very first organs procured for transplant in Japan, back in the late 1960s, may well have been taken from a patient who was not totally dead, so in Japan there is nervousness about procuring organs. The Japanese do not object to procuring organs from a living patient, for instance taking one kidney from a parent to transplant to a child. It is the problem of pronouncing death based on whole-brain death that is the difficulty.[1]

There is one other jurisdiction that still accepts some death pronouncement based on cardiac criteria. That is New Jersey. Policy makers in that state recognize that picking exactly what it means to be dead is not totally a scientific question, that some people could choose one view, some could choose another. In New Jersey, death is based on whole-brain criteria unless the individual had executed a document expressing a religious objection to the use of the whole-brain death concept. This was incorporated primarily to deal with Orthodox Jews, some of whom hold to a cardiac definition. Other groups, including many Native Americans and Japanese, also prefer the more traditional definition.

If his entire brain had been destroyed, as two of the neurologists believed it had been, Yusef Camp would have been dead by whole-brain criteria even though the ventilator was maintaining his heart, respiration, or other bodily integrating functions. Once death has been pronounced, the normal practice would be to stop treatment if it had not already been stopped. Even if one believed that life-supporting treatments should always be provided for living persons (an issue discussed in Chapter 6), many believe there is no reason to provide it if the patient is deceased. Most people hold that treatment can be stopped on one who is dead even against the wishes of the family. Family members have no right, according to this view, to insist that clinicians continue to ventilate a corpse. However, in the case of Yusef Camp, the neurologists could not reach an agreement that the entire brain was destroyed, so they could not use whole-brain death as a way of pronouncing death.

A patient on a ventilator determined to be dead using brain criteria does, of course, make for an unusual corpse. On the ventilator, he is respiring and his heart is beating. But if his whole brain is dead, the law in most jurisdictions says that the patient is deceased.

The Higher-Brain Definition of Death

This brings us to the third definition, sometimes called the **higher-brain-oriented definition**. Suppose a patient were permanently unconscious, with most brain functions gone, but limited reflexes remained in the brain stem. He would not be dead by whole-brain criteria. According to the whole-brain formulation, every last function must be gone. People have begun to say that perhaps there are some brain functions that are not absolutely essential to being considered alive. In that case, we might pronounce somebody dead, if their "higher functions" were permanently lost.

For instance, if the cerebrum is gone, but the brain stem remains so that brain stem reflexes are present, one might, under a higher-brain definition of death, claim somebody is dead. An individual dies, according to this view, when there is an irreversible loss of higher-brain functions.

Defining exactly which functions are critical is controversial. Some have claimed that the critical function is the function of the cerebrum, but it is theoretically possible for some motor functions to remain in the cerebrum even though all sensory function is lost. Most defenders of the higher-brain formulations consider some sensory function to be critical. Some of them simply equate death to an irreversible loss of consciousness. Anybody who is permanently unconscious, according to this newer view, would be considered dead. Since considering someone dead is, in reality, claiming that they have undergone a major change in their moral status, many behaviors appropriate with regard to dead people would become acceptable at this point.

The higher-brain definition of death is not yet legal anyplace in the world. But it is an idea that is debated increasingly. A number of philosophers and neurologists are beginning to endorse this idea. Based on the 2004 Ohio study, it appears that over half (57 percent) of Ohio citizens would consider some people who retain some brain activity to be dead (Siminoff, Burant, and Youngner, 2004). Somebody will eventually propose that it be the legal definition of death. Were it the legal definition of death, Yusef Camp would be dead from the moment he became irreversibly unconscious. Nancy Cruzan and Karen Quinlan (women left in a vegetative state from accidents, whose families led battles for the right to forgo life support) or Terri Schiavo (the Florida woman whose family aired a very public disagreement about withdrawing nutrition) would be dead by this higher-brain definition even though they were legally alive according to the present whole-brain definition.

Definitions and Moral Standing

Almost everyone holds some version of one of these three major definitions of death. They believe that once one has irreversibly lost the critical function—cardiac, whole-brain, or higher-brain—a major moral shift has taken place as well as a biological one. They believe that the individual no longer has the full moral standing that he or she once possessed. Thus, they hold that many behaviors become acceptable that are not appropriate for individuals considered living. They may have lesser moral standing, but full standing no longer exists.

ABORTION

Symmetry Between Definition of Death and Abortion

If calling someone dead is, in fact, a social symbol that we are attributing a major moral status change, the debate over the definition of death is really a great moral debate. Moreover, it may have direct relevance to the even more controversial debate over abortion. Whatever factor signals the end of full moral standing would seem to be relevant to the question of when full moral standing begins. It is possible we can do things before full moral standing is attributed that we will not be able to do later in a human's life. We might, for example, be able to trade off interests, do laboratory manipulations, perhaps even end biological life.

Manipulation of sperm and egg cells are often believed to be less troublesome morally than manipulating a late-term fetus or postnatal infant. It is important to know why that is so. It must be that no matter how we attribute moral status to sperm and egg cells, we view them as having a moral standing that is different from that of the late-term fetus or postnatal infant. If we can identify what is responsible for this perceived shift in moral status, perhaps we can understand better when full moral standing accrues.

Can we use the criterion for end of life as a signal of when full moral standing begins? Some people think this is so. Let us see what the implications of each of the three definitions of death might be for the issue of the moral standing of fetuses. (For a range of well-developed positions on abortion, see Beckwith, 2007; Callahan, 1970; Dworkin, 1994; Feinberg, 1973; Noonan, 1970.)

First, the higher-brain death formulation implies that full moral standing accrues only when the requisite higher functions appear. For many holders of this position that means the capacity for mental function or consciousness. This is late in fetal development, perhaps about twenty-four weeks of gestation. Holders of this view would accept a lesser moral status for fetuses prior to that time, but they would not attribute the same moral status that is assigned to postnatal humans. This concept is probably what underlies the most liberal view on abortion.

Second, the whole-brain death definition implies that full moral standing accrues when capacity for neurological bodily integration or interaction with the environment develops. This is earlier, perhaps in about the eighth to twelfth week. Those who believe that full moral standing accrues at the point at which neurological integrating capacity appears would probably accept abortion up to this point. The exact cutoff would depend on exactly what they understand integration or interaction to mean. They would, thus, be moderates in the abortion debate.

The cardiac definition of death implies that full moral standing accrues when capacity for cardiac function appears. That, in turn, depends on exactly which cardiac function is critical. Full pumping of blood occurs much later, perhaps at a time similar to the occurrence of neurological integrating capacity. Cardiac muscle contraction occurs quite early in fetal development. So do some other somatic integrating functions such as digestion and elimination. If one includes these functions as indicators of life, a more conservative position on abortion is likely.

Each definition of death has a corresponding notion of when full moral standing begins and implications for the moral status of fetuses before that time. None of this implies that a fetus has no moral status before the emergence of the critical function; just as a corpse commands respect even after the critical function ceases, so even liberals on abortion may recognize that early fetuses are not merely meaningless pieces of tissue. There are moral limits on what can be done to a corpse. But those limits are not as constraining as for a being with full moral status. In the case of a dead body, we may transplant organs, do research solely for the benefit of others, perform a respectful autopsy, etc. So, likewise, those who identify a point later in fetal development at which full moral standing begins may still believe fetuses at an earlier stage of development have some intermediate moral status.

Notice that there is no scientific way to choose among these functions to determine which function is critical for maximal standing. This necessarily requires a religious or philosophical judgment. Many in Western society have chosen the whole-brain function as critical in the definition of death. Should they also use that as the critical point in deciding when in fetal development full moral standing accrues? Should those who accept a higher-brain definition of death likewise accept the beginning of these functions as the beginning of full moral standing?

Possible Basis for a Breakdown in the Symmetry

It is striking that none of these positions has anything directly to do with the fixing of the genetic code. None seems to imply full moral standing at the moment of conception. How do conservatives on abortion, those who would oppose all abortion from the beginning, defend their position?

Thus far we have assumed it is the actual capacity to perform some function that is morally critical. That function might be consciousness, neurological integrating capacity, or cardiac function, but it is the *ability to perform* the function that has been taken to be decisive morally. But some people hold that it is the *potential* for these functions that is morally critical. They say that once the genetic code is determined, the eventual development of the critical function is determined. Barring some injury or other untoward event, the capacity will eventually emerge. In death, one loses potential when one loses capacity irreversibility. At the beginning of life, the potential is present long before actual capacity. It is present at conception or soon thereafter. If it is potential for an individual to develop higher-brain, whole-brain, or cardiac function that is morally critical, then full moral standing would arise once that potential has been established.

Liberal critics may claim at this point that potential is present even before conception. The genes are present in sperm and egg, and the potential for combining exists before conception. This claim would appear to give egg and sperm cells full standing, a position almost no one finds plausible. But defenders of the more conservative position claim that what is critical is a potential for these functions occurring *in a unique and individual way*. This occurs only when the genetic code is determined, at least insofar as these functions are determined genetically. If one believes unique potential is what is morally critical to establishing full moral standing, then this moment when the genetic code is fixed becomes critical. A more moderate defender of the potentiality position may recognize that there is at least the possibility for changes in the genetic makeup of an individual for several days after conception (Hellegers, 1970; McCormick, 1991), perhaps up to the point at which twinning can take place. Regardless of when they believe the genetic code is fixed, their ethic is shaped by the belief that full moral standing is contingent on the establishment of the genetically unique individual. This would lead to attributing full moral standing at or near conception no matter which function is critical.

There is one possible exception. If the embryo or fetus has a major defect so that we could determine it could never develop the critical function, then it lacks the potential and would never attain the full moral standing we are discussing. If a fetus is diagnosed as an anencephalic, then holders of a higher-brain view would conclude that the fetus never has the potential for the development of consciousness. Termination of the pregnancy would theoretically be acceptable even for one who was unalterably opposed to abortion of all "living" fetuses. This decision would, of course, require reliance on the higher-brain view and the unique potential view simultaneously. On the other hand, holders of the whole-brain view of which function is critical would still view the anencephalic fetus as having full moral standing. It could not licitly be killed. They would, however, seem logically committed to the view that a fetus so genetically abnormal that had no potential for development of *any* brain function (cerebral or lower) would lack full moral standing. Likewise, the holder of the cardiac or somatic integration view would be committed to the view that a fetus with no potential for any of these functions would lack full moral standing.

HUMAN STEM CELLS

One of the most exciting and controversial developments in recent biology is the emergence of human stem cells as a strategy for medical research and therapy (Gruen, Grabel, and Singer, 2007; *Monitoring Stem Cell Research*, 2008; Monroe, Miller, and Tobis, 2008; National Bioethics Advisory Commission, 1999). Stem cells are undifferentiated cells occurring in multicellular organisms that have the potential to develop into specialized cells of various types. They occur in embryos and in adult organisms and have proven very useful in various kinds of research. They have the potential to be useful in therapy for such diverse conditions as Alzheimer's disease, Parkinson's, strokes, myocardial infarction, and diabetes.

Stem Cells and Moral Standing

Stem cells raise two kinds of moral issues. One arises potentially with both embryonic and adult stem cells. Some people consider that interventions to manipulate the core genetic and cellular structure of humans are too much tampering with nature. They think that generation of replacement cells or organs or conducting research at this level is treading where humans ought not to tread. That issue will be confronted in detail in Chapter 9.

The second issue is more immediate. The production and growth of organisms from stem cells raises issues related to moral standing. That is our focus here. The moral problem arises first in the obtaining of embryonic stem cells. Researchers are also developing the capacity to obtain stem cells from adults (President's Council on Bioethics, 2005), but some insist that embryonic sources are still needed for at least some uses. These come from the inner cell mass of the embryo at the morula or blastocyst stage. This involves destruction of an embryo and thereby the destroying of a human organism that, according to the holders of more conservative views on moral standing, is the immoral killing of a human being. Thus, anyone who is morally opposed to all abortions (even at the earliest stage of embryonic development) would be likely to oppose the destruction of the embryo necessary to obtain embryonic stem cells. Controversy over stem cells is, thus, in part an extension of the controversy over abortion.

A somewhat different issue arises with some efforts to develop stem cells into more differentiated tissues for purposes of research or therapy. The growth of stem cells in some ways produces a new organism, one with the genetic makeup of original stem cell. Whether from adult or a newly formed embryo, some might view the new organism as having enough human characteristics that rights—including potentially the right to life—might be attributed to it.

Stem Cells and Cooperation with Evil

The emergence of stem cells produces a new set of issues for those who would attribute full standing or even high levels of standing less than full to the embryos destroyed in the production of embryonic stem cells. Often the source of these embryos is the in vitro fertilization clinics that intentionally produce human embryos for purposes of treating infertility. Since obtaining the egg cells that are fertilized in these clinics is expensive and burdensome, it is typical that many are procured at the same time. They are fertilized and extras not implanted immediately are stored in case the first efforts fail. This can result in extra embryos not used by the infertile couple that created them.

Assuming that the couple does not wish to donate those extra fertilized eggs for another infertile couple to "adopt" prenatally, these unused embryos would simply be discarded. If, however, they are to be discarded (and thus killed), some might ask whether it would be any more immoral to destroy them in the process of obtaining stem cells and thus creating the possibility that something good would emerge.

Many who would consider the destruction of unwanted embryos immoral would also find the destruction in the process of obtaining stem cells equally unacceptable. Some people, however, might conclude that, as long as the embryos are going to be destroyed anyway, no further wrong is done if they are used as a source of stem cells. Even those who would not themselves be a party to such stem cell procurement may decide that, once the cells have been obtained, it is morally tolerable to make use of cells of a cell line so created.

Critics of the use of embryonic stem cells may argue that the possibility that some good could come from the destruction of the embryos will necessarily add a benign aura to the moral wrong of the original destruction and thus change the moral calculation about obtaining the cells. They may see this as contributing to the condoning of the moral wrong. One who is using the stem cells so obtained is sometimes said to be "cooperating" in the evil of destroying the embryo. There remains some controversy among those who oppose abortion (and thus oppose the destruction of embryos) whether it would be unethical to participate in research on cell lines or in therapies generated by the use of such cell lines. Even if one who is conducting the research had nothing to do with the embryo destruction and was far removed from such activity, there are those who would argue that benefiting down the line would constitute a kind of cooperation that would be unacceptable.

During the administration of George W. Bush, a federal prohibition existed on the use of government funds to create new lines of stem cells although certain cell lines already in existence could still be used in research with federal funding. The Obama administration lifted that ban permitting once again, with certain limits, the production of new cell lines with the use of government funds (Macklin, 2000; Meilaender, 2001).

THE MORAL STATUS OF NON-HUMAN ANIMALS

This discussion of moral standing leads directly into another controversial issue in medicine: the moral status of non-human animals (Council of Europe, 2006; DeGrazia, 2002; Orlans, 1993; Palmer, 2008; Regan and Singer, 1989; Singer, 1975;

Sunstein and Nussbaum, 2004). If clinicians or scientists do research or educational projects using non-human animals, they must confront the question of the moral limits of their use. Radical protestors destroy labs and assault medical personnel fighting over the moral status of non-human animals. In the United States, federal regulations control animal use carefully (U.S. National Institutes of Health, 1985, 1986). The Animal Care and Use Committee must approve animal research just as institutional review boards must approve research on humans.

Do any animals have the "full moral standing" we give to humans, and what would that mean if they did? Western culture has viewed non-human animals as subordinate to humans. They are used for food, medicine, religious ritual, and even sport. This status is reflected in the Judeo-Christian creation story in which humans are to have dominion over the earth and subdue it. This leads to a moral subordination of non-human animals. They are believed to deserve protection from needless suffering, but the interests of humans take precedence. Xenografts (transplantation of organs across species lines) are accepted; in some forms of Judaism they are even imperative. The radical separation between the status of humans and that of animals is seen in the zealous controversy over creation versus evolution. Creationists insist that God has a special relation with humans, who did not merely evolve from other animals.

By contrast, Eastern thought often gives a higher moral status to animals than most Westerners do, and animal suffering causes greater concern. For example, the Hindu doctrine of *ahimsa* (avoidance of suffering) applies to all species. Jains believe no animal should be killed. Their priests actually sweep the ground ahead of them before they walk, to brush insects out of the way.

Western secular thinking has traditionally followed its religious thought in subordinating the moral status of non-human animals, but recently some have taken a different position. Western secular thought is sometimes utilitarian. The focus is exclusively on the amount of good and harm done by an action. Typically, utilitarians treat pain as an evil and pleasure as a good, regardless of the species. An identical kind and quantity of pain counts the same morally regardless of whether it occurs in a human or a non-human. Utilitarians claim that anyone who treats individuals differently solely on the basis of species is guilty of **speciesism** (Singer, 1975). They see it as comparable to racism or sexism or ageism.

Two current views about the moral status of non-humans support concern about animals. One view, the **animal rights perspective** of philosophers such as Tom Regan (1989), holds that sentient animals have a sacredness or right to life just the way humans do. The argument is not driven by concern for consequences. Animals simply have rights, including a right to live. The second position, held by philosophers such as Ray Frey (1989), could be called the "degrees-of-pleasure-and-pain" view. It reflects a **utilitarian perspective**. According to Frey, two animals of different species which experience the same kind and quantity of pain have equal moral claim to be relieved of that pain. But he emphasizes that humans and rats may experience pain differently. Even though a human and a non-human which experienced identical kind and quantity of pain would deserve to be treated equally, if they experience it differently their moral claim would differ.

Frey's view suggests a puzzle: If a chimpanzee has developed mentally to the point that his experiences are richer than those of a severely retarded human, what would justify using the non-human, rather than the human, for research or xenograft or food? How could one defend a priority for the human in such as case? Is species itself a morally defensible dividing line? That is, is speciesism acceptable after all? Or are we prepared to grant to non-human animals which have the functional capacities of severely impaired humans all the moral status we grant humans?

Key Concepts

Cardiac- or Somatic-Oriented Definition of Death   The view that an individual dies when there is irreversible cessation of all cardiac and respiratory functions. If the functions are expanded to include other bodily integrating functions such as digestion, elimination, maintenance of homeostasis, etc., then this is sometimes referred to as the somatic integrating definition of death.

Higher-Brain-Oriented Definition of Death   The view that an individual dies when there is irreversible cessation of all "higher" functions of the brain, often believed to be functions related to consciousness and feelings.

Moral Standing   The status of humans (and other beings) who have moral claims on others or to whom others have duties.

Person (moral definition)   Humans (and other beings) who possess full or maximal moral standing

Person (nonmoral definition)   Humans (and other beings) who possess some critical physical or mental capacity such as self-consciousness, self-awareness, or rationality.

Rights-Based Defense of the Moral Status of Animals   Sentient animals have a sacredness or right to life just the way humans do. The argument is not driven by concern for consequences.

Speciesism   The view in the debate about the moral status of animals that holds that species itself is a morally relevant factor in deciding moral standing, usually in the form of holding that humans, just by being humans, have greater moral standing than non-human animals, even those capable of having similar quantity and quality of experience.

Stem Cells   Cells found in multicellular organisms that are unspecialized and are capable of renewing themselves. Under certain conditions they can become tissue- or organ-specific cells.

Utilitarian Defense of the Moral Status of Animals (the "Degrees of Pleasure and Pain" View)   Animals of different species which experience the same kind and quantity of pleasure or pain have equal moral claim to have the pleasure promoted or to be relieved of that pain.

Whole-Brain-Oriented Definition of Death   The view that an individual dies when there is irreversible cessation of all functions of the entire brain, including the brain stem.

Bibliography

THE DEFINITION OF DEATH

Boucek, Mark M., Christine Mashburn, Susan M. Dunn, Rebecca Frizell, Leah Edwards, Biagio Pietra, and David Campbell, for the Denver Children's Pediatric Heart Transplant Team. "Pediatric Heart Transplantation after Declaration of Cardiocirculatory Death." *New England Journal of Medicine* 359 (2008): 709–714.

Capron, Alexander Morgan. "Death, Definition and Determination of: II. Legal Issues in Pronouncing Death." In *Encyclopedia of Bioethics*, 3rd ed. Ed. Stephen G. Post. New York: Macmillan Reference USA: Thomson/Gale, 2004, pp. 608–615.

Controversies in the Determination of Death: A White Paper by the President's Council on Bioethics. Washington, DC: President's Council on Bioethics, 2008.

Gervais, Karen G. "Death, Definition and Determination of: III. Philosophical and Theological Perspectives." In *Encyclopedia of Bioethics*, 3rd ed. Ed. Stephen G. Post. New York: Macmillan Reference USA: Thomson/Gale, 2004, pp. 615–626.

Harvard Medical School. "A Definition of Irreversible Coma. Report of the Ad Hoc Committee of the Harvard Medical School to Examine the Definition of Brain Death." *Journal of the American Medical Association* 205 (1968): 337–340.

Jonas, Hans. "Against the Stream: Comments on the Definition and Redefinition of Death." *Philosophical Essays: From Ancient Creed to Technological Man.* Englewood Cliffs, NJ: Prentice-Hall, Inc., 1974, pp. 132–140.

Lamb, David. *Death, Brain Death and Ethics.* Albany, NY: The State University of New York Press, 1985.

Law Reform Commission of Canada. *Criteria for the Determination of Death.* Ottawa: Ministry of Supply and Services, 1979.

President's Commission for the Study of Ethical Problems in Medicine and Biomedical and Behavioral Research. *Defining Death: Medical, Legal and Ethical Issues in the Definition of Death.* Washington, DC: U.S. Government Printing Office, 1981.

Shewmon, D. Alan. "The Brain and Somatic Integration: Insights into the Standard Biological Rationale for Equating 'Brain Death' with Death." *Journal of Medicine and Philosophy* 26, No. 5 (2001): 457–478.

Siminoff, Laura A., Chris Burant, and Stuart J. Youngner. "Death and Organ Procurement: Public Beliefs and Attitudes." *Social Science Medicine* 59, No. 11 (December 2004): 2325–2334.

Task Force on Death and Dying, Institute of Society, Ethics and the Life Sciences. "Refinements in Criteria for the Determination of Death: An Appraisal." *Journal of the American Medical Association* 221 (1972): 48–53.

Veatch, Robert M. "The Whole-Brain-Oriented Concept of Death: An Outmoded Philosophical Formulation." *Journal of Thanatology* 3 (1975): 13–30.

Youngner, Stuart J., Robert M. Arnold, and Renie Schapiro, eds. *The Definition of Death: Contemporary Controversies.* Baltimore, MD: Johns Hopkins University Press, 1999.

ABORTION

Beckwith, Francis J. *Defending Life: A Moral and Legal Case Against Abortion Choice.* Cambridge/New York: Cambridge University Press, 2007.

Callahan, Daniel. *Abortion: Law, Choice and Morality.* New York: Macmillan, 1970.

Dworkin, Ronald. *Life's Dominion: An Argument about Abortion, Euthanasia, and Individual Freedom.* New York: Vintage Books, 1994.

Feinberg, Joel, ed. *The Problem of Abortion.* Belmont, CA: Wadsworth, 1973.

Hellegers, A. "Fetal Development." *Theological Studies* 31 (March 1970): 3–9.

McCormick, Richard A. "Who or What Is the Preembryo?" *Kennedy Institute of Ethics Journal* 1 (1991): 1–15, esp. 4, 9, 11–12.

Noonan, John T. *The Morality of Abortion: Legal and Historical Perspectives.* Cambridge, MA: Harvard University Press, 1970.

STEM CELLS

Gruen, Lori, Laura Grabel, and Peter Singer, eds. *Stem Cell Research: The Ethical Issues.* Malden, MA: Blackwell Publishing, 2007.

Macklin, Ruth. "Ethics, Politics, and Human Embryo Stem Cell Research." *Women's Health Issues* 10, No. 3 (May–June 2000): 111–115.

Meilaender, Gilbert. "The Point of a Ban. Or, How to Think about Stem Cell Research." *Hastings Center Report* 31, No. 1 (January–February 2001): 9–16.

Monitoring Stem Cell Research: A Report of the President's Council on Bioethics. Washington, DC: President's Council on Bioethics, 2008.

Monroe, Kristin Renwick, Ronald B. Miller, and Jerome Tobis, eds. In *Fundamentals of the Stem Cell Debate: The Scientific, Religious, Ethical, and Political Issues.* Berkeley, CA: University of California Press, 2008.

National Bioethics Advisory Commission. *Ethical Issues in Human Stem Cell Research Volume I: Report and Recommendations of the National Bioethics Advisory Commission.* Rockville, MD: National Bioethics Advisory Commission, September 1999.

MORAL STANDING OF NON-HUMAN ANIMALS

Council of Europe. *Animal Welfare.* Strasbourg: Council of Europe, 2006.

DeGrazia, David. *Animal Rights: A Very Short Introduction.* Oxford/New York: Oxford University Press, 2002.

Frey, R. G. "The Case Against Animal Rights." In *Animal Rights and Human Obligations,* 2nd ed. Ed. Tom Regan and Peter Singer. Englewood Cliffs, NJ: Prentice Hall, 1989, pp. 115–118.

National Research Council (United States). Commission on Life Sciences. Institute of Animal Resources. *Guide for the Care and Use of Laboratory Animals.* Washington, DC: National Academy Press, 1996.

Orlans, F. Barbara. *In the Name of Science: Issues in Responsible Animal Experimentation.* New York: Oxford University Press, 1993.

Orlans, F. Barbara, et al. *The Human Use of Animals: Case Studies in Ethical Choice.* New York: Oxford University Press, 1998.

Palmer, Clare, ed. *Animal Rights.* Aldershot, Hampshire, England/Burlington, VT: Ashgate, 2008.

President's Council on Bioethics. *Alternative Sources of Human Pluripotent Stem Cells.* Washington, DC: President's Council on Bioethics, 2005.

Regan, Tom, and Peter Singer, eds. *Animal Rights and Human Obligations,* 2nd ed. Englewood Cliffs, NJ: Prentice Hall, 1989.

Regan, Tom. "The Case for Animal Rights." In *Animal Rights and Human Obligation,* 2nd ed. Ed. Tom Regan and Peter Singer. Englewood Cliffs, NJ: Prentice Hall, 1989, pp. 105–114.

Singer, Peter. *Animal Liberation: A New Ethics For Our Treatment of Animals.* New York: Avon Books, 1975.

Sunstein, Cass R., and Martha C. Nussbaum, eds. *Animal Rights: Current Debates and New Directions.* Oxford/New York: Oxford University Press, 2004.

U.S. National Institutes of Health. "Laboratory Animal Welfare: Public Health Service Policy on Humane Care and Use of Laboratory Animals by Awardee Institutions; Notice." *Federal Register* 50, No. 90 (May 9, 1985): 19584–19585.

U.S. National Institutes of Health. Office for Protection from Research Risks. *Public Health Service Policy on Humane Care and Use of Laboratory Animals.* Bethesda, MD: Office for Protection from Research Risks, September 28, 1986.

U.S. President's Council on Bioethics. *Controversies in the Determination of Death: A White Paper by the President's Council on Bioethics.* Washington, DC: President's Council on Bioethics, 2008.

Notes

1. Denmark has an ongoing debate. It has been the primary site of controversy on this issue in Europe. In Denmark it is legal to pronounce death by brain criteria, but some scholars and policy makers there are not willing to accept that conclusion.

Problems in Benefiting and Avoiding Harm to the Patient

4

Historically, ethics for the health professions has been dominated by the maxim of the Hippocratic Oath: Benefit the patient and protect the patient from harm. In later chapters we shall see that much of biomedical ethics of the past generation has been devoted to questioning that it is always wise or morally appropriate to follow that maxim. We shall see that there are times when many believe it would be morally wrong to benefit the patient (e.g., when the patient has not consented to the benefit or when protecting from harm might involve intentionally killing the patient out of mercy). There are times when social concerns may legitimately challenge the health professional who would try to do everything possible for the patient.

COMPLICATIONS IN DETERMINING WHAT BENEFITS PATIENTS

Even if a health professional decided to remain committed to the Hippocratic principle of benefiting the patient and protecting the patient from harm, he or she would still face some serious problems. Some of these problems are increasingly difficult to solve. Four areas of concern are particularly troublesome: the subjective nature of the Hippocratic commitment, the trade-offs that must be made between medical and other elements of personal welfare, the different kinds of medical benefit that a physician might pursue, and different strategies for combining assessments of benefits and harms to reach a single course of treatment. Following the discussion of these four issues, we will need to confront the problem of paternalism to decide whether it is always morally right to benefit the patient.

Subjective Versus Objective Estimates of Benefit and Harm

First, if a health professional is to be Hippocratic and work only for the welfare of the patient, he or she must face the problem of whether to rely on subjective or objective assessments of benefit. A judgment of benefit is *subjective* if it is based on the perspective of the one who is making the assessment. On the other hand, a judgment can be considered *objective* if it would be true regardless of who was making it. There is considerable dispute over whether valuative judgments (such as judgments about whether something is a good or a harm) can be thought to be objective at all. Some people believe that, by their very nature, value judgments are always subjective. They might define the "good" as "desired by the speaker" or as "preferred by the speaker." Others believe that at least some values are objective, that certain states are good or bad independent of anyone making the assessment. If we believe that some value judgments, including some medical value judgments, can be objective, we might seek to discern what is truly a good outcome. We might do this by trying to eliminate or at least neutralize biases and special perspectives when we decide what a good outcome would be. We might do this, for example, by involving many different people in the assessment, by using the consensus of a large group of people rather than relying solely on the judgment of an individual physician about what counts as a good outcome.

For our purposes, the important point is that there are different ways of assessing how good or bad an outcome is. If we are striving to determine what is objectively good, we will probably use a different method of assessing than if we are striving to determine the good subjectively. In the case of subjective assessments, in medicine we have traditionally relied on the physician's judgment, but, as we shall see later, we might also consider the judgment of the patient or some other party.

CASE 5

The Physician Who Favors Hysterectomies

Dr. Morton Westerman is a gynecologist who has been in practice for thirty years. He sees an ambiguous pap smear with some abnormal cell development, something that he has seen for thirty years. In such cases his rule is: When in doubt, do a hysterectomy. Recently his professional peers have done studies that reveal that there is no documentation that a hysterectomy does any good in these circumstances. But Dr. Westerman has been in practice for a long time, and his gut feeling is that it is better for this woman to have a hysterectomy—better to be safe than sorry. The Hippocratic Oath tells us that the physician is to benefit the patient according to the physician's ability and judgment. Thus, the oath is telling Dr. Westerman that, even if his colleagues disagree with his clinical judgment and have an abundance of empirical studies and data to support their position, it is his moral duty to do what he thinks is beneficial. Should he follow his own judgment or that of his peers?

The view that the physician should decide on the basis of subjective criteria grounded in his or her own judgment is increasingly hard to defend today. In fact, Dr. Westerman could be sued for malpractice for doing a hysterectomy that none of his colleagues thinks is worth doing. The mere fact that he believes something subjectively is not enough to settle the matter.

One can refer to the approach in which the physician bases a decision about patient benefit on his or her own judgment as **subjective Hippocratic utility**. *Utility* refers to assessments of benefit and harm. The principle of *utility* holds that an action is morally right insofar as it increases net utility, that is, the net amount of good taking into account the harm that may be done as well. Sometimes the benefits and the harms are considered separately, and we then refer to the principles of **beneficence** and **nonmaleficence** (that actions are, respectively, morally right insofar as they increase the good and avoid harm). *Beneficence* is the philosopher's word that simply means doing the good. *Nonmaleficence* means avoiding doing harm. Taken together we can speak of utility. Subjective Hippocratic utility, then, is based on the clinician's individual judgment.

Figure 8 shows that the principles of medical ethics can be formulated with two dichotomous variables. The two columns of the chart represent the fact that some ethics are **consequentialist** (meaning they focus on producing benefits and avoiding harms, doing good and avoiding evil), whereas others are **duty-based** (i.e., they hold that some actions are morally required as one's duty regardless of the consequences). This latter group of ethics is sometimes called **deontological ethics**, which is a term derived from the Greek word for duty. The Hippocratic ethic is consequentialist in that it focuses on benefiting the patient. Both consequentialist and duty-based ethics can apply either to the individual or to the society or community. Hippocratic utility is individual and consequentialist. The physician's duty is to pay attention only to consequences, but only for the individual patient.

The individual, consequentialist quadrant, that is, the upper left quadrant of the two-by-two table, is labeled Hippocratic utility. The original form of Hippocratic utility is subjective. The clinician's judgment is what counts. Increasingly, this emphasis on personal physician judgment is being replaced with a more **objective form of Hippocratic utility** in which judgment of outcomes are based on peer review,

	Consequentialist Principles	Duty-Based Principles
Individual	Subjective 1. Beneficence 2. Nonmaleficence —Hippocratic Utility— Objective 1. Beneficence 2. Nonmaleficence	
Social		

FIGURE 8 Where Hippocratic Utility Fits in a Grid of Types of Ethical Principles

utilization review, quality assurance, outcomes research, and treatment protocols—all examples of more collegial consensus about what the objective consequences of a particular treatment decision will be. If the consensus of his colleagues is that there is no evidence that a hysterectomy would have an effect on the patient, the more modern form of Hippocratic utility requires the clinician not to do the hysterectomy. He must be guided and influenced by the more objective data about outcomes. This is no major moral change. It is still consequentialist, and it still focuses on the individual patient. But now the clinician is no longer the sole standard of benefit. There is normally no reason to assume, according to this new view, that the individual physician's judgment of benefit is right when his or her colleagues disagree.

There is a remaining problem: Even if the community of clinicians can agree on an outcome, it must still evaluate whether the outcome is beneficial. Even if the determination of the outcome can be considered a matter about which the medical community has expertise and can strive to determine objectively, evaluating how good or how bad an outcome is turns out to be a different matter. What happens if the entire medical profession reaches a consensus about what is beneficial that conflicts with the convictions of other groups or individuals in the society?

Physicians must not only estimate the outcome of the hysterectomy (the decrease in probability that the patient will develop uterine cancer), but also whether that decrease in the risk of cancer is worth the psychological and physical effects on the woman. Deciding how good it is to reduce the risk of cancer and how bad the side effects are involves value judgments. There is no reason to assume that the value judgments of the community of physicians are the correct ones. Maybe the physicians place unusually high value on reducing the risk of cancer or judge the side effects, such as the loss of reproductive capacity, to be less harmful than others in the society.

Here an important distinction must be made. The claim that a hysterectomy is beneficial really involves two different kinds of propositions. First, it involves an empirical claim about medical science: that the operation will reduce the probability of the patient developing cancer of the uterus. That is a scientific claim about which we generally recognize an expertise. Physicians and other medical scientists are usually presumed to be more expert in judging such factual claims. It is these kinds of scientific claims about which objective evidence, peer review, and outcomes research are considered legitimate.

But the claim that hysterectomy will benefit the patient also involves a second proposition: that the outcome of the surgery will produce a change that is beneficial. Sometimes the judgment that the outcome of medical intervention is beneficial may be obvious, but that is not always the case. For example, a hysterectomy has the potential not only to reduce the risk of cancer developing, but also can have profound side effects—leaving a woman unable to bear children, changing her capacity for sexual relations, and producing potentially serious psychological effects. Deciding that these side effects are justified by some reduction in risk of cancer is not something medical science can determine. It is a value judgment pure and simple. It is not an issue about which physicians or other experts and medical science can be expected to be authorities.

Thus there are two separate questions at stake here. The first, determining the effects of the hysterectomy, is increasingly seen as requiring an objective standard. Recent years have seen a shift from a subjective basis rooted in the individual physician's judgment to a more objective basis as articulated by a physician's peers, in the scientific literature, and in the peer review process. The second issue is how people should go about making judgments about the value of the expected outcomes. One pattern has been a shift away from relying on the subjective value judgments of the individual physician in favor of more objective standards of evaluation, such as by relying on a consensus of medical experts. But simultaneously, critics are questioning whether even a community of clinicians can be relied upon to make these value judgments objectively. Even if peer review is gaining acceptance as the standard for making scientific determinations of outcomes, that peer review is increasingly questioned when it comes to making the judgments of the value of the agreed-upon outcomes. The patient's own evaluation is increasingly given priority over either that of the individual clinician or that of the physician community as a whole. (For a full discussion of this problem, see Veatch, 2009.)

Medical Versus Other Personal Benefits

There is a second problem. Is the goal really to promote the total well-being of the patient? Or is the goal to promote only *medical* well-being? Either way, there is a major problem for a physician. If the goal is total well-being, no physician can be expected to be able to be skilled in all aspects of living well. Total well-being involves all aspects of a person's life: education, religion, social relations, aesthetics, entertainment, and plumbing, for example. But if the goal of the physician is medical well-being, one has to recognize that no rational patient wants to maximize his or her medical well-being. People have goals for well-being that have nothing to do with their health. Health is an important goal, but not the only one. Sometimes marginal gains in medical well-being can come at the price of serious losses in other spheres. Sometimes those small medical gains are simply not worth it to the patient. What should the physician do when patients say they understand that a certain behavior—smoking or eating fatty foods or mountain climbing—is not good for their medical well-being, but that they nevertheless get such pleasure from it that the medical risks are justified? If the physician's duty, following the Hippocratic Oath, is to promote the total well-being of the patient, he or she should recognize that determining what will maximize the patient's total well-being requires skill well beyond that of the ordinary health care professional. Patients may not need the physician's medical skills to increase their well-being; they may need a chef, an art critic, a book salesman, or a television repair person. In some cases they may even be willing to take some risks with their medical well-being in order to promote their total well-being.

Suppose that the circle in Figure 9 represents total personal well-being. This pie can be divided into several slices, or subspheres, of well-being. Let's call one organic and another psychological. There are also legal, economic, religious, social, and aesthetic areas of well-being, as well as others that are grouped in one subsphere. According to the Hippocratic formula, the physician's duty is to promote the total well-being of the patient. But that is an unrealistic demand in light of the skills that physicians possess. No one pretends that a physician will be an expert on aesthetic, religious, and economic well-being as well as medical. On the other hand, if a physician focuses only on organic well-being, he or she is obviously attending to only one area of the patient's concerns.[1]

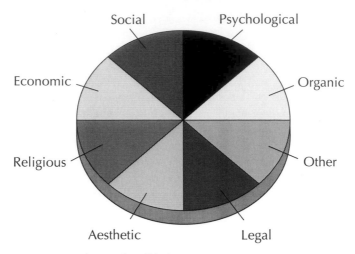

FIGURE 9   Spheres of Well-being

It becomes increasingly clear that it would be irrational for the patient always to maximize one sector of this pie at the expense of the others.

At first, one might be inclined to reject this conclusion. We sometimes think we need to follow the physician's recommendation about what will maximize our health in order to be able to enjoy any other spheres of well-being. But that really is not true. Consider a person who is diagnosed as suffering from diabetes. Imagine what a physician would recommend if she were committed to doing literally what was medically best for the patient. The absolutely best course might include an impossibly strict diet, a terribly disrupting exercise program, frequent monitoring of blood sugar, and perhaps multiple daily injections of insulin to maintain tight control. Now a rational person would take these recommendations seriously and would try to comply with most of them most of the time. But no rational person would at all times follow what is literally the perfect diet; no one would monitor blood sugar quite as often as the best possible regimen. If the physician recommends what is absolutely the best possible course, the reasonable patient will perhaps come close to following those recommendations, but will back off a little from time to time in order to accomplish other valued experiences in life.

The reasonable person will also be receiving advice from advisors in other spheres of life: from a lawyer, dentist, accountant, clergyperson, insurance agent, auto mechanic, and so on. If each recommended literally what was best in their sphere, the poor person would face impossibly complex demands—probably consuming more time than is available in a normal day. Moreover, no obviously correct formula exists for exactly how much one should back away from the recommended course for making one's life "best" in each sphere. One thing is clear, however: No person will lead an ideally perfect life in any sphere if the goal is to maximize overall well-being rather than merely well-being in one sphere.

It is the patient's job to balance these spheres against one another so that the total size of the pie, or total well-being, is as large as possible.

In contrast to the Hippocratic Oath, members of the World Medical Association pledge to work only for the *health* of their patients. The problem here is that if they focus on only one piece of well-being, they have to recognize that rational patients will trade off that piece against all the others. The total resources a person needs to maximize well-being in all spheres are going to exceed the total available. The rational patient will have to conclude that the advice given by a physician targeted on maximizing health is advice that ought not to be followed completely. Whether the goal is medical well-being or total well-being, all professional advisors have to realize that rational patients should not follow professional advice completely.

Conflicting Goals Within the Medical Sphere

A third problem that Hippocratic physicians will face is deciding what counts as a benefit within the medical, or organic, sphere. Even if we accept the position that the physician's duty is to focus on medical benefits, no consensus exists about what counts as a medical benefit. The notion of medical benefit turns out to be incredibly vague. As seen in Figure 10, there are no fewer than four different goals that a physician or a patient may want to pursue. Before about 1960, the gold standard was that the purpose of medicine was to preserve life. It had not always been that way, but for most of the twentieth century that was the goal. On this basis, keeping oxygen flowing into permanently unconscious Yusef Camp's lungs would count as a benefit. This notion had become controversial by the late 1960s.

In addition to preventing death, medicine strives to cure disease, relieve suffering, and promote the well-being of the patient. The problem is that sometimes one cannot accomplish all four of these goals in a given patient at the same time. The only way to relieve suffering in the metastatic cancer patient with pneumonia may be to withhold the penicillin and let the patient die. The goal of preserving life has not been achieved, but the goal of relieving suffering has.

No definitive way exists to combine all four of these goals of medicine into a single all-purpose goal that will indicate definitively what the health professional ought to do for each patient. Some may see it one way; some another. Different

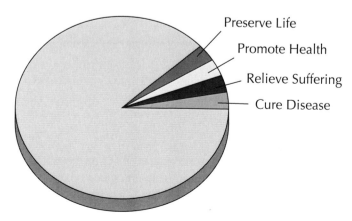

FIGURE 10 Elements of Medical Well-being

physicians will balance these goals differently just as patients will. Even if there are objective facts upon which a physician must base judgments about possible outcomes of treatments, there may be no such thing as an objective, factual way to determine which types of benefits to pursue or no definitive way to correctly balance these four competing medical goals.

Ways to Balance Benefits and Harms

Even if the decision maker determines whether to pursue subjective or objective benefits, whether to pursue total well-being or only medical, and which medical goals deserve priority, there is still a fourth problem in assessing benefits. For each possible intervention alternative, the benefits and harms have to be combined in some way (at least by rough intuition) into a single estimate so that the clinician can attempt to do that which produces the best outcome. But there is no single definitive way for these benefit and harm estimates to be combined. At least three major possibilities exist.

BENTHAM AND ARITHMETIC SUMMING   Jeremy Bentham was a late-eighteenth-century philosopher who is often considered the father of **utilitarianism**, the moral philosophy that is committed to the view that the correct action or rule is the one that produces the best consequences. Classical utilitarianism is like Hippocratic ethics except that, while Hippocratic utility focuses only on the individual patient, classical utilitarians would consider the effects on all parties. Classical utilitarianism is thus **social consequentialism**. Its proponents often put forward a specific method of calculating net benefits (sometimes called utilitarian or Benthamite "calculus").

Bentham proposed that a decision maker should consider the amount of benefit to each person affected and then the amount of harm. The envisioned harm should then be subtracted from the benefit to reach a net figure for that individual. After repeating this calculation for each person affected, the individual numbers should be summed to get an overall estimate of the effect of that option. Then the whole process should be repeated for every alternative course being considered—for example, every treatment option. The decision maker morally ought to choose the option with the greatest net aggregate good consequences.

In one form of Hippocratic medicine, the same process of combining estimated benefits and harms is undertaken except that the estimate is made only of the net benefit to the individual patient. Properly speaking, this should be undertaken after deciding whether it is medical good or total good to be estimated and after deciding what counts as medical good. The method used in each case is adding and subtracting. Hence, the approach is referred to as "arithmetic."

COMPARING THE RATIO OF BENEFITS TO HARMS   Adding and subtracting is not the only way one could determine what course is the most beneficial. Some would prefer to compare ratios of benefits to harms. Consider the following problem faced by a physician who is contemplating placing her patient into a randomized clinical trial of a new chemotherapeutic combination for her patient's cancer.

CASE 6

Risks and Benefits in a Randomized Clinical Trial

Dr. Sally Satherwaite had cared for Mr. Jerome Jenkins for some years. He had been diagnosed with cancer of the prostate two years ago. Dr. Satherwaite was in contact with the Oncology Center of a nearby teaching hospital, which had offered to place Mr. Jenkins in a randomized clinical trial.

If he entered the trial he would be placed in either the standard treatment (control) group or the group given an experimental combination of potent new agents. The standard treatment posed only minor risks, but, unfortunately, offered only modest benefits. Two-year survival rates were as low as 3 percent. Based on this information, Dr. Satherwaite figured that the benefits were nonetheless greater than the risks—perhaps two times as great. If she had only the standard treatment available, she would recommend it to Mr. Jenkins.

The experimental agent was more promising. Preliminary data showed better two-year survival rates, perhaps ten times as great. Unfortunately, the side effects were also greater, about ten times as bad as the standard treatment. Mr. Jenkins asked her for her recommendation about whether to enter the trial.

On the basis of Dr. Satherwaite's estimates, the standard treatment has an expected benefit that is twice the expected harm (considering both severity and probability). But so does the experimental treatment. The clinician could view this as a choice between two options, which, if we used some imaginary unit of benefit and harm, could be said to offer the choice presented in Figure 11.

One choice has a benefit of 2 and harm of −1. The other choice has a benefit of 20 and a harm of −10. Of course these are only rough intuitive estimates, but often that is all the bedside clinician has to go on.

If Dr. Satherwaite follows Bentham's method of calculating, subtracting harms from benefits in each case, she reaches the surprising conclusion that the standard treatment has a net good of one while the experimental treatment has a net good of ten. In general, when comparing high-risk/high-gain options with low-risk/low-gain ones, the difference between plausible alternatives will be greater in the high-risk/high-gain option. Bentham's arithmetic combining has the surprising effect of tending to

	Standard	Experimental
Benefits	2 units	20 units
Harms	1 unit	10 units

FIGURE 11 High-Risk/High-Gain vs. Low-Risk/Low-Gain Therapy Choices

favor more aggressive interventions. Dr. Satherwaite would probably urge Mr. Jenkins to enter the trial with the hope of getting the experimental treatment. She might even try to get it for him off protocol so he does not have the risk of being randomized to the standard treatment.

However, Dr. Satherwaite might try to integrate her estimate in a different way. She could calculate the ratio of benefits to harms in each case. Strikingly, she would find that the ratios of benefit to harm for the two options are the same. She would presumably be at the "indifference point" (the point at which she had no basis for favoring one treatment or the other) and, since she has no basis for preferring one or the other options, might endorse entry into the trial on a randomized basis. It is when benefit/harm ratios of treatment options seem the same that many consider the randomized trial to be morally acceptable. Likewise, many health planners attempt to arrange limited health resources so as to maximize the ratio of benefits to harms. Because it uses ratios, this method of combining benefits and harms is sometimes called "geometric." (This method of allocating scarce resources will be discussed further in Chapter 8.)

FIRST OF ALL, DO NO HARM   There is still a third possibility for combining benefits and harms that is even more conservative than using ratios. The folk ethics of physicians often includes the slogan *primum non nocere* or "first of all, do no harm." It is a slogan popular among physicians and is meant to address problems of comparing benefits and harms of alternative treatments. It gives priority to avoiding harms. Often it is presumed to come from the Hippocratic Oath, but, as we have already seen, all the oath says is to benefit *and* do no harm; a coordinating conjunction indicates no priority for avoiding harm. Those who have looked for the origins of this slogan cannot find it prior to the nineteenth century, at which time medicine began to realize that sometimes physicians' interventions caused harm rather than good (Jonsen, 1978; Sandulescu, 1965; Veatch, 1991). A recent publication claims that it dates back only to 1860 (Smith, 2005), a time when physicians were beginning to realize that their treatments (such as bloodletting and mercury tablets) often hurt patients severely.

Giving priority to avoiding harm, clearly, is the most conservative of all the methods of combining benefits and harms. It implies pursuing good for the patient only if one has ruled out the possibility of harming. If loyal to this particular method, Dr. Satherwaite would have a clear preference for the standard treatment. She would direct her attention to the second line of the table in Figure 11, paying attention to minimizing the amount of harm. In fact, taken to the extreme, she would not even recommend the standard treatment, since it would pose the risk of at least some harm. Locking oneself in the office and never doing anything would guarantee that no harm would be done. Of course, much good would be foregone as well.

Perhaps what some who invoke the *primum non nocere* slogan mean is that the physician should *intend* no harm. That would at least be more plausible than an instruction to *do* no harm. This is part of the idea behind what is sometimes called the *doctrine of double effect*, a notion we shall discuss in Chapter 6. If that is what is meant, it is quite different from the injunction to do no harm; much harm can be done even if it is not intended. The doctrine of double effect holds that harms may even be foreseen and still be morally tolerable provided they were not intended.

We are left with the question of whether a physician can ever be permitted to do harm in the process of doing good for patients and, if so, how one ought to combine the benefits and the harms: whether one should look at the arithmetic result, calculate ratios, or give an absolute priority to avoiding harm. None of these methods of combining benefits and harms is obviously the correct one. Different physicians and patients with different risk aversiveness will use different methods. It seems that, even if the data with which physicians can predict outcomes could be made more or less objective through peer review, there is, in principle, no way that quantifying benefits and harms and combining those into an integrated estimate of the value of alternatives can be made objective. In such cases a critical question is whether it is the physician's judgment that should count rather than the judgment of the professional group, the larger social community, or the individual patient.

THE PROBLEM OF MEDICAL PATERNALISM

In addition to the practical problems of identifying which types of benefits and harms count and how they should be compared, a serious moral issue raised by the Hippocratic ethic has come to light in the current generation of medical ethics. We have seen that there are good reasons why the typical physician, especially one who does not know the patient well, ought not to be able to figure out what will benefit the patient. If different people have different values and priories, it would be expecting too much for even the very talented and dedicated physician to be able to figure out what will really promote the patient's well-being the most. But even if the physician can succeed in that difficult task, there still remains a problem. The Hippocratic ethic, even at its best, is paternalistic.

Paternalism, as we saw in Chapter 1, is an action taken to benefit a person and done for the welfare of that person, but against his or her will. It should not be assumed that all paternalistic actions are necessarily immoral. Most people, for example, favor some instances of what is often called "weak" paternalism, that is, paternalism regarding persons who are not (or may not be) mentally competent to make substantially autonomous choices—small children, the severely mentally retarded, and the incapacitated, for example. Moreover, even among those who usually find "strong" paternalism (i.e., paternalism toward those who are substantially autonomous) morally troublesome, there may be overriding considerations that could justify it.

The Hippocratic Oath tells the clinician, whether using his own personal judgment or that of peers, to do what appears to benefit the patient. The oath does not require the patient to be in agreement. In fact, the patient may not even want the benefit offered. Other ethical systems have other principles that move beyond consideration of the consequences to the patient. These other principles may require that physicians, in some circumstances, refrain from trying to benefit the patient. One such principle is the principle of autonomy, which requires respecting the patient's right to be self-determining.

Medical paternalism is rampant in the old Hippocratic tradition. The health care professional was instructed to do what is beneficial according to his ability and judgment. It did not factor in benefit based on the patients' judgment of what was good. It did not consider the possibility that the patient might have a right to choose even if that choice did not produce the most good for the patient.

The Hippocratic Oath says that the physician should benefit the patient and protect him or her from harm. However, scholars have asked, "What is this harm with which the Hippocratic position is concerned?" Some suggested that it was harm instigated by enemies. In Greek medicine, occasionally an enemy of the patient would bribe a physician to prescribe a medicine for the patient that was actually a poison. But it is not a great moral insight if the Hippocratic tradition merely requires that one not take bribes from the patients' enemy in order to poison the patient. In fact, there is no historical evidence that this is what the Hippocratic author meant. Another possibility is somewhat more promising. Sometimes the Hippocratic Oath is interpreted to mean that patients may have family and friends that come around in a time of illness who mean well, but actually do more harm than good. Remember the view of knowledge in the Pythagorean system: Well-meaning uneducated do-gooders may do more harm than good. So when lay people gather around the patient and start to make recommendations, it is the physician's duty, according to this interpretation, to make sure they do not harm the patient unintentionally.

That at least makes a little more sense, but there is no evidence that that is what the Hippocratic writer meant, either. Edelstein (1967), the scholar mentioned earlier, believes that what the Hippocratic author meant was that the physician's duty is to protect patients from harm that patients may do to themselves. Remember, the patient is ignorant; he or she does not have the knowledge that comes with initiation into the cult.

The best interpretation of the Hippocratic Oath was that the physician's duty was to protect patients from themselves. Even if one shifts to a more objective standard of what counts as a benefit by using peer review, one still may end up being paternalistic. The peers may not reach the same conclusion about the hysterectomy that the patient reaches. And to the extent that modern philosophical thought is skeptical about paternalism, problems will arise in taking the Hippocratic Oath at face value. To get us oriented toward the alternative to Hippocratic beneficence, consider the following case that arose in 1970 just as birth control began to be widely used and medical paternalism emerged as problematic. It is a case that changed the history of medical ethics, at least in the Anglo-American West.

CASE 7

Is Birth Control Bad for One's Health?

In 1970 Doctor Robert Browne, a kindly, 63-year-old British general practitioner, had been the family physician of a 16-year-old woman since this young woman's birth. This young woman thought she should get some contraceptive counseling. She realized that Dr. Browne might not look too favorably upon this plan, so she went to a place called the Birmingham Brook Advisory Centre. This was a local birth control counseling clinic. She got contraceptive counseling, a physical examination, and a prescription for oral contraceptives. It is standard medical practice to inform a family physician if one writes a prescription for someone who normally sees another physician. The clinic's physician asked if he could notify her physician, Dr. Browne. Perhaps without thinking, she gave her approval.

Dr. Browne received in the mail, unsolicited, a letter informing him that his patient was on the pill. Dr. Browne expressed two concerns. First, he was concerned about her pharmacological well-being. In 1970 the pill had not been on the market very long. Nobody understood what the effects might be, especially in a 16-year-old. But he was also worried about her total well-being: in particular, about what he called her "moral health."

Dr. Browne consulted with some colleagues, got their advice, and finally came up with a plan. One day when the young woman's father was in the doctor's office, Dr. Browne told him the whole story.

The young woman was not pleased with this turn of events. The clinic physician was not pleased either. Dr. Browne was charged before the General Medical Council in Great Britain with the violation of patient confidentiality (General Medical Council, 1971). Dr. Browne in his defense introduced two documents: the Hippocratic Oath and the British Medical Association (BMA) code. The oath says that the physician should not disclose "that which should not be spread abroad." That, in turn, has traditionally been interpreted as confirming the core Hippocratic principle, that his moral duty is to do what he thinks will benefit the patient. Likewise, the BMA code explicitly permitted disclosures when doing so was believed to be for the benefit of the patient. Dr. Browne, having struggled with his conscience and consulted with colleagues, claimed he did what he thought was best for his patient. He may have had a somewhat archaic view about what would benefit her, but he really believed that this was the most beneficial course. Should the General Medical Council exonerate him?

Dr. Browne was acquitted of any violation of the British standard of confidentiality. He followed both the Hippocratic Oath and the British medical code. If he had been an American physician, he could have consulted the American Medical Association code in effect at the time. This code was consistent with the Hippocratic Oath and British code: The physician's duty was to keep confidence with certain exceptions, including when the physician believes that it is in the patient's interest to disclose.

The current generation of medical ethics has seen a dramatic move away from Hippocratic paternalism toward a new set of principles, based on duty rather than maximizing good consequences for the patient.[2] When dealing with the individual patient, these principles involve respect for autonomy, fidelity to promises, veracity, and sometimes, the duty of avoiding killing. Sometimes they are collected together under the heading "respect for persons." These duty-based principles give physicians much less leeway to act paternalistically. Together they offer an alternative to Hippocratic beneficence when dealing at the level of the individual. In the next chapter, we shall see how the first three of these principles affect the patient–physician relation. The fourth, avoiding killing, will be the subject of Chapter 6.

Key Concepts

Beneficence   The moral principle that actions or practices are right insofar as they produce good consequences (cf. Nonmaleficence).

Consequentialist Ethics   Normative ethical theories that focus on producing good consequences (see Hippocratic Ethics; Social Consequentialist Ethics; Utilitarianism).

Deontological (Duty-Based) Ethics   Any of a group of normative ethical theories that base assessment of rightness or wrongness of actions on duties or "inherent right-making characteristics" of actions or rules rather than on consequences. (See also Formalism [Key Concepts, Chapter 5]. Compare Duty-Based Principles; Consequentialism)

Duty-Based Principles   Ethical principles based on formal obligations to act in certain ways toward others regardless of the consequences. These are sometimes referred to as "deontological," a term derived from the Greek term for duty. Among the deontological or duty-based principles are fidelity, autonomy, veracity, and avoidance of killing (sometimes collectively referred to as the principles of "respect for persons") as well as the social ethical principle of justice. See Justice (Key Concepts, Chapter 8).

Hippocratic Ethics   Consequentialist ethics that limits the relevant consequences to those that affect the individual patient.

Nonmaleficence   The moral principle that actions or practices are right insofar as they avoid producing bad consequences (cf. Beneficence).

Objective Hippocratic Utility   The principle that the physician should benefit the patient and protect the patient from harm as the benefits and harms are determined by standards that are objective rather than based on the physician's personal judgments (cf. Subjective Hippocratic Utility).

Paternalism   Action taken to benefit another person done for the welfare of that person, but against his or her will. "Strong paternalism" involves taking such action even though the individual benefited is mentally competent; "weak paternalism" involves actions taken for the benefit of an individual who is either known to be incompetent or who is suspected of being so.

Social (or Classical) Consequentialist Ethics   Consequentialist ethics that include all consequences for all parties affected by an action.

Subjective Hippocratic Utility   The principle that the physician should benefit the patient and protect the patient from harm as the benefits and harms are determined by the physician (cf. Objective Hippocratic Utility).

Utilitarianism   The normative ethical theory that is committed to the view that the correct action or rule is the one that produces the best consequences considering all parties affected; often limited to those forms of consequential ethics that envision calculations of anticipated benefits and harms by subtracting expected amount and probability of harm from expected amount and probability of benefit for each affected party and then summing the net benefits for all those affected.

Bibliography

Bentham, Jeremy. "An Introduction to the Principles of Morals and Legislation." In *Ethical Theories: A Book of Readings*, ed. A. I. Melden. Englewood Cliffs, NJ: Prentice-Hall, 1967, pp. 367–390.

Edelstein, Ludwig. "The Hippocratic Oath: Text, Translation and Interpretation." *Ancient Medicine: Selected Papers of Ludwig Edelstein*, ed. Owsei Temkin and C. Lilian Temkin. Baltimore, MD: The Johns Hopkins Press, 1967, pp. 3–64.

"General Medical Council: Disciplinary Committee." *British Medical Journal* Supplement, No. 3442 (March 20, 1971): 79–80.

Jonsen, Albert R. "Do No Harm." *Annals of Internal Medicine* 88 (1978): 827–32.

Kamm, F. M. *Intricate Ethics: Rights, Responsibilities, and Permissible Harm*. Oxford/New York: Oxford University Press, 2007.

Katz, Jay. *The Silent World of Doctor and Patient*. Baltimore, MD: Johns Hopkins University Press, 2002.

Sandulescu, C. "*Primum non nocere*: Philological Commentaries on a Medical Aphorism." *Acta Antiqua Hungarica* 13 (1965): 359–368.

Smith, Cedric M. "Origin and Uses of *Primum Non Nocere*—Above All, Do No Harm!" *Journal of Clinical Pharmacology* 45 (2005): 371–377.

Veatch, Robert M. *Patient, Heal Thyself: How the New Medicine Puts the Patient in Charge*. New York: Oxford University Press, 2009.

Veatch, Robert M. *The Patient-Physician Relation: The Patient as Partner, Part 2*. Bloomington, IN: Indiana University Press, 1991.

Notes

1. It is debatable whether the medical sphere includes both organic and psychological dimensions of well-being. A case can be made that the psychological and organic dimensions are different and that medicine in its traditional form is restricted to organic well-being. Under that view, psychiatry would be an interdisciplinary specialty that deals with the problems at the borderline between psychological and organic well-being. Of course, the physician, as a specialist in organic well-being under this view, would be responsible for recognizing patient problems in other spheres of life including psychological well-being, but just as the clergyman should be aware of the possibility of an organic cause of what might at first appear to be a religious problem (but not attempt to treat the organic problem), so the physician should be aware of the possible links between organic and psychological well-being, but not claim expertise in the treatment of the psychological problem. The psychiatrist or psychologist should deal with these. However, regardless of whether the medical sphere ought to include psychological well-being, the problem remains the same: Some elements of well-being will clearly be beyond the physician's expertise and, even within the medical sphere, there will always be potential goals that can conflict with one another.

2. For two recent discussions of the limits on promoting good consequences for patients and others, see Katz (2002) and Kamm (2007).

The Ethics of Respect for Persons: Lying, Cheating, and Breaking Promises and Why Physicians Have Considered Them Ethical

In the case at the end of the last chapter, Dr. Browne felt justified (and indeed was exonerated by the British General Medical Council) in breaking a confidence because he followed the Hippocratic dictum that the clinician should always act in a way that he believes will benefit the patient and protect the patient from harm. Reflection on cases such as this one has increasingly led critics of the Hippocratic ethic to doubt that the physician's subjective judgment of patient benefit is the definitive standard for clinician action. The ethic focuses only on the welfare of the patient, that is, patient-centered beneficence and nonmaleficence, excluding any consideration of the welfare of other parties. The problem of the interests as well as the rights of other patients is to be taken up in Chapter 8. The Hippocratic principle also poses problems even if we focus only on the individual patient. Increasingly critics are insisting that medical ethics must take into account duties and rights in the patient–physician relation as well as benefits and harms. The general problem is one of whether sometimes an action can be morally wrong even if it produces good consequences.

An ethic based on duty is increasingly replacing or supplementing one focusing exclusively on consequences. When that ethic focuses on duties to individuals it is often called an ethic of **respect for persons**. The ethics of respect for persons is one that derives to a great degree from the philosopher Immanuel Kant (1964). Kant stressed that it was important to treat human beings as ends-in-themselves and not mere means. He affirmed the intrinsic value of human life and therefore that humans deserve respect independent of the consequences of actions. We show respect for them by observing certain duties toward them.

The ethic of respect for persons, being a type of ethic based on duty, differs from ethics that focus on production of good consequences and avoiding evil ones. While consequentialist ethics determines what is morally right by examining the consequences of actions, an ethic of respect for persons considers certain behaviors simply to be one's duty—regardless of the consequences. If an action includes a lie, a broken promise, or a violation of another's autonomy, then these features tend to make it morally wrong—even if the consequences are good. Such an ethic focuses on the intrinsic nature of the action, its moral structure or form, and hence is sometimes called **formalism**. According to this view, actions (or sets of actions) are right or wrong, not based on the consequences they produce, but on their inherent content or form. Certain actions are simply one's duty regardless of the consequences. Some people also call this kind of ethic *deontological*, derived from the Greek word for duty. Deontological or formalist approaches to ethics such as an ethic of respect for persons stand as a major alternative to ethics that decide what is morally right or wrong on the basis of consequences.

In modern Western society those who emphasize more deontological or formalist approaches sometimes use the language of *rights* rather than duties, but, as we saw in Chapter 1, there is a close connection between the two. If one person has a right, for example a right to refuse medical treatment, then other people have a reciprocal duty, in this case, the duty to leave the individual alone when he or she refuses treatment.

For a discussion of the "basics of bioethics," we will present a shorter list of core principles (with the assumption that all of the UNESCO principles can be accounted for as specifications of this list). Figure 12 modifies the Figure 8 of Chapter 4 by adding the principles of ethic of respect for persons as an alternative to the Hippocratic ethic. The figure indicates four principles that are sometimes included under the rubric of respect for persons. The first is the principle of **fidelity**, that is, fidelity to commitments made in relations with others, to promises made and contracts to be kept. Anyone who feels some moral duty to keep a promise, even if the consequences are not the best, is reflecting this principle. But this is only one aspect of respecting persons. The second is the principle of **autonomy**. The notion of informed consent can be derived from this principle. Third is the principle of **veracity**, or simply the duty to tell

	Consequentialist Principles	Duty-Based Principles
Individual	**Subjective** 1. Beneficence 2. Nonmaleficence **—Hippocratic Utility—** **Objective** 1. Beneficence 2. Nonmaleficence	**The Ethic of Respect for Persons** 1. Fidelity 2. Autonomy 3. Veracity 4. Avoidance of Killing
Social		

FIGURE 12   Types of Ethical Principles

the truth. The fourth, which we will take up in detail in Chapter 6, is the principle of avoidance of killing. In some religious systems, this is referred to as the sacredness of life or the ideal that life is precious and to be respected. Kant derived from that the idea that not only should one not kill other people, but even that one should not take one's own life. So for Kant, suicide was prohibited because suicide was failing to show adequate respect for one's own person, for one's own life, or for failing to treat life as an end in itself.

The ethic of respect for persons stands in contrast with the ethics of Hippocratic benefit. The problem was encountered in the case of Dr. Browne at the end of Chapter 4. The general form of the problem is that one course of action is believed by the physician to be most beneficial for the patient while another course, often expressed in terms of either rights or duties, appears to be morally required by some principle related to respect for persons. The cases are ones in which the clinician feels required to do something other than what he or she believes is the most beneficial course.

Many people, when reflecting on Dr. Browne's choice to disclose the use of contraceptives to the young woman's father, believe he simply had a duty of confidentiality. Or to put it in other language that amounts to the same thing, the girl had a right to confidentiality. Whether duties or rights language is used, it conveys that Dr. Browne is obliged to do something other than merely do what he thinks will benefit his patient. This obligation appears to be related to the element of respect for persons that can be called the principle of fidelity.

THE PRINCIPLE OF FIDELITY

The general idea of the principle of fidelity in the patient–physician relation is one of loyalty. A special type of relationship exists between a patient and a physician. Each owes the other some loyalty.

Fidelity and the Notion of Loyalty

Most attention is focused on the loyalty of the physician to the patient, but in some settings we are increasingly talking about the obligations or duties of loyalty of the patient to the physician as well (Benjamin, 1985). The troublesome cases are those in which keeping a commitment to the patient is not the way to produce the best consequences for the patient. Consequences incline one toward one action, duty another.

CASE 8

The Promised Internship

A senior medical student, using the national matching program, is promised what she considers the perfect residency position. She receives and signs a contract for the position. But just before July 1, the day when residency programs begin, the physician/administrator from the hospital calls and says, "I'm very sorry to tell you this, but we have found somebody we think will be better for our hospital and our patients.

Even though you have excellent skills, this candidate is just exactly what we need. He has already done a clerkship in the area where we have special need. We're sorry, but we won't be able to accept you after all."

The medical student may feel she has a legal claim against the hospital. That may depend on the exact wording of the legal contract. But she may also feel she has been wronged morally. Given the traditional Hippocratic ethical notion that physicians have a duty to do what is best for their patients, the physician who administers the program claims that, regardless of the legal implications, he was merely doing what his professional ethics requires. Assuming the physician/administrator really believed that the other person would be better for the patients of his hospital, does this medical student have any moral grounds for protest?

Many would feel at that point that the medical student had been treated improperly. Something was promised, and the hospital's administrators reneged. Anyone who has such a feeling has the idea of ethics of fidelity. Something was promised; a commitment was made. The general idea is that one owes something to the person to whom a promise has been made. Those who hold to the principle of fidelity claim that the mere fact that better consequences will result if one reneges on the promise does not necessarily justify breaking the promise. The striking thing about this case is that many feel like the hospital administrators owe something to this medical student even if the hospital's patients really will be somewhat better off if the promise is broken.

Fidelity gives rise to an independent duty to keep promises or contracts. This is an ethic that is particularly visible in classical Judeo-Christian ethics. The ethic of contract or covenant keeping is the central motif of ancient Jewish ethics. This ethic of fidelity has carried into secular ethics of Immanuel Kant and others in the formalist or deontological tradition in the notion that there is reason to keep a promise simply because it is a promise.

The Ethics of Confidentiality

The ethics of confidentiality is closely related to the principle of fidelity and the obligation to keep promises. Hippocratic and non-Hippocratic ethics imply quite different promises about keeping medical information about patients confidential. They each permit some disclosures and prohibit others. It is important to understand the significant differences.

THE HIPPOCRATIC APPROACH TO CONFIDENTIALITY   The Hippocratic Oath commits the physician not to disclose "that which ought not be spread abroad." This implies that some things may be spread abroad, perhaps even that some things should be. Thus, the Hippocratic tradition cannot be seen as unambiguously requiring that medical information be kept confidential.

If one asks how to determine what should be spread abroad, the answer is found in the Hippocratic principle: benefit the patient and protect the patient from harm. Hippocratic confidentiality is driven by beneficence. Whenever it will serve the patient's good to keep information confidential, then it should not be disclosed. But, on the other hand, in the standard Hippocratic stance, whenever, according to the clinician's judgment, disclosure would be better for the patient, the physician should release the information. Any confidentiality commitment is voided. That was also the ethic of the British Medical Association (BMA) before the Dr. Browne case. It was the position of the American Medical Association (AMA) until 1980. It remains the ethic of some codes such as that of the St. George's University School of Medicine. That oath is essentially Hippocratic, saying, "all things seen or heard in the exercise of my profession, which ought not to be divulged, I will keep secret and will never reveal." So far, that sounds like an oath or a promise for confidentiality. But then a final clause appears: "excepting for most weighty reasons." If one interprets the "most weighty reason" to be the benefit of the patient, then it becomes Hippocratic. And given that many of the elements of the St. George's oath are Hippocratic, it is open to this paternalistic interpretation.

According to the Hippocratic interpretation, confidences should not be broken to benefit other people. For instance, if a patient were to acknowledge to a physician that child abuse had occurred, that information could not be disclosed (unless it was for the benefit of the patient making the disclosure), but the Hippocratic physician is free to disclose even against the wishes of the patient if some benefit to the patient were discerned.

NON-HIPPOCRATIC APPROACHES TO CONFIDENTIALITY   A number of codes have more rigorous confidentiality requirements. They prohibit disclosure even if the breaking of confidence is believed to benefit the patient. One might ask, Why a physician should not break confidence if he or she believed it would benefit the patient in the end? Confidentiality, according to the "respect for persons" view derived from fidelity to commitments, involves more than patient benefit. The duty to keep medical information confidential is part of fidelity to the patient. A promise of confidentiality is, at least by implication, made when the relation is created. Views that find a duty of confidentiality that goes beyond patient benefit hold that there is a duty to keep confidences when confidentiality is promised.

The World Medical Association (WMA) Declaration of Geneva is generally Hippocratic; it is a rewriting and modernizing of the Hippocratic Oath. On this issue, however, it breaks with the Hippocratic Oath. It gives a flat pledge of confidentiality. No exception clauses are included.

In 1971, just after the Dr. Browne case, the BMA rewrote its code to deal with cases such as Dr. Browne's in which the physician believes it is in the patient's interest to disclose confidential information to a third party. In 1971 it said that in such cases "it is the doctor's duty to make every effort to persuade the patient to allow the information to be given to the third party, but where the patient refuses, that refusal must be respected."[1]

Some more-recent codes go beyond the Hippocratic Oath in *requiring* or *permitting* disclosure of confidential information, not to benefit the patient, but to protect others from serious harm. The BMA, for example, says that, according to its opinion, confidences may be broken when the law requires it or when the physician has an overriding duty to society. Depending on the jurisdiction, this might include the legal duty to report gunshot wounds, venereal or other infectious diseases, or a diagnosis of epilepsy. It is the physician's obligation to make sure the patient understands that exception.

An issue of controversy today is whether the law should require reporting of HIV diagnoses. Some jurisdictions require reporting; others do not. When a physician is facing a patient in whom tests for HIV are contemplated in a jurisdiction that requires reporting, fidelity to the patient requires mentioning the reporting requirement. A physician who is committed to practicing within the constraints of the law and who is practicing in a jurisdiction with a reporting requirement will have to disclose a positive diagnosis. If the patient at that point cannot continue the relation on that basis, he or she has the right to end it.

The new (2005) UNESCO Universal Declaration on Bioethics and Human Rights is unfortunately vague on the issue of confidentiality. Like the WMA, it offers no exceptions to the confidentiality requirement, but includes the statement that patient information should not be disclosed without patient consent "to the greatest extent possible." That offers no opening to disclose to protect third parties, but seems to imply that sometimes withholding information might not be possible.

If confidentiality is part of the ethics of promise keeping, what is crucial is what the clinician promises the patient. The corollary is that physicians should not promise more than they can deliver. Consider the following case in which a physician may imply too much to his patients (Based on Veatch, 1977):

CASE 9

The Case of the Homosexual Husband

A family physician had a general practice at the time when the law still required physical exams as part of a premarital medical examination. He had a 21-year-old male patient whom he had known for a long time. Because he had previously treated him for sexually transmitted diseases, the physician was aware of the patient's sexual history and knew he was gay. Over the course of the years, the patient had discussed his lifestyle with the physician.

When this patient came to the physician requesting a premarital physical examination, the physician was surprised, but he believed it was really none of his business. He knew that, at least sometimes, persons living a gay lifestyle are bisexual, so perhaps the marriage would work out.

Just to make conversation, he asked the patient who his fiancée was and was shocked to discover it was one of his own patients, someone he had known for many years. He began to realize he was facing a dilemma. If he followed the Hippocratic principle, it was his duty to do what he believed would be beneficial to the patient. In this case, the woman who was about to marry this man was herself a patient. On the other hand, if he had promised confidentiality, it was his duty to the male patient not to disclose without the man's permission.

At this moment the physician found himself in a bind. He believed that the young woman was at some risk. First, he knew her future husband had a history of sexually transmitted diseases. If he remained actively bisexual, he was going to bring those diseases into the marriage. Second, from what he knew of the man, the physician was rather confident that this woman was going to be in for a very unpleasant marriage. Her marrying someone whom the physician knew was gay seemed to him to doom the marriage to a quick divorce.

This physician concluded it was his duty to his female patient to find out from the man whether his fiancée knew about his lifestyle, and, if she didn't, to inform her. He might be lucky and discover that she already knew the situation or that the man was willing to have the physician help the couple discuss it. If, as seems more likely, he was not willing to discuss it with his fiancée, then the physician's problem would remain because he also concluded that his duty to his male patient was to keep confidentiality.

The physician believed he had implicitly promised confidentiality to the male patient and Hippocratic beneficence to the female, but he could not deliver on both promises. He found himself in a spot in which he had two duties and had to determine which one should prevail. Once he has made two contradictory commitments, there is no ideal solution to the problem. If he had been more cautious in what he promised to either the woman or man—for instance, if he had promised to the woman that he would work for what was in her interests unless it involved breaching confidentiality with another patient, or, alternatively, if he had promised to the man to keep information confidential unless it was crucial to the welfare of another patient—then the problem would have been solved. But this physician had gotten himself into a bind by making commitments on which he could not deliver simultaneously.

The striking thing about this case is that the Hippocratic solution of doing what will benefit the patient does not satisfy most people. First, it poses a serious problem because the clinician has two patients who may have significantly different interests. In that case, it is impossible to be Hippocratic to both patients simultaneously. Second, even if that problem is avoided, as long as the clinician believes it is in the woman's interest to know about her fiancé's sexual orientation, he has a duty to tell her, and that does not square with his duty to keep the implied promise of confidentiality with the male patient.

Those who hold that the promise of confidentiality must be kept must yield on their commitment to the Hippocratic notion that the physician's primary duty is to benefit the patient. If there is reason to keep the confidence, it must stem from the obligation owed to the male patient, one best understood as deriving from a promise made. Respect for persons and the principle of fidelity under that notion appears to generate obligations, in this case the obligation of confidentiality, that cannot be overridden by mere considerations of the consequences to another patient.

There is another dimension to the confidentiality controversy. Even if confidences cannot be broken merely to do what the clinician believes will be beneficial to the patient, it is possible they may be broken in some cases to benefit others. The AMA's Principles of Medical Ethics have been interpreted by its Judicial Council (1984, p. 19) to permit disclosure when "a patient threatens to inflict serious bodily harm to another person and there is a reasonable probability that the patient may carry out the threat."

This is clearly not a Hippocratic paternalistic provision.[2] It could easily justify breaking confidence when it is not in the patient's interest to do so. Contrary to the Hippocratic perspective, it introduces a social dimension: consideration of other persons. Whether it is the rights or the interests of the other party that justifies disclosures is a matter that we will take up in Chapter 8. Now we need to see how, at the level of an individual patient, there may be other principles derived from the notion of respect for persons that place limits on the health professional's duty to do what he or she thinks will benefit the patient.

THE PRINCIPLE OF AUTONOMY AND THE DOCTRINE OF INFORMED CONSENT

Keeping faith in relations, called for by the principle of fidelity, is not the only principle entailed in respect for persons. But once one understands the relation between duties derived from fidelity and those derived from beneficence and nonmaleficence, the implications of the other principles under the rubric of respect for persons will be easy to grasp. The most visible principle of the medical ethics of the past generation has been the principle of **autonomy**—another aspect of showing respect for persons. In fact, respecting autonomy is so central to respect for persons that some (see Beauchamp and Childress, 2006) are inclined to treat autonomy as the only principle of this sort. It seems clear, however, that even persons who are not substantially autonomous can still command respect.[3] For instance, the principle of fidelity requires that promises made to the nonautonomous still must be kept. Likewise, in the following sections, we shall see that many people hold that respect for persons implies two further principles: veracity and avoidance of killing. They entail duties to deal honestly and to avoid killing humans, even if those humans are not substantially autonomous or may not technically be "persons."

The Concept of Autonomy

The principle of autonomy comes, not from the Hippocratic tradition, but from the traditions of Kant and liberal political philosophy. Liberal political philosophy (the very term *liberalism* focuses us on liberty) has dominated the medical ethics of the United States and much of the rest of the Western world since the radical rethinking of medical ethics began about 1970. The liberty of the individual is very frequently a key part of the principle of autonomy. We see it dominating liberal political philosophy (though not medical ethics articulated by the medical profession) from the eighteenth century. We frequently see this kind of thinking represented by the use of "rights" language. As was noted in the first chapter, rights have a reciprocal relation with duties. If one person has a right, then others normally have duties. Controversy remains over whether rights or duties are conceptually prior (Macklin, 1976), but they are clearly closely related. Normally, when an appeal is made to a *right*, this claim is seen as having a special priority or standing such that mere appeals to consequences cannot be used to override the right.

We often talk about the right of a patient to give informed consent before being touched, for example, prior to surgery. That's just an example of playing out this respect for the autonomy of the patient. We can either express this in duty language or rights language, but in either case, the language signals a priority for the claim being made. Sometimes philosophers will say that rights "trump" appeals to consequences, implying that they believe that the principles upon which the rights claim is based take priority over appeals to consequences. Thus, when philosophers say rights and duties are correlative, they mean that this priority might be expressed in two different ways. I can say that a physician has a duty to get informed consent before touching the patient, or I can say the patient has a right to give informed consent before being touched. They mean exactly the same.

Sometimes, in Western thought, people talk about a woman's *right* to procure an abortion. When a woman expresses this right, she is claiming that under the principle of autonomy she should be free to proceed. Of course, if one believes that the fetus has full moral standing so that duties such as the duty to avoid killing it apply, then the woman would be acting in a way that is depriving someone else of their rights. We would, once again, have a clash between two principles, in this case between the principles of autonomy and avoidance of killing.

Positive and Negative Rights

Rights come in two different forms: **negative** and **positive**. Autonomy is primarily related to negative rights. A negative right is a right to be left alone, to be free from the interference of others to act autonomously. A positive right implies much more, a right not only to act autonomously, but also to have access to the means necessary to carry out one's actions. Some people talk about liberty rights and entitlement rights, implying the same distinction. For our purposes we can assume they mean the same thing.

We can illustrate the difference in the case of an abortion. In the United States, following the 1973 decision of *Roe v. Wade*, a woman has a legal right to an abortion—meaning she has a liberty right, or a negative right. All that means is that she is legally free to pursue an abortion using whatever means she has available within the constraints of the law. If she can find a physician and has enough money to pay for the procedure, she has the autonomy, or liberty, to make an arrangement with that physician to get an abortion. She is free from state interference.

That does not imply a positive entitlement right. If she had an entitlement right, she would have the right, not only to engage the physician, but also to the resources necessary, such as the funds to pay the physician. One may believe that a woman ought to have both a liberty right and an entitlement right, but that is not presently the federal law in the United States. Certain states and certain insurance plans may provide such funding. Legal cases since *Roe v. Wade* have clarified that what *Roe* established was a liberty right, that is, the legal freedom to try to make a deal with a physician to procure an abortion. Of course, the existence of a legal right, in either a liberty or entitlement form, does not settle the question of whether either form of right exists at the moral level. A liberty right gives a woman the right to be left alone, free from state interference, to try to make whatever arrangements in private she is able to make. Claiming an entitlement right is a more extensive claim; it implies that the state or some other body has the obligation not only to refrain from interfering, but also to provide the resources. Liberty rights are generally grounded in the principle of autonomy, that is, the duty to permit others to live their lives according to their own life-plans. By contrast, a claim to an entitlement right is not grounded in autonomy; it is based on some principle that imposes an affirmative duty to act, perhaps the principle of beneficence or justice.

Although the principle of autonomy receives full expression in liberal political philosophy, Judeo-Christianity figures in a complicated way in its prehistory. Early Judaism and Christianity had no principle of autonomy any more than any other ancient culture did. No culture in that day held a moral principle that required respecting life-plan choices made by individuals. That required the evolution of a concept of individual choice that did not emerge until much later. Until this day, Jewish Talmudic ethics has no principle of autonomy, at least in the most traditional forms of rabbinical interpretation. Thus, in more traditional Talmudic interpretation, a patient does not even have the moral right to refuse a recommended treatment (Bleich, 1979).

Early Christianity had no principle of autonomy in a full-blown sense, but what it did have was a remarkable recognition of the importance of the individual and of personal decisions, even when the religious choice of the individual caused separation from one's family. That seems to be the historical precursor to the development of the principle of autonomy. By the Protestant era in the sixteenth century and the centuries immediately preceding, we begin seeing developments pointing to the affirmation of the individual as a decision maker. In the fourteenth century John Wycliffe and John Hus as well as the Catholic mystic Johann Tauler recognized this idea of the importance of the individual. The Protestant Reformation went further in affirming the authority of the individual. We were headed toward a concept of autonomy even though it did not surface full-blown until the eighteenth century.

Kant, writing in the eighteenth century, is a manifestation. Kant was a German Pietist, and many people believe this Protestant affirmation of the authority of the individual is the basis for Kant's secular affirmation of autonomy.

By contrast, a number of other philosophical and religious systems in the world do not emphasize autonomy. Marxism does not; neither do Hinduism, Buddhism, Confucianism, and Islam. Of course, in any tradition certain individuals who have been exposed to views outside their own culture may have adopted some amalgam of cultural commitments. Thus, in modern Japan a Western-educated physician or lawyer may use language that is constantly peppered with expressions such as "the right of self-determination" and "individual autonomy." They are not getting that from Buddhism or Shintoism; it comes from their Western exposure.

Informed Consent, Autonomy, and Therapeutic Privilege

Informed consent is a critical element of any theory that gives weight to autonomy. Hippocratic beneficence might incorporate some minimal informed consent, but only when the clinician believes informed consent will benefit the patient. For example, if a physician is about to write a prescription for diphenylhydantoin, a seizure medication, she might feel obliged to say to that patient that one of the side effects of diphenylhydantoin is that it can make one drowsy. She might warn the patient not to drive a car or operate dangerous equipment until he is sure he knows how he responds to this drug. This informing occurs, however, only because she is worried that the patient might injure himself or somebody else. The physician must provide certain information just to protect the patient.

In liberal political philosophy, the key idea is that meaningful information must be disclosed even if the clinician does not believe that it will be beneficial. By contrast, Hippocratic ethics includes what is known as **therapeutic privilege**. It is the privilege that a Hippocratic physician will claim when withholding information that the physician believes would be harmful or upsetting to the patient. That privilege makes sense in an ethic based on paternalistic patient benefit, but is contrary to an ethic giving important place to the principle of autonomy.

In the conflict between liberal political philosophy and Hippocratic ethics a major clash emerges over informed consent. The case of *Natanson v. Kline* suggests the continuing evolution of the principle of autonomy as a replacement for the Hippocratic ethic and the related doctrine of therapeutic privilege.

CASE 10

Natanson v. Kline: When May Information Be Withheld?

In 1960 in the state of Kansas, a woman named Irma Natanson suffering from breast cancer needed radiation following a radical mastectomy. She suffered terrible radiation burns, after which she sued her doctor, Dr. Kline, for the injury. One of the counts was that she had not consented to the risk of the radiation burn.

Dr. Kline defended himself claiming therapeutic privilege. He did not deny that he had failed to tell Mrs. Natanson about the risk of the burns. Often physicians in this position claim that such information might disturb the patient; perhaps even irrationally lead her to refuse consent to the needed treatment. Did Dr. Kline have the right to withhold this information if he believed it would upset her or make her do something irrational? Or, alternatively, did he have a duty to explain about those risks anyway?

Justice Schroeder, the judge in this case, gave the definitive response of Anglo-American liberal political philosophy:

> Anglo-American law starts with a premise of a thorough-going self-determination. It follows that each man is considered the master of his own body, and he may, if he be of sound mind, expressly prohibit the performance of life-saving surgery or other medical treatment.

It followed that, if this information was relevant to her decision about whether she wanted the radiation, she had a right to be informed. When she charged

Dr. Kline with failure to get informed consent, the dispute was not over whether she had signed a form. The issue was whether the consent was informed and voluntary. We don't really care, from the point of view of the ethics, whether a piece of paper has a signature. The piece of paper with a signature may help to demonstrate that the patient has at least seen the paper. It will not prove that the patient read the paper; much less that the signer understood it. The court will, in some cases, throw the consent form out if it is believed that the patient never understood what was on the paper.

Thus, back as far as 1960, Justice Schroeder appeared to be rejecting the therapeutic privilege. In 1960, we were just at the beginning of the era when liberal political philosophy was exerting its influence on medical ethics and challenging the therapeutic privilege. We were in a period of transition in which judges and others sometimes reverted to Hippocratic language and sometimes talked as if autonomy were all that counted. Additional text from Justice Schroeder's opinion reveals the confusion. In spite of the bold appeal to autonomy, Justice Schroeder also said:

> The physician's choice of plausible courses should not be called into question if it appears, all circumstances considered, that the physician was motivated only by the patient's best therapeutic interest and he proceeded as a competent medical man would have done under a similar situation.

That sounds very much like the therapeutic privilege doctrine of an earlier era and appears to reject a "thorough-going self-determination." It sounds like the judge is about to say that as long as the physician was worried about Mrs. Natanson's welfare, he had acted acceptably. Justice Schroeder said both that the patient has an absolute right to self-determination and that the physician should not be questioned if he had the patient's best therapeutic interest in mind and acted as competent medical men would have in the circumstances. The latter sounds like therapeutic privilege; the former, more like the principle of autonomy.

Just before the latter sentence, however, there is an opening clause that conveys that, even as far back as 1960, autonomy was really dominant in Justice Schroeder's mind. He introduced the therapeutic privilege language with the clause, "So long as the disclosure is sufficient to assure an informed consent." On balance he appears to be insisting on an adequately informed consent, not just a consent without potentially disturbing information. But in 1960 therapeutic privilege was so common that the judge was still inserting therapeutic privilege language. He was part of the way down the road toward a conversion to autonomy, and he liked to talk self-determination language, but he still lapsed into the talk of therapeutic privilege. In the end, the judge insisted that the consent be informed. The case presents an ambiguous combination of two points of view and, on balance, it seems to be tipping in the direction of requiring information, even if it is upsetting to the patient and even if it is not the common practice among physicians of the day.

It was a series of cases from 1969 to 1972 that really set the pattern of the shift from the more paternalistic Hippocratic basis for consent to one grounded squarely in respect for patient autonomy (*Berkey v. Anderson*, 1969; *Canterbury v. Spence*, 1972; *Cobbs v. Grant*, 1972). *Canterbury v. Spence* (1972) is a good example.

CASE 11

Canterbury v. Spence

A 19-year-old youth named Canterbury suffered from back pain. He had an operation called a laminectomy to repair a ruptured disc. Afterwards he fell from bed and suffered an injury that resulted in lower-body paralysis. In the court case, the critical question was whether Dr. Spence should have explained to Mr. Canterbury the risk of falling out of bed. Dr. Spence made a therapeutic privilege claim, saying he did not think that disclosure was appropriate. Disclosure might irrationally lead the patient to refuse to consent to the procedure he really needed, and might have produced "adverse psychological reactions which could preclude the success of the operation."

The court affirmed the right of self-determination, holding that the patient needed to have the information necessary to make an informed decision. At this level the court did not say that Dr. Spence needed to inform about the risk of falling out of bed. That question was referred back to a lower court. What the higher court said was that Dr. Spence had to tell the patient everything that the patient would deem significant to his decision. Dr. Spence still had available the possibility that he could convince a lower court that falling out of bed was so rare or the risk so obvious that the patient would not need to be told about it to make a rational decision. What this court said was that the physician could not use therapeutic privilege to justify withholding of relevant information.

Standards of Disclosure for Consent to Be Adequately Informed

No one is insisting that consent be "fully" informed. It is not even clear what that could mean. Telling the patient everything about a treatment is an impossible task. All that is being called for is adequate information. The key question addressed in this series of court cases is what standard should be used in deciding how much information must be transferred for a consent to be adequately informed. Three different standards are considered: the professional standard, the reasonable person standard, and the subjective standard.

THE PROFESSIONAL STANDARD   The **professional standard** is the traditional standard. It requires that a physician disclose what colleagues similarly situated would have disclosed in similar circumstances. This standard appears to be built on the presumption that deciding how much information to disclose is something that only professionals can know. It is related to the Hippocratic ideology. This, however, does not necessarily serve patient autonomy. It could be that colleagues would not disclose everything about a procedure that a patient would find important. The physician accused of failing to get an informed consent might be able to bring in a number of colleagues who might testify that they also would not have disclosed the disputed information. On the basis of the old professional standard, their testimony would settle the matter in court.

THE REASONABLE PERSON STANDARD   *Canterbury v. Spence* and other cases of that period introduced a new standard called the **reasonable person standard**. (It used to be called the reasonable man standard.) It requires that the physician must disclose what a reasonable patient would want to be told or find significant, even if none of the physician's colleagues would agree.

Ruth Faden and her colleagues (1981) conducted a study in a seizure clinic at Johns Hopkins Hospital in Baltimore. She asked the physicians in the clinic how many side effects to the medicine Dilantin they would disclose. At least for adult patients, the majority of the physicians identified three: ataxia (defective muscle coordination), sedation, and skin rash. These side effects required some immediate patient action— care in operating equipment or checking with the physician—to control them.

Dr. Faden then went to the patients in the clinic waiting room and gave them a long list of possible side effects, asking which of them they would like to have been told about. The patients said that they wanted to know about a lot more than those three side effects. For example, one of the risks is hirsutism; Dilantin will make hair grow, a problem that could be of concern, especially to some female patients. They might agree that this was not a crucial problem and that, if necessary, in order to prevent epilepsy, it was a risk worth taking, but most patients said they wanted to know about it anyway. By contrast, the majority of the physicians believed patients did not need to know about it. Patients also said they wanted to know about very serious effects, even if they were rare, such as drug-related mortality, lupus, and teratogenic effects (developmental malformations).

Thus, it is now documented that the patients said in the survey that they wanted to know certain risks that the physicians in the same clinic said were not appropriate to disclose. Studies such as this one suggest that reasonable lay people may want to know certain information that the professional standard would not require. If a patient were to sue a physician for failure to disclose certain side effects, the reasonable person standard would support the patient. If reasonable patients want the information, then, according to the reasonable person standard, the clinician is obliged to disclose it.

Self-determination of the patient is not promoted by the professional standard. Surely, the fact that a physician's colleagues would not disclose does not establish that patients would not want the information. Disclosing what the reasonable person would want to know seems to come closer. Of course, some patients may not be "reasonable." They may need more or less information than typical, reasonable people. That suggests a third standard of disclosure.

THE SUBJECTIVE STANDARD   If the goal is to give the patient the information he or she would personally find meaningful, then, to the extent that is known or can be known, it seems that the standard should be more subjective. It should fit with the life-plan and interests of the individual patient. This is what is called the **subjective standard**. It is subjective in that it is based on the actual subjective interests of the patient, not those of some more hypothetical reasonable person, whether patient or physician. Thus, even if the ordinary reasonable person might not want to know of a one-in-a-hundred-thousand risk of paralysis of the fingers, the patient who is a concert pianist might.

Of course, this creates a difficult, if not impossible, task for the clinician. In order to know which risks and benefits to present, the clinician would have to learn all of the patient's idiosyncratic interests and tastes. He or she cannot just tell the patient "everything" because there is an enormous, perhaps infinite, amount of information that could be said about any treatment. In addition to information about the side effects of any particular treatment, information about all available options would have to be provided. Some treatment options that are conceivable are terribly implausible. Indeed, they may even be immoral in the eyes of most people. Nevertheless, they might be very important to some people with unusual lifestyles and preferences. For every condition, suicide is theoretically an option although normally clinicians will not suggest that possibility.

There is no way that a clinician can guess at all of the possible areas of concern for each patient. He or she can, however, take into account what is known about the patient. If he or she knows unusual interests, such as the career of the concert pianist, then the clinician must take that information into account. Moreover, the clinician must encourage the patient to make special interests known.

Perhaps the optimal approach for deciding what information must be transmitted would be a combination of the reasonable person and the subjective standard. The clinician would disclose what the reasonable person would want to know adjusted by what the clinician knows or should know about the unique interests of the individual patient.

THE PRINCIPLE OF VERACITY: LYING AND THE DUTY TO TELL THE TRUTH

A third way to show respect for persons is by being truthful with them. In addition to the principles of fidelity and autonomy, the principle of **veracity** is an essential characteristic of human action that shows respect. (It is the third element of respect for persons in Figure 12.) Moral conflicts involving the principle of veracity follow the same pattern as the other principles grouped under the heading of respect for persons. Once again, we have a conflict between doing what is best for the patient in terms of benefit and harm and fulfilling some general obligation, in this case the obligation to tell the truth.

The Change in Physician Attitudes

In the United States, two studies of physician attitudes about telling the truth to patients reveal an intriguing pattern. In 1961, Donald Oken published a study in which he asked U.S. physicians what their usual policy was about telling the truth to terminally ill cancer patients. Eighty-eight percent of the physicians surveyed said it was their usual policy not to tell the patients if the patient was diagnosed with a malignancy. The reason is easy to understand if one understands the Hippocratic principle and the depth of the commitment of 1960s physicians to that principle. They were afraid that if they told the patient, the patient would become psychologically upset, and the Hippocratic Oath says not to do things that will upset the patient. Almost uniformly, as recently as the 1960s, physicians would not tell patients about cancer.

Something dramatic happened in the late 1960s and early 1970s. This is the period when respect for persons emerged as a dominant consideration in medical ethics—the time of the *Roe v. Wade* case involving abortion, the *Natanson* case involving informed consent, and the Karen Quinlan case involving the right to refuse life support. In 1979, Dennis Novack and a group of colleagues published a study in which they replicated Oken's questions, asking an essentially similar population of physicians. Less than twenty years later they found 98 percent followed a usual policy of telling.

Accounting for the Change in Attitudes

CHANGES IN JUDGMENTS ABOUT BENEFIT AND HARM The question is, What accounts for this moral shift? Why are physicians now inclined to tell the truth? The original Hippocratic approach stressed doing what will benefit the patient, so that Bernard Meyer (1968), a physician writing in the 1960s, gave the following explanation. (Notice the Hippocratic quality.)

> What is imparted to the patient about his illness should be planned with the same care and executed with the same skill that are demanded by any potentially therapeutic measure. Like the transfusion of blood, the dispensing of certain information must be distinctly indicated, the amount given consonant to the needs of the recipient, and the type chosen with a view towards avoiding untoward reactions. (Meyer, 1968, p. 172)

According to this Hippocratic ethic, the physician should tell only things that are going to help the patient and should withhold those things that are going to hurt. The logic is identical to the old idea of the therapeutic privilege, radically different from the attitude found by Novack's group. Now, how did the change come about?

One possibility is that physicians remained consequentialist, but had recalculated the consequences. The medical ethicist Joseph Fletcher (1954) illustrates an early example of the kind of change that could take place without abandoning the focus on consequences. He was a consequentialist; he believed in benefiting patients and protecting them from harm. But according to him, awful things will happen if the physician does not tell the patient the truth. Particularly as we move to complex medicine in a hospital setting, maintaining the fiction of a dishonest diagnosis becomes exceedingly difficult. Everybody on the health care team has to maintain the same story, and eventually, something goes wrong. Fletcher said that to benefit the patient, in the long run, the consequences are better if the truth is told. That is still staying within the Hippocratic principle, but the consequences are recalculated for a period of high-technology, complex hospital-based medicine. As early as 1903 pioneering physician, Richard Cabot, was arguing against virtually all his colleagues that patients would be better off if they are told the truth (*See* Cabot, 1978, reprint).

A POSSIBLE SHIFT TO AN ETHIC OF RESPECT FOR PERSONS The other possibility is that, at about this same time, people began saying that something was simply inherently wrong about not being honest with patients. Particularly if one is already committed to informed consent, relevant information must be disclosed. How can one get informed consent for chemotherapy if the patient does not know he has cancer? He would be crazy to consent to radiation or chemotherapy believing all that was wrong was that he had a benign lump. He could not give an adequate consent, because he would not be adequately informed.

CASE 12

Limits on the Physician's Duty to Promote Health

Jim Sullivan in his early thirties comes to Dr. Tom Wordsworth's office for a routine exam in conjunction with a new job. Dr. Wordsworth starts taking the history. It is obvious that Mr. Sullivan is grossly overweight. He tells the physician that he does not get any exercise, smokes two packs of cigarettes a day, and has done so since he was fourteen. He drinks a lot and generally does not take very good care of himself.

Dr. Wordsworth feels that he should encourage his patient to change his lifestyle. He realizes he is not very likely to change anything simply by telling the patient that he should not drink as much and should quit smoking. This is a man who is not likely to take up an exercise routine simply because this physician says so.

Dr. Wordsworth contemplates another approach. He decides to do a chest x-ray, suspecting that some opacity will appear that will do the trick. He sees nothing terribly alarming on the x-ray, but notices some spots that would serve his purpose: to shock his patient into changing his lifestyle. With an air of great alarm he brings the x-ray to his patient saying that the spots indicate precancerous developments. He says that if Mr. Sullivan stops smoking now, there is a good chance he can stop this development. But if he keeps smoking he is headed for lung cancer. Intentionally overstating, Dr. Wordsworth rationalizes that it is true that Sullivan's chances of developing lung cancer are higher if he continues to smoke and that it is an innocent, benevolent stretching of the truth to point to the meaningless spots and exaggerate the probability that the smoking would cause cancer. He believes that overstating the risk will benefit his patient. It is the only thing he can think of that will shock him into a new lifestyle.

Here is a physician lying to a patient about the risk of lung cancer and the meaning of his x-ray, but his purpose is to benefit the patient. If one is Hippocratic, he or she must at least sympathize with what this doctor is doing. But many people react saying that what Dr. Wordsworth did is still wrong. He told a lie to this patient. He deceived him. Those who include the principle of veracity in their list of ethical principles hold that it is simply wrong to tell a purposeful lie even for the benefit of the patient.

The philosopher Immanuel Kant (1909 [1797]), classically associated with this "respect for persons" view, wrote an essay in the eighteenth century called "On the Supposed Right to Lie from Altruistic Motives." He argued that "to be truthful or honest in all declarations is therefore a sacred and absolutely commanding decree of reason limited by no expediency." *Expediency* was the word of the day for calculation of benefits and harms. So no calculation of benefits and harms was relevant to deciding when a patient should be told, according to this "respect for persons" or Kantian view.

Not everyone who believes lying to be wrong takes as rigid a stand as Immanuel Kant. Most can imagine a situation so extreme that the only plausible course of action would be to lie. In military situations, prisoners captured by an enemy may feel obliged to lie when asked to disclose the position of their colleagues. In medicine, a physician may feel that there are special cases such as a mentally ill, temporarily suicidal patient who asks if a tumor is malignant. A physician may feel that consequences of a truthful disclosure of the malignancy would be so severe in this case that a lie is justified, especially if it is only for a period necessary to overcome the suicidal tendencies. A moral principle such as veracity indicates a characteristic of actions that tends to make actions morally wrong. In Chapter 10 we will discuss how some actions may involve two different principles simultaneously. A physician's communication with a patient may, for instance, involve both lying to a patient and attempting to protect the patient from harm. We will see in that chapter that there are several different approaches for attempting to resolve such conflicts.

For many years the AMA has realized that physicians have sometimes justified lying to patients in order to attempt to protect them. The earlier, more Hippocratic stance accepted lying to patients or withholding the truth from them on these grounds. In 1981 the AMA published a new version of its principles that says that "a physician shall deal honestly with patients and colleagues." There were no qualifications. That remains the current AMA position in their principles.

What did the AMA have in mind here? It could have been adopting a new Kantian view, that it is simply a duty to tell the truth. Or the AMA spokespersons could have been recalculating the consequences of lying and deception thus holding to traditional consequential reasoning, but now believing that honesty tended to be beneficial to the patient.

The AMA's principles fit on one page at the beginning of a much larger document. The principles are adopted by the AMA's House of Delegates, but that group leaves interpretation to its Council on Ethical and Judicial Affairs. The principles are published at the beginning of a larger volume of the Council's interpretations. Those interpretations suggest the reasoning of the council members. The interpretations say if disclosure poses such a serious psychological threat of detriment to the patient as to be "medically contraindicated," then the physician may withhold the truth (AMA, 2000, p. 165). The Council reopened a consequentialist justification for dishonesty that the House of Delegates had apparently closed. One explanation is that the House of Delegates, when it adopted the revised principles, was merely saying that it now believes that usually the way to benefit the patient is to deal honestly with him or her, and the Council simply made clear that sometimes calculating consequences will lead to exceptions. The other possibility was that the House of Delegates was making a more fundamental shift to the view that there is simply a duty on the physician's part to deal honestly with patients, but the Council misunderstood that change, posing an interpretation that fails to take seriously the House's commitment to honesty.

Medically contraindicated is a term that arises frequently in medicine, especially in pharmacology. When someone claims a treatment (or a piece of information) is medically contraindicated, it sounds as if someone is stating a medical fact, but, on reflection, the term *medically contraindicated* is much more complex. Research may show that a drug or a disclosure may have a certain effect—that disclosure may be very depressing to the patient, for example. Still, it is a value judgment whether it is wrong to disclose a diagnosis because it will cause depression. Likewise, research may show that a drug has an effect most people do not like. Nevertheless, calling that effect a "side" effect or saying that the effect makes the drug "contraindicated" requires a value judgment. It is merely a way of saying that the speaker believes on balance that the effect is undesirable (see Veatch, 1991).

In the case of disclosure of a diagnosis, the AMA's Council is saying that some information can apparently produce effects that the clinician should consider so bad that, in someone's judgment, the information should not be disclosed. That makes good sense from a Hippocratic perspective, but would be rejected by one who holds to a strong principle of veracity.

The three principles that give rise to duties and rights that have been discussed thus far—the principles of fidelity, autonomy, and veracity—are three important constituent parts of the notion of showing respect for people, the main alternative to Hippocratic medical ethics. There is a final element that is sometimes included—the notion that respecting persons requires that they not be killed even if hypothetically it would do no harm and might even do them good to kill them. That principle, the principle of avoidance of killing, is the subject of the next chapter.

THE UNESCO UNIVERSAL DECLARATION ON BIOETHICS AND HUMAN RIGHTS

The most important new ethical codification for health care is the UNESCO Universal Declaration on Bioethics and Human Rights (2005). It is strongly committed to rights and duties as well as consequences and is therefore closely associated with the "respect for persons" view outlined in this chapter. Adopted by the UNESCO General Conference October 19, 2005, it is the first bioethics document adopted by a organization that can claim to be worldwide and accountable to all citizens (rather than merely to health professional organizations such as the WMA, the group that is responsible for the Declaration of Geneva). This declaration, which continues quite self-consciously the tradition of human rights, applies the 1948 Universal Declaration of Human Rights to matters of health care. It sets out a series of principles that closely parallel the principles described in this book in Chapters 4 through 8. It sets out not only principles of benefit and harm (what in Chapter 4 we called beneficence and nonmaleficence), but also autonomy, confidentiality, and equity—principles that are covered in this chapter and in Chapter 8. See Figure 13 for the parallels between the UNESCO Declaration and the principles covered in this book. The terminology is not exactly the same, but the similarities should be apparent. The striking differences are that the UNESCO document contains no mention of the principle of veracity or avoiding killing. It turns out, as we have seen in this chapter, the idea that there is a duty to tell the truth is among the most controversial in contemporary bioethics. We shall see in the next chapter that a duty not to kill patients is similarly controversial in an era when euthanasia and physician-assisted suicide are gaining supporters. The committee drafting the UNESCO Universal Declaration took up both topics but could reach no agreement on them. The UNESCO Universal Declaration also includes some additional principles, such as "respect for cultural diversity and pluralism," "solidarity and cooperation," "social responsibility and health," "sharing of benefits," "protecting future generations," and "protection of the environment, the biosphere and biodiversity." These seem to be more explicit specifications of the principles of beneficence, autonomy, and justice rather than independent ethical principles.

Key Concepts

Autonomy   A formalist or deontological moral principle that holds that actions or rules are morally right insofar as they involve respecting the autonomous choices of individuals. (Note: autonomy is also a psychological state of an individual who is capable of being self-determining or self-legislating. The moral principle of autonomy holds that one has a duty to respect the self-determined choices of autonomous individuals.)

Fidelity   A formalist or deontological moral principle that holds that actions or rules are morally right insofar as they involve keeping commitments, promises, or contracts.

Formalism   A type of normative ethical theory that holds that actions or rules are morally right insofar as they conform to a specified form rather than based on the consequences they produce (similar to Deontological ethics, Chapter 4).

Negative Right (sometimes called a liberty right)   A right to be left alone, to be free from the interference of others to act autonomously. Negative rights are often based on the principle of autonomy.

Positive Right (sometimes called an entitlement right)   A right not only to act autonomously, but also to have access to the means necessary to carry out one's actions. Positive rights must be based not on the principle of autonomy, but on the basis of some other principles such as beneficence or justice.

Professional Standard   The standard for informed consent that requires that a physician disclose what colleagues similarly situated would have disclosed in similar circumstances.

Reasonable Person Standard   The standard for informed consent that requires that the physician must disclose what a reasonable patient would want to be told or find significant, even if none of the physician's colleagues would agree.

Respect for Persons   A term referring to a type of deontological or formalist normative ethics in which the principles of moral rightness specify certain duties owed to individuals (such as respect for autonomy, fidelity, veracity, or avoidance of killing).

Subjective Standard   The standard for informed consent that requires that physicians disclose what the individual patient would want to know or find significant.

Therapeutic Privilege   The privilege that a Hippocratic physician will claim in order to withhold information when the physician believes the information will be harmful or upsetting to the patient.

Veracity   A formalist or deontological moral principle that holds that actions or rules are morally right insofar as they involve communicating truthfully and avoiding dishonesty.

Bibliography

American Medical Association. *Current Opinions of the Judicial Council of the American Medical Association*. Chicago, IL: American Medical Association, 1981.

American Medical Association, Judicial Council. *Current Opinions of the Judicial Council of the American Medical Association—1984: Including the Principles of Medical Ethics and Rules of the Judicial Council*. Chicago, IL: American Medical Association, 1984.

American Medical Association, Council on Ethical and Judicial Affairs. *Code of Medical Ethics: Current Opinions with Annotations*. Chicago, IL: American Medical Association, 1994.

American Medical Association, Council on Ethical and Judicial Affairs. *Code of Medical Ethics: Current Opinions with Annotations, 2000–2001 Edition*. Chicago, IL: American Medical Association, 2000.

Beauchamp, Tom L., and James F. Childress, eds. *Principles of Biomedical Ethics*, 6th ed. New York: Oxford University Press, 2006.

Benjamin, Martin. "Lay Obligations in Professional Relations." *Journal of Medicine and Philosophy* 10 (1985): 85–103.

Berkey v. Anderson. 1 Cal. App. 3d 790. 82 Cal. Rptr. 67 (1969).

Bleich, J. David. "The Obligation to Heal in the Judaic Tradition: A Comparative Analysis." In *Jewish Bioethics*, ed. Fred Rosner and J. David Bleich. New York: Sanhedrin Press, 1979, pp. 1–44.

Cabot, Richard C. "The Use of Truth and Falsehood in Medicine." *Connecticut Medicine* 42, No. 3 (1978): 189–194.

Canterbury v. Spence. United States Court of Appeals, District of Columbia, 464 F.2d 772, 150 U.S.App.D.C. 263 (1972).

Cobbs v. Grant. 502 P.2d 1, Cal. (1972).

Council on Ethical and Judicial Affairs, American Medical Association. *Code of Medical Ethics: Current Opinions with Annotations*. Chicago, IL: American Medical Association, 1994.

Faden, Ruth R., Catherine Becker, Carol Lewis, John Freeman, and Alan I. Faden. "Disclosure of Information to Patients in Medical Care." *Medical Care* 19, No. 7 (July 19, 1981): 718–733.

Fletcher, Joseph. *Morals and Medicine*. Boston, MA: Beacon Press, 1954.

General Medical Council. *Professional Conduct and Discipline: Fitness to Practise*. London: The Council, 1990.

Kant, Immanuel. "On the Supposed Right to Tell Lies from Benevolent Motives." Trans. Thomas Kingsmill Abbott and reprinted in Kant's *Critique of Practical Reason and Other Works on the Theory of Ethics*. London: Longmans, 1909 [1797], pp. 361–365.

Kant, Immanuel. *Groundwork of the Metaphysic of Morals*. Trans. H. J. Paton. New York: Harper and Row, 1964.

Macklin, Ruth. "Moral Concerns and Appeals to Rights and Duties." *Hastings Center Report* 6, No. 5 (1976): 31–38.

Meyer, Bernard C. "Truth and the Physician." In *Ethical Issues in Medicine*, ed. E. Fuller Torrey. Boston, MA: Little Brown, 1968, pp. 159–177.

Natanson v. Kline. 186 Kan. 393, 350 P. 2d 1093 (1960).

Novack, Dennis H., Robin Plumer, Raymond L. Smith, Herbert Ochitill, Gary R. Morrow, and John M. Bennett. "Changes in Physicians' Attitudes Toward Telling the Cancer Patient." *Journal of the American Medical Association* 241 (March 2, 1979): 897–900.

Nys, Thomas, Yvonne Denier, and Toon Vandevelde, eds. *Autonomy & Paternalism: Reflections on the Theory and Practice of Health Care*. Leuven/Dudley, MA: Peeters, 2007.

Oken, Donald. "What to Tell Cancer Patients: A Study of Medical Attitudes." *Journal of the American Medical Association* 175 (April 1, 1961): 1120–1128.

UNESCO General Conference. "Universal Declaration on Bioethics and Human Rights," October 19, 2005, [accessible on the Internet at http://portal.unesco.org/en/ev.php-URL_ID=31058&URL_DO=DO_TOPIC&URL_SECTION=201.html, accessed January 25, 2010].

Veatch, Robert M. "Case Studies in Bioethics: The Homosexual Husband and Physician Confidentiality." *Hastings Center Report* 7 (April 1977): 17.

Veatch, Robert M. "The Concept of 'Medical Indications.'" *The Patient–Physician Relation: The Patient as Partner, Part 2.* Bloomington, IN: Indiana University Press, 1991, pp. 54–62.

Notes

1. Central Ethical Committee. *British Medical Journal Supplement* (May 1, 1971), p. 30. The BMA appears to have since backtracked on its overturning of the paternalistic exception, perhaps attempting to conform to the General Medical Council, which in Britain has the legal authority to discipline physicians. The BMA by the 1980s (*Handbook of Medical Ethics.* London: British Medical Association, 1981, p. 12) was publishing a list of five exceptions to the duty of confidentiality. One was when the patient consented to disclosure. Three additional exceptions all involve disclosing to serve various interests of society (research, legal requirements to disclose, and "the doctor's overriding duty to society"). The fifth exception can only be seen as paternalistic: "When it is undesirable on medical grounds to seek a patient's consent, but is in the patient's own interest that confidentiality should be broken." This is compatible with the British General Medical Council's position, which reads, "only in exceptional cases should the doctor feel entitled to disregard his [the patient's] refusal." (See General Medical Council, 1990.)

2. In 1994, in a little-noticed modification, the AMA's Council on Ethical and Judicial Affairs (the new name for the Judicial Council) changed the wording to read "Where a patient threatens to inflict serious bodily harm to another person or *himself or herself...*," thus reverting to the older notion of Hippocratic paternalism, while still including the non-Hippocratic authorization to break confidence to protect third parties (Council on Ethical and Judicial Affairs, 1994, p. 72).

3. In fact, some humans who are technically not "persons" may also command respect. As we saw in Chapter 3, many commentators define "person" to refer to any being who is capable of self-consciousness or self-awareness. That would surely exclude many living humans (such as babies, the severely retarded, or individuals with advanced Alzheimer's disease). Since most of us believe that these "human living nonpersons" still deserve respect, it is not entirely accurate to refer to "respect for persons" as the foundation for the duties we are addressing. We could speak of "respect for humans," but that would exclude some non-humans who may also command respect. As we saw in Chapter 3, some believe that higher primates and perhaps others also deserve the kind of respect we are discussing here. We shall continue to use the common term *respect for persons* realizing that the same principles that derive from the notion of respect for persons may also apply to some living humans and others who may not have the capacity for self-consciousness or self-awareness.

6 The Principle of Avoiding Killing

In Chapter 5 we looked at three ethical principles that are elements of the notion of respect for persons. A fourth element has generated a great deal of controversy in recent medical ethics. Many religious and philosophical commentators as well as health care professionals have held that human beings have a moral status that requires that life, especially innocent life, not be taken by human hands. The idea is sometimes expressed that life is sacred, that it is to be preserved (even preserved at all costs), or that one must refrain from killing. In this chapter we discuss this notion as the principle of avoiding killing and examine the differences among the various formulations.

The principle of avoiding killing is another duty-based principle. It can conflict with the consequence-based principles of beneficence and nonmaleficence, just as fidelity, autonomy, and veracity do.

The ethics of death and dying has in recent years included a significant controversy over exactly what it means to be dead. The definition of death debate, as it is sometimes called, has led to a shift in favor of a brain-oriented definition of death. These issues were taken up in Chapter 3.

Here we take up the question of how we treat patients who are critically or terminally ill, but are still alive according to the legal definition of death. Suppose a still living but critically ill patient raises the question of whether it is necessary for his or her life to continue. This kind of case challenges us to get clear on the meaning of terms like *killing*, *allowing to die*, **forgoing treatment**, and **extraordinary means**. It also forces us to clarify ethical questions, including whether it is acceptable to actively kill for mercy or to forgo treatment allowing the patient to die. If forgoing treatment is sometimes acceptable, we need to know just which treatments. Here we confront the ethics of caring for the critically ill. In order to discuss this, four distinctions are crucial: the distinctions between active killing and allowing to die; between withdrawing and withholding treatment; between direct and indirect killing; and between ordinary and extraordinary means (Figure 13).

I. Active Killing vs. Letting Die
   (Action vs. Omission)

II. Withholding vs. Withdrawing

III. Direct vs. Indirect

IV. Ordinary vs. Extraordinary Means

FIGURE 13   Four Basic Distinctions in
Death and Dying

ACTIVE KILLING VERSUS ALLOWING TO DIE

The first distinction is the difference between actively killing the patient, on the one hand, and simply allowing the patient to die by forgoing treatment, on the other. This distinction is widely held throughout the world of medicine (Figure 14). It is generally believed that a moral difference exists between actively killing the patient and simply letting the patient die. It has been accepted by the AMA (2000, p. 55, 72), Roman Catholic moral theology (Congregation for the Doctrine of the Faith, 1980), and the U.S. President's Commission for the Study of Ethical Problems in Medicine and Biomedical and Behavioral Research (1983).

The distinction is not accepted by Orthodox Judaism. In Judaism, letting a patient die is violating the sacredness of life just as much as actively killing (Bleich, 1979). An Orthodox Jewish patient who decides not to turn off a ventilator or to forgo some other treatment is expressing a long-standing Jewish position that all life is a gift from God and to be preserved, even if it is for a short period. Only when the patient is

Actions that kill are morally wrong while forgoing life support may be acceptable depending on the circumstances

Traditions tending to recognize this distinction:

Roman Catholicism

The President's Commision for the Study of Ethical Problems in Medicine and Biomedical and Behavioral Researsch

American Medical Association

Traditions seeing no difference between killing and forgoing life-support:

Judaism

Right-to-life Groups

Groups Supporting Active Euthanasia

FIGURE 14   Active Killing Versus Forgoing Life Support
(Actions vs. Omissions)

goses (moribund) will traditional Talmudic scholars accept the termination of life support. In fact, in that case it becomes a moral duty not to interfere with God's plan for the patient.

Distinguishing Active Killing from Allowing to Die

INVALID ARGUMENTS FOR KEEPING THE DISTINCTION BETWEEN ACTIVE KILLING AND LETTING DIE   Is there really a valid distinction between these two? Some arguments for the distinction really do not make much sense (Figure 15). For example, the argument that killing the patient just intuitively feels morally very different from letting the patient die cannot prove that there is truly a moral difference. It may be that they feel different only because people have been taught all their lives that it is worse to actively kill than it is to let die. If a feeling has been taught over the years by people who think there is a difference, that feeling cannot be used as evidence that a difference really exists. That would be a circular argument.

Second, it is sometimes argued that active killing is illegal in almost all jurisdictions while letting die is legal everywhere, at least under some conditions. It is true that active killing, even on the request of the patient, is illegal in almost all jurisdictions of the world. In the Netherlands, for many years an informal arrangement existed between the prosecutors and the medical profession so that if physicians follow agreed-upon rules they would not be prosecuted even though active killing remained illegal. In 2001 the Dutch Parliament passed a bill that still makes active mercy killing by physicians illegal, but physicians now will be exempt from prosecution if they follow certain requirements. The Northern Territory of Australia in 1995 was the first jurisdiction in the world to legalize active killing for mercy, but that action was overturned by the national legislature. Since then active killing for mercy has become legal in Belgium and Luxembourg. In addition, by 2010, assistance in suicide (aiding someone in killing themselves) was legal in Switzerland and in the states of Oregon, Washington, and most recently in Montana (*Baxter v. State*, 2009).

Regardless of the state of the law, one cannot use what the law says to determine what is ethical. Imagine legislators in a jurisdiction trying to figure out what the right law is to pass. They cannot argue that because it is illegal, it should stay illegal. It is

Invalid Argument	Reason It is Invalid
They intuitively feel different	They may feel different because we have always been taught they are morally different.
Active killing is illegal while forgoing treatment is legal.	The fact that one is legal and the other is illegal does not establish that there is a moral difference or that there should be a legal one.
Active killing would change the role of the physician	Physicians need not be the ones doing the killng.

FIGURE 15 Invalid Arguments for the Omission/Commission Distinction

possible that it is presently illegal, but ethical. In that case, perhaps the law should be changed. Or recently in Montana, where the Supreme Court ruled physician-assisted suicide was not prohibited, legislators faced the question of whether they should make it illegal.

Third, sometimes it is argued that active killing is different from letting die because, if physicians were allowed to actively kill, their role would be changed in a way not entailed in simply letting critically ill patients die. But it would theoretically be possible to legalize active killing while still prohibiting physician participation. We could prohibit physician participation, leaving the role of euthanizer to other people. The law could authorize some other group to actively kill. If one believes that the physician's role is healing and that healing is incompatible with killing, then we might say, "No one in this special role should kill, but other people could." Likewise, if active killing for mercy were legalized, we might also want to exclude people in certain other social roles from the practice. Elementary school teachers, for instance, might have responsibilities that would make it difficult aesthetically and practically to permit them to moonlight as euthanizers.

CONSEQUENTIALIST ARGUMENTS FOR AND AGAINST DISTINGUISHING ACTIVE KILLING AND LETTING DIE   Are there more valid arguments for the distinction between omissions and commissions? Some think they can defend or oppose the distinction by arguing from consequences. Some consequentialists argue that the result is going to be the same whether the terminally ill patient is actively killed or is simply allowed to die. The patient is going to be dead soon either way, so it really does not make any difference. Other consequentialists reply that the consequences of actions and omissions may not really be the same. The consequences to the society, they argue, are actually worse if we permit active killing than if we continue to forbid it and permit only forgoing of treatment. That is an empirical question. What will the world be like if we legalize active killing? Will there be spillover effects, so that some people get killed who should not be killed?

An important series of studies was conducted by the Remmelink Commission, a governmental commission established to examine the effects of the Dutch tolerance for active physician euthanasia (Netherlands Ministry of Welfare, Health and Cultural Affairs, 1992; also see van der Maas et al., 1991). The commission made its best estimate of the number of physician interventions to end life in a twelve-month period. In the Netherlands euthanasia is defined as a physician intervention to kill the patient after a persistent and voluntary request. The report estimated there were 2300 such interventions. This does not include about 400 assisted suicides, which were already considered legal in the Netherlands. The critical finding was that the commission estimated that 1000 additional life-terminating acts occurred *without* an explicit and persistent request from a competent patient (Netherlands Ministry of Welfare, Health and Cultural Affairs, 1992). Thus, almost one in three life-terminating interventions by physicians did not conform to the stipulated terms of the arrangement, which included that the request from the patient had to be explicit and persistent. Moreover, the commission also found that, of the total of 3724 actions by physicians to provide medical assistance in actively ending life, only 486 were reported as required on death certificates. The net result is only 16 percent of the acts in which physicians actively assisted in causing the death of a patient were completely within the terms of the agreement. It is not possible to know whether the quasi-legalization of active euthanasia in the Netherlands increased the number of nonvoluntary and extralegal killings by physicians, but critics of the law claim that these nonvoluntary deaths increase when voluntary mercy killing is made acceptable.

THE ARGUMENT FROM IMPLICATIONS FOR INCOMPETENT PATIENTS   Those who favor legalizing active killing attempt to guard against these bad outcomes by limiting the cases in which it would be permitted. They insist that the patient make a voluntary request while competent and that the patient be certified to be terminally ill. They propose that a second physician confirm the diagnosis and certify the patient's competence and the voluntariness of the patient's choice. But those very safeguards may have unexpected implications.

These requirements could actually make it more difficult for incompetent patients to be treated humanely. Most commentators agree that it is morally justifiable to withdraw life support from incompetents using the same criteria that are used for competents. If, however, those who claim there is no difference between omissions and commissions carry the day, then there would be no reason to use different criteria for deciding when to accept omissions and commissions. If we are committed to the view that active, merciful killings are only justified when the patient is terminal and voluntarily requests to be killed while competent and if the same criteria apply to omissions, then it would always be unacceptable to withdraw life support from incompetent patients. In fact, it would even be unacceptable to withdraw life support for competent persons who were not terminal. The premise that there is no difference between omissions and commissions combined with the belief that commissions are acceptable only for terminal, competent patients leaves the incompetent and the nonterminal not only without active killing, but also without relief that would come from forgoing life support. They are condemned by the logic of the premise that there is no difference between omissions and commissions. The only other option is for the defenders of active killing for mercy to revise their belief that active killings are only acceptable when patients are terminal and voluntarily ask to be killed after being certified competent. In fact, many more honest defenders of active killing for mercy acknowledge that there is no logical way to limit such killings to the terminal and the competent. The same concern for compassion in the face of suffering would seem to support mercy for the nonterminal and incompetent as well. If there is no difference between active killing and letting die, then either both are acceptable for everyone or neither is acceptable for the nonterminal and the incompetent. This leads some people to conclude that, even though the distinction is hard to maintain, there must be something to it. Two other arguments have been put forward to attempt to sustain that claim.

THE ARGUMENT FROM A PRINCIPLE OF AVOIDING KILLING   A third argument in defense of the traditional distinction between active killing and letting die rests on the belief that there is a principle of avoiding killing. According to this view, there is something inherently wrong about killing a human. (Whether this principle extends to non-human species was a question raised in Chapter 3, where we also considered exactly who counts as human with this full moral standing such that it would be wrong to kill them.)

The principle of avoiding killing is, according to many, a fourth part of "respect for persons." Just as there is something inherently wrong with violating fidelity or autonomy or veracity, so, according to this view, respect for persons entails the idea that killing a human being is morally wrong even if, hypothetically, it would be in that person's interest to be killed and even if that person voluntarily requested to be killed. This is the position held by Jews and ancient Christians. It is also held by Muslims, Buddhists, and Hindus and is accepted by many secular thinkers, including Marxists, and by many physicians.

Some versions of this commitment to avoid killing extend to treating all human life as sacred; so it is not only wrong to actively kill, but also to let any preventable death occur. Sometimes, in this form, this position is referred to as the *principle of the sacredness of life*. Holders believe all life is sacred and must be preserved whenever possible.

Taking such a view literally, however, would require extremely rigorous demands: preserving as long as possible the lives of the terminally ill and comatose and actively intervening to prevent all deaths not only in war and violence, but also in famine and natural disasters. Most believe that it is not one's moral duty in the strict sense to prevent all preventable deaths no matter how remote and how difficult to prevent. They accept the naturalness of death, but interpret the principle of avoiding killing to stand against any actions that will hasten death. If this principle of avoiding killing applies only to active interventions to hasten death, then there would be a basis for distinguishing between active killings (commissions) and omissions.

Surely, some omissions that lead to death are morally wrong as well. Someone who had an affirmative duty to save a life and failed to do so would have violated some moral principle. A parent who fails to feed his child or an emergency room physician who fails to deliver basic emergency care that could be life-saving would have violated specific duties to act affirmatively. Perhaps this can be viewed as violating the principle of fidelity—that is, failing in a fiduciary relation.

THE ARGUMENT FROM AUTONOMY   A fourth way of arguing that commissions and omissions that result in the death are morally different can be called the argument from *autonomy and informed consent*. Letting die at the request of the patient or surrogate is always required by respect for autonomy. By contrast, autonomy never requires that a physician kill a patient. Autonomy is an ethical principle requiring noninterference with the life-plans of others. It does not require that one facilitate those plans. Autonomy, as we have seen, generates a *negative right* or the right to be left alone. It does not produce a *positive* right by which one would have a claim to goods or services or resources needed to carry out one's plans. At least in the law, many negative rights do not entail positive rights. Hence, as we saw in Chapter 5, women legally have a negative right to abortion, but not an entitlement to the resources necessary to obtain one. Thus omissions, according to this view, are morally different from commissions in that they are mandated by the principle of autonomy while commissions never are.

New Legal Initiatives for Physician-Assisted Suicide

DISTINGUISHING HOMICIDE ON REQUEST FROM ASSISTANCE IN SUICIDE   Recently, advocates of more active interventions to hasten death have made some additional conceptual distinctions. They have separated cases in which one person would actively kill another at that person's request from cases in which the one helping would merely assist in the person's suicide (Balkin, 2005; Gorsuch, 2006; Mitchell, 2007; Quill and Battin, 2004). The key, they argue, is whether the helper takes the last critical step that causes the death. On the basis of this distinction, injecting a lethal drug would be homicide. (If it were done at the patient's request, it would be called **homicide on request**.) On the other hand, prescribing an oral form of the drug that was then taken by the patient would be considered assistance in suicide since the last key step (taking the drug) was done by the patient. In the 1990s there was a significant movement attempting to legalize **assisted suicide**, in which the assistance is provided by a physician to a mentally competent, terminally ill patient who has requested the assistance. This is what is now legal in the states of Oregon, Washington, and Montana as well as certain European countries including Switzerland and those that have legalized active killing for mercy.

Part of the moral argument is that if the cases are limited to patients certified as terminally ill who have documented requests for assistance and if the patient must physically take the key step that results in death, the risk of abuse is lessened. In the early 1990s the reformist physician Jack Kevorkian developed a "suicide machine" that could be transported in a van. He reportedly assisted in the suicide of at least 130 people, some of whom were apparently not even terminally ill. The Michigan Supreme Court has confirmed that the law prohibiting assisting in suicide was not unconstitutional (*People v. Kevorkian*, 1994). Nevertheless, in spite of several prosecutions, he was never convicted of assisting in a suicide, in part because it was difficult to prove what he had done and in part because some jurors in Michigan were sympathetic. Not content with assisting in suicide and wanting to press the issues further, he injected Thomas Youk, a 52-year-old man in the end stages of amyotrophic lateral sclerosis (ALS), with a lethal drug to end his life. He videotaped the events making clear that Youk appeared mentally competent and desired to end his life. His ALS paralyzed him so he was unable to take medication himself. When the videotape was shown on the television program *60 Minutes*, Kevorkian was prosecuted. He was convicted in 1999 and sentenced to ten to twenty-five years in prison.

INITIATIVE PETITIONS   Assisted suicide was also pursued through an "initiative petition," a process that permits citizens to place issues on a state ballot. Initiative 119 in the state of Washington in 1991 was the first recent attempt to legalize physician-assisted suicide. It did not pass, but it got 46 percent of the vote and was a sign of things to come (McGough, 1993). The next year another citizens' initiative was attempted in California, and it did about as well (Capron, 1993).

In Oregon in 1994, a referendum legalizing physician assistance in suicide for competent, terminally ill patients was passed by a close vote (Oregon Death with Dignity Act, 1994) and has been sustained in challenges all the way to the

U.S. Supreme Court, making it the first law in the United States legalizing physician participation in active assistance in suicide. It still does not legalize actual killing by physicians.

Meanwhile proponents of assisted suicide made two unsuccessful attempts to legalize it, one arguing that state laws prohibiting such assistance violated constitutionally protected liberty (*Compassion in Dying v. Washington*, 1994), the other, that it violated the equal protection clause of the Constitution by supporting persons who wanted to end their lives by terminating life support while prohibiting those who wanted to end their lives with physician-assisted suicide (*Quill et al., v. Vacco*, 1995). The U.S. Supreme Court rejected both of these. The result in the United States is that individual states have the authority either to ban or permit physician-assisted suicide. In 1997, Oregon legalized physician-assisted suicide using a voter initiative. Washington used a similar process in 2008 and the Montana Supreme Court found assisted suicide legal in 2009. Other states continue to consider the question.

The ethics of physician assistance in suicide is now four-square on the agenda for moral and public policy debate. One issue raised is whether there is any principled difference between physician assistance in suicide and physician killing for mercy. Many are claiming that if physicians may assist in suicides of patients, they may, for the same reasons, actually intervene to commit the lethal act. A patient (Thomas Youk, for example) who is mentally lucid but so immobilized by disease as to be unable to take any action on his or her own seems to be deprived of the alternative available to terminally ill persons who could take lethal medications. This could lead to a right to have assistance not merely by providing information or writing a prescription, but actually by having the physician do the injection.

One practical argument remains for a distinction between actually committing the active euthanasia and merely assisting in suicide. If we are concerned about the potential for abuse and about some physicians who might irresponsibly attempt to pressure difficult patients into ending their lives, then possibly it makes sense to hold on to the requirement that the patient must himself or herself actively take the decisive step in ending his or her own life. Of course, some are concerned that even permitting physician assistance will run the risk that patients will be pressured into committing suicide. Some, pointing to Dr. Jack Kevorkian, are concerned that the personality of many physicians prepares them to intervene aggressively, taking matters into their own hands. This is the personality that is ideal for an emergency room when a patient has a blocked airway and needs instant, aggressive intervention to save a life, but it could be just the wrong personality type for terminally ill patients who are candidates for having their lives ended.

Many of those who oppose such interventions do so on ethical grounds rooted in the principle of avoiding killing or the doctrine of the sacredness of life. They are unlikely to be persuaded that pragmatic checks that will minimize abuse are relevant in deciding the matter. Some who continue to hold out for a difference between all active killings (both homicides on request and assisted suicides) and merely letting die may appeal to the difference between the negative rights autonomy provides and the positive rights that are beyond its grasp. It is likely that the matter of legalization of active life-ending interventions will remain controversial.

STOPPING VERSUS NOT STARTING

Besides the basic distinction between omission and commissions, a second distinction complicates the ethics of the care of the dying. It is common to feel that it is morally worse to withdraw a treatment once it has begun than to avoid starting it in the first place. To those physicians and nurses who physically must withdraw a ventilator or other treatment, it feels psychologically as if they are actively killing just as certainly as if they had injected an air embolism. But it makes no sense as a practical matter or if the moral basis for drawing lines is between what is derived from autonomy as a negative right and what is based on positive rights. It seems wiser to follow a policy of trying a treatment and then withdrawing it if it is not working.

The law treats stoppings as "forgoing treatment"; that is, it views them as the same as not starting in the first place. Withdrawing is comparable to withholding, not as active killing. The argument from autonomy explains why stopping treatment is morally the equivalent of not starting. Stopping is morally required by autonomy when consent to treatment is canceled. By contrast, killing is never obliged by the autonomous action of the patient or surrogate. If the principle of autonomy is significant in understanding why commissions are different from omissions in the first place, it should help us understand why withdrawing a treatment is morally like an omission rather than a commission. Now most commentators, legal judgments, and hospital policies that recognize the legitimacy of the omission/commission distinction will classify withdrawing as comparable to withholding. That is the position of The President's Commission for the Study of Ethical Problems in Medicine and Biomedical and Behavioral Research (1983, pp. 73–77) and other groups such as the AMA and Roman Catholic theologians. It is also the view of Talmudic scholars although they, by contrast, find both withholdings and withdrawings morally unacceptable.

THE DISTINCTION BETWEEN DIRECT AND INDIRECT KILLING

A third distinction is often confused with active/passive or commission/omission distinction: that is the distinction between direct and indirect effects. This notion is also sometimes referred to as the **doctrine of double effect**. The basic idea is that in some situations an action can lead to two effects, one intended and desirable, the other unintended and undesirable. The doctrine of double effect holds that the unintended, undesirable effect is morally tolerable if the action itself is not immoral, the undesirable consequence is not a means to the desirable one, and the desirable effect produces a great enough amount of good to be proportional to the undesirable effect. A killing that is "direct" results from an action (or omission) in which the intention of the actor is the death of the individual. A nurse who refused to answer a code because he wanted the patient dead is direct killing by omission.

An indirect effect, such as a death, results from an action (or omission) in which the effect may be foreseen by the actor, but is not intended and is not a means to a desired effect. An anesthesia accident in high-risk surgery would certainly not be intended although it might be foreseen as a possible outcome. Deaths in such cases are morally tolerable according to those who subscribe to the doctrine of double effect.

Consider a physician who is morally opposed to abortion and who is caring for a pregnant woman with cancer of the uterus. Removing a cancerous uterus in a pregnant woman would certainly be known to cause the death of the fetus. That outcome is foreseen with absolute certainty. Nevertheless, even opponents of abortion, such as those who subscribe to the main tenets of Catholic moral theology, would find such a death morally tolerable although they would oppose all directly intended abortions. In this case, if they could save the fetus, they would do so, but in the case of the pre-viable fetus that would not be possible. The death of the fetus would not be the intended purpose of the action. Defenders of the removal of the uterus who nevertheless oppose directly intended abortion would say that, in this case, the physician was performing the act of removing the uterus. The physician could say that this act has a double effect: that is, two consequences—one desired and intended, the other undesirable and foreseen but not intended.

Giving high doses of narcotic for the purpose of relieving pain may also be known to run the risk of respiratory depression and even death. Once again, that death is morally tolerable according to the doctrine of double effect if it had not been intended even though it might be foreseen. If an analgesic could have been used that would have avoided the risk of death, then it would have been used. The Catholic Church opposes all direct killing, as does the AMA. The courts generally accept the distinction as well.

Critics of the doctrine claim that it is important to distinguish between the morality of the behavior and the morality of motivation. They acknowledge that the character of the actor who wants to see someone dead may be different from that of the person who merely knows that death may be an inevitable, unintended outcome. They insist, however, that these judgments about the character of actors not spill over into assessments of the behavior itself. They hold that giving an effective dose of a narcotic that is known to run the risk of death must be deemed morally right (or wrong) behavior regardless of the intention of the actor. If someone malevolently wanted the patient dead and took advantage of his severe pain to give a narcotic that was known to run the risk of killing, the critics of the doctrine of double effect might simply say that this person did the morally right thing for a morally wrong reason. Thus, not everyone who accepts actions known to run the risk of bad consequences does so based on the double effect doctrine.

THE DISTINCTION BETWEEN ORDINARY AND EXTRAORDINARY MEANS

The Meaning of the Terms

Having made the previous three distinctions, we can limit our attention to forgoing of treatments in situations in which the death is not directly intended, whether the treatment is withheld or withdrawn. We need to try to determine which among the treatments that are possible are morally required. The traditional term for those treatments that could acceptably be foregone was **extraordinary means** while those that were morally required were called **ordinary means**.

That language was unfortunate and confusing. There are at least three ways to distinguish ordinary from extraordinary treatments. The first two are older, largely rejected meanings. Treatments could be distinguished statistically by separating common from uncommon ones and considering the common ones "ordinary." That would seem to be the normal meaning of the term *ordinary*. They could be distinguished by the complexity of the technology separating simple from complex, high-tech interventions.

Neither distinction provides a plausible basis for making a moral distinction. Just because a treatment is common, it is not necessarily morally required for every patient. For some patients, even common procedures may be inappropriate. They may serve no purpose, or the patient may be known to react poorly to them. Likewise, some very unusual procedures may be just right for some patients. By the same token, it makes no sense to decide which treatments are required by asking how complex the technology is. Some everyday, simple procedures may not be right for certain patients while complex, high-tech ones may be exactly what some patients need. Medical ethicists have never used the term *ordinary* to mean either common or simple; they have not used *extraordinary* to mean either uncommon or complex. Rather the terms have been used to refer to morally required (ordinary) and morally expendable (extraordinary) treatments.

Currently, the terms *ordinary* and *extraordinary* are being abandoned and replaced by language that makes more clear the inherently normative character of the distinction that needs to be made. We are increasingly simply referring to *appropriate* and *inappropriate* treatments. That language does not reveal the criteria for appropriateness, but it at least makes clear that the reference is not to how common or how complex the treatment is.

This new terminology does not constitute a real change in meaning. The terms *ordinary* and *extraordinary* have always had the normative meaning among the philosophers and theologians using them. The terms simply refer to treatments that are morally required or fitting and those that are not. The key question is, What are the criteria that make the treatment appropriate?

The Criteria for Classifying Treatments Morally Expendable

USELESSNESS   Traditionally, a treatment has been considered morally expendable if it does not serve a useful purpose. That judgment just seems like common sense. But, as we shall see, figuring out whether a treatment serves a useful purpose turns out to be more complicated than it may appear.

GRAVE BURDEN   Even if a treatment serves a useful purpose, such as prolonging life, it may still be expendable if it involves a *grave burden*. Both these criteria are cited by The President's Commission for The Study of Ethical Problems in Medicine and Biomedical and Behavioral Research (1983, p. 84).

The language came from Catholic moral theology and was used by Pope Pius XII in a statement on prolonging life in which he said:

> But normally one is held to use only ordinary means—according to circumstances of persons, places, times and culture—that is to say, means that do not involve any grave burden for oneself or another. Pius XII (1958, pp. 395–396)

In this statement Pius XII refers only to grave burden. Other Catholic moral theology literature includes uselessness as a criterion as well. Note, however, that he includes burden to others as well as burden to the patient, a foreshadowing of the social medical ethics that we shall encounter in Chapter 8. For the remainder of this chapter we shall focus on the burden to the patient as a basis for forgoing life-sustaining medical treatment.

PROPORTIONALITY   In considering both useless and grave burden we are really dealing with the question of benefit/harm ratios. An absolutely useless treatment is one with a zero benefit and therefore one that always has an unfavorable benefit/harm ratio.[1] A gravely burdensome treatment could be one that would have some benefits, but whose benefits would be exceeded by the burdens.[2] Recognizing that both these criteria reduce to a notion of a favorable benefit/harm ratio, the Vatican Declaration of 1980 (Sacred Congregation for the Doctrine of Faith, p. 8) urged the adoption of a single criterion of **proportionality** as the basis for deciding which treatments may morally be omitted.

This notion was accepted by the U.S. President's Commission (1983, p. 88), but in characteristic American fashion, it has given the criterion a patient-centered twist, emphasizing that the values that underlie the judgments of benefit and burden are subjective and must be the patient's values:

> Extraordinary treatment is that which, *in the patient's view*, entails significantly greater burdens than benefits and is therefore undesirable and not obligatory, while ordinary treatment is that which, *in the patient's view*, produces greater benefits than burdens and is therefore reasonably desirable and undertaken. [italics added][3]

The Subjectivity of All Benefit and Harm Assessments

The emphasis in the President's Commission Report on the subjectivity of the value judgments in all benefit and harm assessments is becoming a critical dimension in all judgments about the appropriateness of medical treatments. As we saw in Chapter 4, determining whether an effect is a benefit or a harm, and, in either case, how much of a benefit or a harm, is invariably subjective. There is no reason why being an expert in medicine gives one special expertise in making these judgments. Of course, being an expert in medicine helps in knowing what the effects are likely to be, but once the effect is specified, a positive or negative value must be assigned. It is this task that is inherently subjective and beyond the expertise of the health professional. In fact, insofar as we are concerned about the benefit or harm to the patient, it is not going too far to say that the health professional cannot know whether the treatment will be beneficial and, if so, how beneficial without asking the patient (Veatch, 2009). It is the patient who is likely to be the authority on making the assessment insofar as it is the effects on him or her that are concerned. If one includes the principle of autonomy in any assessment of the morality of a treatment option, then, even in those cases in which it seems clear that the patient is not the best judge of how beneficial the treatment is, it may still be the patient's right to decide whether it is provided. The patient's point of view is determinative.

Determining when a burden is a grave burden is perhaps more obviously subjective. Two patients, medically identical, may have very different subjective responses to treatments. One may experience dialysis as unpleasant, but bearable, while another experiences it as intolerable. For the latter the burden is surely greater than for the former. When the burden gets great enough, then, using the criterion of proportionality, the treatment becomes expendable.

It may be somewhat harder to understand that uselessness is also a subjective judgment. Uselessness sounds like a matter of objective fact. But uselessness must be defined as a function of what counts as worthwhile. Consider the possibility of using a ventilator to maintain a patient in a permanent vegetative state. If the purpose is to restore the patient to consciousness, then the ventilator is totally useless. If, however, someone views even vegetative life as precious and worth maintaining, then the ventilator could be thought of as very useful.

Withholding Food, Fluids, CPR, and Medications

If the morality of a treatment is a function of benefit/harm ratio from a patient's point of view, are there any universally required treatments? What about antibiotics for infection, CPR (cardiopulmonary resuscitation), fluids, nutrition, and routine nursing protocols such as turning a patient?

Three views can be considered: (1) these are simple, therefore required, (2) these can be expendable as objectively useless, or (3) their usefulness is a function of patient (or surrogate) preferences. Controversy exists over whether there is some abstract sense in which there is an objective theory of value for determining whether these treatments are serving a worthwhile purpose. Even if there is, it seems obvious that mere mortal, finite human beings, whether they be physicians or philosophers, are incapable of rendering a definitely correct account of whether these are useful or useless in a given case.

Increasingly these are seen, like all other medical treatments, as requiring benefit/harm determinations. In many cases providing food, fluid, CPR, antibiotics, and routine nursing procedures will be very worthwhile on balance and, in those cases, they should be provided. In other cases, however, they may actually do no good for the patient—from the patient's perspective. They may even produce burdens that exceed expected benefits. In those cases, according to the proportionality view that now prevails, they are morally expendable. They are "extraordinary" means no matter how routine and simple.

This means there can be no such thing as a routine DNR (do not resuscitate) order or an inherently necessary provision of fluids and nutrition. As a matter of law, the Baby Doe regulations may require that all infants must be provided with antibiotics, fluids, and nutrition—apparently even when they serve no purpose or offer substantially grave burden. Many observers, however, including the authors of the President's Commission Report, spokespersons for the Catholic Church, and other conservative commentators, are now acknowledging that there are times when these serve no purpose and can be omitted (President's Commission, 1983, p. 90; May et al., 1987).

With the incorporation of all medical treatments into the framework of benefit and harm assessment under the criterion of proportionality, there is increasing agreement on how to analyze decisions involving competent patients and how patients should go about making those decisions. The real controversies for the future center on the problem of active intervention by health professionals to assist in suicide and to kill for mercy and on how these difficult life-and-death decisions can be made on behalf of incompetent patients.

Key Concepts

Assisted Suicide   Providing help to a person to facilitate his or her suicide—normally by education or supplying the means for committing suicide.

Doctrine of Double Effect   The doctrine that when an action can lead to two effects, one intended and desirable and the other unintended and undesirable, the unintended, undesirable effect is morally tolerable if the action itself is not immoral, the undesirable consequence is not a means to the desirable one, and the desirable effect produces a great enough amount of good to outweigh or be proportional to the undesirable effect.

Extraordinary Means   Medical treatments that are not morally required.

Forgoing Treatment   The term often used to refer to either withholding or withdrawing of treatment.

Homicide on Request   Killing of another person at his or her request—in medicine normally as an act of mercy—such as by injecting a lethal drug.

Ordinary Means   Medical treatments that are morally required.

Proportionality   The criterion for determining whether a medical treatment is required or expendable by assessment of the benefit/harm ratio. Treatments are disproportional if the benefits do not exceed the harms (i.e., if the ratio is 1 or less).

Bibliography

American Medical Association, Council on Ethical and Judicial Affairs. *Code of Medical Ethics: Current Opinions with Annotations*. Chicago, IL: American Medical Association, 2000.

Balkin, Karen F., ed. *Assisted Suicide*. Detroit, MI: Greenhaven Press, 2005.

Battin, Margaret P., Leslie P. Francis, and Bruce M. Landesman, eds. *Death, Dying and the Ending of Life*. Burlington, VT: Ashgate, 2007.

Baxter v. State, No. DA 09-0051 (Mont. December 31, 2009).

Beauchamp, Tom L., and Robert M. Veatch, eds. *Ethical Issues in Death and Dying*, 2nd ed. Upper Saddle River, NJ: Prentice-Hall, 1996.

Bleich, J. David. "The Obligation to Heal in the Judaic Tradition: A Comparative Analysis." In *Jewish Bioethics*, ed. Fred Rosner and J. David Bleich. New York: Sanhedrin Press, 1979, pp. 1–44.

Capron, Alexander-Morgan. "Even in Defeat, Proposition 161 Sounds a Warning." *Hastings Center Report* 23, No. 1 (January–February 1993): 32–33.

Compassion in Dying v. State of Washington, No. C94-119R, United States District Court, W.D. Washington, at Seattle, May 3, 1994.

Congregation for the Doctrine of the Faith. *Declaration On Euthanasia*. Rome: The Sacred Congregation for the Doctrine of the Faith, May 5, 1980.

Gorsuch, Neil M. *The Future of Assisted Suicide and Euthanasia*. Princeton, NJ: Princeton University Press, 2006.

May, William E., et al. "Feeding and Hydrating the Permanently Unconscious and Other Vulnerable Persons." *Issues in Law and Medicine* 3, No. 3 (1987): 203–217.

McGough, Peter M. "Washington State Initiative 119: The First Public Vote on Legalizing Physician-assisted Death." *Cambridge Quarterly of Healthcare Ethics* 2, No. 1 (1993, Winter): 63–67.

Mitchell, John B. *Understanding Assisted Suicide: Nine Issues to Consider*. Ann Arbor, MI: University of Michigan Press, 2007.

Netherlands Ministry of Welfare, Health and Cultural Affairs. *Medical Practice with Regard to Euthanasia and Related Medical Decisions in the Netherlands: Results of an Inquiry and the Government View*. Rijswijk, Netherlands: Ministerio van WHC, 1992.

Oregon. "Oregon Death with Dignity Act [Ballot Measure 16]." *Trends in Health Care, Law and Ethics* 9, No. 4 (1994): 29–32.

People v. Kevorkian, 447 Mich. 436, 527 N.W.2d 714 (1994).

Pope Pius XII. "The Prolongation of Life: An Address of Pope Pius XII to an International Congress of Anesthesiologists." *The Pope Speaks* 4 (Spring 1958): 393–398.

President's Commission for the Study of Ethical Problems in Medicine and Biomedical and Behavioral Research. *Deciding to Forego Life-Sustaining Treatment: Ethical, Medical, and Legal Issues in Treatment Decisions*. Washington, DC: U.S. Government Printing Office, 1983.

Quill et al. v. Vacco et al., Docket No. 95-7028, United States Court of Appeals for the Second Circuit (1995).

Quill, Timothy E., and Margaret P. Battin, eds. *Physician-Assisted Dying: The Case for Palliative Care and Patient Choice*. Baltimore, MD: Johns Hopkins University Press, 2004.

Shannon, Thomas A., ed. *Death and Dying: A Reader*. Lanham, MD: Rowman & Littlefield, 2004.

Van der Maas, Paul J., Johannes J. M. Van Delden, Loes Pijnenborg, and Casper W. N. Looman. "Euthanasia and Other Medical Decisions Concerning the End of Life." *The Lancet* 338 (September 14, 1991): 669–674.

Veatch, Robert M. *Patient, Heal Thyself: How the New Medicine Puts the Patient in Charge*. New York: Oxford University Press, 2009.

Notes

1. We can view an unfavorable benefit/harm ratio as one that is 1 or less. If the benefits equal the harms then the ratio is 1. Most would assume that such a treatment is not worth pursuing and not morally required. A ratio less than 1—that is, a treatment with greater harms than benefits—is surely expendable. An older, more conservative interpretation of grave burden implies that the harms must substantially exceed the benefit before a treatment is morally expendable. According to this view, if a life could be saved with burdens only modestly greater than benefits, apparently one would have a duty to preserve life. However, if one includes life preservation itself as one of the benefits, presumably a great benefit, it is hard to imagine why the burdens would have to greatly exceed the benefits in order for a treatment to be expendable.

2. One can imagine a treatment that has grave burdens and even greater benefits. One interpretation of the grave burdens criterion is that, in this case, there is only so much we can ask of a person, so if the burdens are great enough, the treatment is expendable even if the benefits are larger. Most secular commentators, however, would accept the idea that

whenever the burdens exceed the benefits the treatment is expendable, even if the burdens are not great, while in any case in which the benefits exceed the burdens, the treatment is morally appropriate, at least until we consider the right of the patient to refuse and the interests of the society.

3. The President's Commission still retains the older notion that the burdens must "significantly" exceed the benefits, implying that a treatment would be *ordinary* or "required" if the burdens merely equaled the benefits. Newer analyses question this view. Some would argue that a treatment should be expendable if the benefits were not larger than the burdens, even if they were not smaller either.

7 Death and Dying: The Incompetent Patient

A fair amount of agreement exists today about the things said about competent patients in the previous chapter. Although debates occur about the ethics of active killing including assisted suicide, people generally accept with relatively little controversy the framework presented in Chapter 6 for analyzing decisions made by competent patients. For incompetent patients, by contrast, the situation is one of moral chaos, where physicians and others often do not know how to handle the treatment stoppage decisions.

One reason for the chaos is that there are three separate kinds of incompetent patients. Each must be handled differently. This chapter first considers formerly competent patients, then never-competent patients without family, and finally never-competent patients who do have family. The ethical principles and legal standards used to guide decisions for each group are summarized in Figure 16.

FORMERLY COMPETENT PATIENTS

Some patients who are presently incompetent were once competent. Some of them may have expressed their wishes while competent. The first task in caring for the incompetent patient is to find out whether that is the case. This can be done orally, by talking to other people who know the patient or increasingly today it is done with what is called an **advance directive** (Cantor, 1993; President's Commission, 1983). An advance directive is a written expression of the patient's wishes. A **substantive directive** records the patient's substantive wishes about medical treatment. Usually, but not always, it is designed to apply when the patient is terminally ill or in a permanent vegetative state (also sometimes called a persistent vegetative state). Patients can write out certain things they would not like. Ventilators, chemotherapy, medically supplied nutrition and hydration, and other means of aggressive life support are often mentioned. They can also record certain treatments that they would want to

Type of Patient	Ethical Principle	Legal Standard
Formerly competent	Autonomy extended	Substituted judgment
Never-competent without family	Hippocratic utility	Best interest
Never-competent with family	Limited familial autonomy	Limited familial autonomy

FIGURE 16 Types of Incompetent Patients and the Standards Used in Surrogate Decisions

have provided. These may include palliative care, but could also include medically supplied nutrition. If a patient has unusual desires to receive life-sustaining technologies, it is important that those wishes be recorded because, increasingly, the norm is not to provide them for terminally ill and permanently unconscious patients.

A **proxy directive** specifies the person to serve as a surrogate decision maker in the event the patient is unable to speak for himself or herself. An advance directive naming a proxy is particularly crucial for those who do not want their legal next of kin to be their agent. Because legally the spouse is the next of kin, feuding spouses may want some other relative or friend to function as decision maker. A person with an incapacitated spouse or one for whom taking an active role as decision maker would be too much of a burden may wish to name someone else: A brother or sister, an adult son or daughter, a friend, or someone else may be so named.

One can combine these two forms of directives into a single document that serves both to specify the general types of treatment one would want and names someone to interpret one's wishes in cases of ambiguity.

The Principle of Autonomy Extended

A decision that is made while competent is usually deemed valid and binding when one lapses into incompetency. It is extended into the period of incompetency. The moral principle underlying this form of advance decision making could be called the **principle of autonomy extended**. Whether it is legitimate to extend that autonomy has recently become a matter of increasing controversy. Cases in which the patient has become so incompetent that no memory of the former self remains pose a particular difficulty. The advanced Alzheimer's patient may be quite content with a new lifestyle even though the former self who wrote a treatment refusing advance directive would have militantly refused to continue life in the patient's present form. We usually assume today that the advance directive is still binding, but some would argue that in some cases the contrary policy should be followed (Buchanan and Brock, 1989, pp. 184–189; Dresser and Robertson, 1989). The issue is whether the autonomous decisions of the individual made while competent should continue to control after the individual's life and values have changed radically and the individual has become incompetent. If one thinks of the present person as radically different from the one who wrote the directive, the tendency will be to question the authority of the directive. Some go so far as to say that the incompetent one may actually have become a "new person" to whom the advance directive written by the "other person" does not apply. It is in those cases, in particular, that questions have arisen about the status of advance directives. On the other hand, one might view the entire life of the writer of the directive as a biosocial whole so that there is continuity even if the person cannot presently remember the writing of the directive. Then one will be more inclined to want the directive to control the decisions of the now-incompetent one.

Substituted Judgment

For formerly competent persons, we talk in law about **substituted judgment**. A substituted judgment is one made by a proxy based on the patient's beliefs and values. It fills the gaps, the ambiguities, in an advance directive by drawing on what is understood to be the patient's value framework. For example, if a proxy knows the patient would not want a ventilator even though the proxy would find the ventilator appropriate, the proxy must refuse the ventilator for the patient.

An advance directive is supposed to express the patient's own unique beliefs and values. Some of them will make no sense to the physician at the bedside who may not understand the patient's values. The clinician needs to rely on the surrogate's substituted judgment, drawing on the patient's own beliefs and values to try to do what the patient would have chosen had he or she been able to speak competently. When there is ambiguity or doubt about what the patient would have wanted, we give the benefit of the doubt to the surrogate, but the surrogate who seems clearly to misinterpret the patient can be challenged in court and overruled in cases of well-established error.

Going Beyond Advance Directives

A patient may be in a jurisdiction without a statute authorizing an advance directive. Some countries have no relevant statutes at all. All states in the United States now have statutes or case law that authorize advance directives (Choice in Dying, Inc.), but some of those states cover only very special circumstances. For instance, in many states the law only applies when the patient is terminally ill.

That limitation may not appear to be a problem, but the law usually defines terminal illness very narrowly. To be terminally ill, a person must be dying in a relatively short time period *regardless of life-supporting therapy.* A person who is stable in a permanent vegetative state is technically not terminally ill, yet someone anticipating the possibility of ending up in that situation may still want the advance directive to apply. Is there a way advance directives can be used even though they are not covered by state statute?

Whether the patient is terminally ill or not, if the correct moral principle is autonomy extended and the patient's wishes can be surmised, then those expressed desires ought to be followed. Under common law in British and U.S. legal traditions, the choice of the patient to refuse a treatment is binding, even though not in writing. In the U.S. Supreme Court decision in *Cruzan (Cruzan v. Director, Missouri Dept. of Health,* 110 S.Ct. 2841 [1990]), the court said, "For the purposes of this case, we assume that the United States Constitution would grant a competent person a constitutionally protected right to refuse lifesaving hydration and nutrition." While this is not a definitive conclusion from the court, it suggests where the court will come out, and it extends even to nutrition and hydration, so refusal of other, less controversial treatments would almost certainly be protected. Especially, if the patient's wishes are not in writing, the clinician needs to make sure that the next of kin or the surrogate really is expressing what the patient wanted. In rare cases, if doubt exists about what the patient wants and there is no agreement among the relevant parties, they may actually have to go to court to clarify whether the surrogate is interpreting the patient's wishes correctly.

CASE 13

Terri Schiavo: The Role of Relatives in Refusing a Feeding Tube

On February 25, 1990, 27-year-old Terri Schiavo suffered a cardiac arrest. At the hospital it was determined that she was experiencing hypokalemia, a potassium imbalance. It may have resulted from an eating disorder. There were also unsubstantiated charges of abuse that were discounted in later hearings. She suffered massive brain damage (anoxic-ischemic encephalopathy).

On June 18, 1990, Michael Schiavo, her husband, was appointed guardian. In November he took her to California for unsuccessful experimental rain stimulator treatment. Eventually, tensions emerged over treatment decisions. In May 1992 Michael, who had been living with Terri's parents, moved to another residence. In November of that year a million dollar malpractice award was granted related to the inadequate care Terri received when she first received emergency treatment. An amount of $300,000 was awarded to Michael; $750,000 was used to create a trust fund for Terri's future care.

In May 1998 Michael Schiavo petitioned the court asking that her feeding tube be removed, claiming this was based on her expressed wishes about how she would want to be cared for. He claimed his wife was in a persistent vegetative state. Both this diagnosis and the view that she would want the feeding tube removed were challenged by Terri's parents, Bob and Mary Schindler.

Many court reviews followed. Over the next seven years twenty judges reviewed the case. By the year 2000 the court had concluded that she was indeed in a persistent vegetative state and that her previously expressed wishes had been that the feeding tube should be removed in such a circumstance.

After many years of court review including appeals to the U.S. Supreme Court and after several temporary removals of the feeding tube, it was removed for a final time on March 18, 2005. Terri Schiavo died on March 31.

This case illustrates many of the issues in decision making for a critically ill, no-longer-competent patient. Her next of kin, her husband Michael, was presumed to be her guardian. He could have been disqualified if he had been found abusive or if he was being influenced by a conflict of interest related to the existence of a trust fund that he might inherit. These issues were reviewed many times and the courts decided that he should remain her guardian. Terri's parents, though not her next of kin, had a relevant interest in her well-being and were given ample opportunity to try to show that she was not in a vegetative state or that she would not have wanted the life-supporting feeding tube removed. After careful review, neither of these claims was found proven by the court.

It is noteworthy that, if the court can determine what Terri's wishes were, neither her husband's nor her parents' views about what would be best for her are decisive. The role of the family members was to help determine her wishes. In doing so, her guardian's opinion is given a special place (although he could have been disqualified if the suggestions that he had a conflict of interest were sustained).

It is unclear what the courts would have done had, contrary to fact, they had determined she was not truly vegetative, but in what is sometimes called a "minimally conscious state." Although some might assume that if she were even minimally conscious, then the life support should continue, others might claim that this would be even stronger reason to want the feeding tube withdrawn. The court would have to first try to determine if she had expressed her wishes about such a decision. If not, the choice would pass to her valid surrogate—a role discussed later on in this chapter.

The principle of autonomy suggests that a person ought to be able to decline treatment even if he or she is not dying rapidly, even if he or she has not reduced her views to writing, and even if he or she is refusing something that is not covered under a state advance directive statute.

Mechanisms for Expressing Wishes

ADVANCE DIRECTIVES

The Euthanasia Educational Council's "Living Will"   The written advance directive had its origins in proposals for what was originally called a "Living Will." First proposed by Luis Kutner in the 1930s, the written instruction directive was promoted starting in the 1970s by the Euthanasia Educational Council. It used the language of "artificial or heroic means," terms that we have seen now are thought to be too ambiguous for such documents. The model implies that one type of refusal is the answer for all persons and that refusing treatment was the only thing one would ever want to do. (Now we understand that people may have varying and idiosyncratic preferences regarding terminal care—including a desire to have aggressive life support continue. They may consider writing a directive insisting on treatments.) It and other advance directives are prospective rather than ad hoc; that is, they normally state wishes while one is still healthy, before one knows exactly how one will die. They are therefore often rather vague and fail to speak to specific issues of an individual's terminal care.

One physician, who had an unusual capacity to understand the nature of the choices involved, was able to be more specific. He refused life support in the event of a cerebral vascular accident, but then excluded "cerebral vascular accidents of the subarachnoid space." Another physician, in his advance directive, rejected artificial respiration to prolong life "if I have lost the ability to breathe for more than two or three (not five or six) minutes." Most of us would know the difference between three and five minutes of anoxia well enough to write such specific instructions. It is for problems such as this that a proxy who understands the patient's values is often needed.

An advance directive was in its original form permissive rather than mandatory. It authorized the physician to stop rather than instructing that he or she must stop. Now most advance directives are more firm in specifying what the patient wants, giving instructions rather than mere permission.

Catholic Health Association The Catholic Health Association at one time produced a document in which the operative sentence was identical to that of the Euthanasia Council's living will. It stated that if "there is no reasonable expectation of my recovery from physical and mental disability, I request that no extraordinary means be used to prolong my life." That document has now been replaced by a pamphlet that assists people in preparing their own advance directives (United States Catholic Conference, n.d.). Since advance directive forms are now state specific, a general form is no longer useful. Many state Catholic Conferences now have their own forms that reflect the laws of the individual states. The U.S. Catholic Conference pamphlet continues to affirm the right of patients to make their own decisions about forgoing life support (including nutrition and hydration) while explicitly rejecting physician-assisted suicide and what it calls "euthanasia," by which it means intentionally acting to end life.

The President's Commission for the Study of Ethical Problems in Medicine and Biomedical and Behavioral Research The 1983 report on *Deciding to Forego Life-Sustaining Treatment* of the U.S. President's Commission (p. 136) endorsed a combined substantive and proxy directive. Such proposals had existed since the mid-1970s (Bok, 1976; Veatch, 1976). Other national bioethics groups including the Bioethical Advisory Committee (1988–1990), National Bioethics Advisory Commission (1996–2001), and the President's Council on Bioethics (2001–2009) have not pursued the issues of terminal illness decision making further.

Problems with Advance Directives A number of problems have been raised with advance directives. One of the first was whether wishes of the author necessarily remain valid when one lapses into incompetency. Another was need to permit variation in wishes. This has been addressed by encouraging an individually tailored advance directive, by using forms permitting recording of explicit patient preferences in a range of medical scenarios (Emanuel and Emanuel, 1989), or by using value assessments that attempt to produce a written record of the patient's values pertaining to terminal care (Doukas and McCullough, 1991; Kielstein and Sass, 1993).

LEGISLATION As an alternative to individually prepared advance directives, some people have advocated legislation clarifying the legal options for terminal care decisions.

Attempts to Legalize Active Mercy Killing and Assisted Suicide Some of the boldest, if most crude, attempts at legislation have been designed to legalize active killing for mercy. This was tried without success in Great Britain in 1937, followed in 1947 by an equally unsuccessful attempt in New York, then in Idaho in 1969, in Montana in 1973, and in Oregon in 1973. None had gotten anywhere until recently when, as described in Chapter 6, the strategy has shifted, attempting to legalize only physician assistance in suicide of terminally ill, competent patients. At that point the Washington Initiative (1991) and the one the following year in California, both of which were limited to assisted suicide, were narrowly defeated before Oregon passed such an initiative in 1994, a decision re-affirmed by the state in 1997. Since then the state of Washington has legalized physician-assisted suicide by an initiative placed before the voters (November 2008) and Montana has legalized it through a court decision the following month.

Legalizing Active Killing for Mercy   Meanwhile, international developments in the Netherlands, Belgium, and Luxembourg have, in effect, legalized active killing for mercy exempting physicians from prosecution for committing euthanasia provided proper procedures are followed.

Natural Death Act Legislation   Before this recent legal activity directed toward physician-assisted suicide and voluntary active euthanasia, most legal activity had been designed to clarify the status of advanced directives for terminally ill, formerly competent patients. All U.S. jurisdictions now have this type of legislation, providing either substantive or proxy directives. They generally make clear that an advance directive written while the individual is competent is valid and must be obeyed provided certain conditions are met (including provision for confirmation of diagnosis and prognosis). More generally, in the United States competent patients have the legal right to refuse medical treatment offered for their own benefit and valid surrogates have the right to make such decisions on behalf of incompetent persons.

Issues to Be Addressed in an Advance Directive

The most important lesson from the past two decades of discussion of advance directives is that they need to be specific to values and desires of the individual person. However, several categories of information should be covered.

WHAT TREATMENTS ARE BEING REFUSED?   If the writer of an advance directive simply refuses "extraordinary" means, he or she is begging for trouble in interpretation. *Extraordinary* can mean many different things to different people. Such language should be avoided. Even references to "machines" are ambiguous. Specific machines should be named, if they are to be excluded. Is an intravenous drip a "machine" or is the reference only to ventilators and dialysis machines? Does a refusal of machines imply a desire for other kinds of treatment such as antibiotics for infection, surgery that is meant to be an attempt to cure, or radiation? If one refuses CPR (cardiopulmonary resuscitation), is that refusal meant to apply to temporary and potentially reversible situations resulting from choking, an anesthesia accident, or an accidental drug overdose?

Another traditional term is *gravely burdensome.* It makes sense to say that one wants to refuse gravely burdensome treatments, but one must be aware that such terms are subject to tremendous variation in interpretation. At least one should designate whose judgment about grave burdens should be governing. If someone writes an advance directive refusing gravely burdensome treatments, does that mean the writer refuses only if the burden is very large, only if the burden is much larger than the benefits, or all treatments with an excess of burden over benefit?

Advance directives should make clear whether the writer is refusing (or accepting) food, fluids, antibiotics, and CPR and under which circumstances. Since it is very difficult to anticipate all possible circumstances, it is particularly important that someone be named to interpret what the patient really wants.

WHAT TREATMENTS ARE DESIRED   It is at least as important to specify which treatments are desired and when. Does the writer of the advance directive want medically supplied nutrition? What about oral nutrition? Is fluid necessary for the purpose of keeping the patient alive or only for comfort and who is to determine whether it is needed for comfort? If the person has refused surgery, does that include pain relieving surgery?

A new problem has arisen with advance directives that refuse life support. Many who would normally refuse such treatment also would like to be organ donors if the circumstances permit. In some cases, however, organs are preserved better if some life-extending treatments are provided temporarily—ventilator support or vasopressors, for instance. Many who write directives refusing all life support would really want these measures to help preserve organs even if it briefly extended life. In such case, an advance directive should include a proviso that life support can be administered temporarily for the purpose of preserving organs. Otherwise, the treatment team may feel forced to follow the treatment-refusing directive and damage potentially valuable organs.

WHEN SHOULD THE DIRECTIVE TAKE AFFECT?   The standard language of an advance directive is that it should take effect only when the patient is terminal and is dying imminently. That may be what some people have in mind, but for others that is the time when an advanced directive becomes irrelevant. If the patient is going to die soon regardless of treatment, then it is too late to make the decision to avoid prolonged dying. Does the advance directive include cases in which the person might be permanently vegetative, but not terminally ill in the sense of dying imminently regardless of treatment? Does it ever come into effect when the person is neither dying nor vegetative, such as when the patient is in prolonged painful illness or is suffering from decline of mental capacity? Should it come into play whenever the surrogate decides, regardless of patient diagnosis as long as the patient is not competent to speak for himself or herself? Recent medical literature recognizes that some people previously thought to be permanently unconscious are actually "minimally conscious." Should an advance directive ever come into effect in such a case or would the writer want life support to continue?

IS A DURABLE POWER OF ATTORNEY TO BE APPOINTED?   Is a durable power of attorney (a proxy or surrogate) to be appointed and, if so, is there a secondary proxy? If two or more are named, must their decision be unanimous or can anyone authorize nontreatment? What happens if they disagree? Some people may have special concerns that will lead them to include other items in their advance directive such as the hospital (or jurisdiction) in which the person wants to receive treatment, which physicians or lawyers should be consulted, which ethics consultants the individual would like involved, whether there should be consultation with a priest, neighbor, teacher, or other trusted confidant, and whether treatment refusal is based on common law or statute or both.

NEVER-COMPETENT PATIENTS WITHOUT FAMILY OR OTHER PRE-EXISTING SURROGATES

Among incompetent patients, cases of those who were formerly competent are not the most difficult to resolve. A second group, those who have never been competent and are without family who could act as surrogates, may pose a greater challenge. These could be elderly people with no living relatives, adults estranged from family, or even isolated, orphaned, or abandoned children. We shall take up this group before turning to never-competent patients with family. We can include in this group those without surrogates who were once competent but have left no record of their wishes upon which a substituted judgment could be made. In terms of what we know about their wishes, it is as if they had never been competent.

The Principles

Morally, the principle to be used with the familyless, never-competent patient cannot be autonomy. By definition, autonomy is impossible in this group. We must revert to the next principle, which is to maximize the patient's net welfare, that is, the principle of individual (Hippocratic) utility (see Figure 16).

Using this principle, however, requires some assumptions. It requires assuming that incompetent persons have interests. In the case of the most severe cases of incompetency (anencephaly, for example), some would question whether it is meaningful to speak of the interests of the incompetent one at all. Even if an incompetent can be said to have interests, there must be agreement on what counts as welfare for the patient. We must believe enough agreement exists on a theory of value to determine what is in this incompetent one's interest. We are not merely interested in medical welfare (although that, by itself, would be difficult to determine). We saw in Chapter 4 that reasonable people will normally want to trade off medical for other kinds of welfare.

No legal or moral basis exists for someone in the role of physician to decide to stop treatment on a patient in this group. On the other hand, clearly some treatments that physicians think of are not worth pursuing. Someone has to decide and some standard has to be used for that decision.

The Legal Standard

Legally the standard is called the **best interest standard**. The goal is to do what is best for the patient—at least until we move to the level of social ethics and consider whether social utility or justice can ever dictate limits on pursuing the best interest of such patients. Some people are beginning to doubt whether we must do literally what is best for such patients. Not only social considerations but also pragmatic patient considerations suggest possible limits. It seems unlikely that we would be required to fly a patient to Bethesda for the latest research protocol or to call in the best surgeon in the world to treat an almost certainly fatal condition if doing so created enormous burdens for others. Whatever decision maker is identified, it is possible that the agent will come up with a treatment plan that will provide somewhat less than the absolute best possible outcome for the patient. If the agent has missed by very far what to others seems like the best treatment, some review will be needed, but small deviations will probably be overlooked.

Who Should Be the Surrogate?

The critical question is who the surrogate should be for the never-competent patient without family. Presently no clear answer exists. As we have seen, there is no basis for assuming that the attending physician (or anyone else) has the authority to speak for this group of patients. We have two options. First, we could pass a law naming the primary physician the default surrogate. Still, there is no reason why a physician assigned to the patient should be authoritative in deciding the patient's best interest. In fact, physicians may have systematic biases inclining them toward certain decisions that may be contrary to the patient's real interest. In the 1950s and '60s, for instance, physicians tended to have a strong commitment to preserving life at all costs. More recently, tendencies may be appearing to avoid what clinicians deem to be "futile treatments." Even if there are no systematic biases in the physician population as a whole, individual biases will always be present. One physician may be aggressively pro-treatment while the one on duty on the next shift may be equally militant in his or her decision to transfer the patient to a hospice. There is no reason why this group of patients should be subject to these random variations.

A second argument against using the attending physician as de facto surrogate concerns the physician's role as one to protect patients from irresponsible surrogates. The primary physician is in the best position to be a check on the surrogate, whoever that may be. While he or she should not have the authority to override a surrogate, he can certainly insist on outside review of the surrogate's judgment. If the physician becomes the surrogate that check is lost.

The alternative is to insist that a guardian be appointed legally for this one narrow class of patients. If someone believes that a patient who has never been competent and has no family would be better off dead, perhaps a guardian should be formally appointed before that belief is acted upon. This group of patients is particularly vulnerable. They deserve special precautions, and many argue that this is the type of case where it would be better to err on the side of caution.

NEVER-COMPETENT PATIENTS WITH FAMILY SURROGATES

This leaves us with a third group of patients for whom a decision-making structure must be found: those who have never been competent (or have never expressed themselves while competent) but have family members available to function as surrogates. The consensus is that the next of kin should be the presumed surrogate in such cases (Areen, 1987; President's Commission, 1983). They should serve until they are demonstrated (normally to a judge) to be too foolish, too malicious, or simply unwilling to serve. It seems clear that the family should try to serve the best interest of the patient. What happens, however, when there is a difference of opinion about what is in the patient's best interest?

This seems to have been the situation in the case at the beginning of this volume of the youngster named Yusef Camp who ate a pickle and was found unconscious, presumably because someone had laced the pickle with drugs causing respiratory depression. When he was diagnosed as being permanently unconscious in a vegetative state, his parents refused to agree to terminating life support. Are there any objective grounds to which physicians can appeal to challenge this decision?

The clinicians would have to admit ventilatory support might be effective in changing the dying trajectory of this patient. And the family can make a case for benefit, at least from their point of view. There seems no medical basis on which to refute the claims that unexpected results can occur. Nor are there any grounds for refuting the family's claim that all life, even permanently unconscious life, is precious. The clinicians can counter with the claim that further life support will almost certainly not permit the patient to emerge from a coma, but that is not the same as proving that the treatment will do no good. The latter claim is surely not a scientific medical fact; it is a value judgment—a widely accepted one, but one not universally held. The physicians might try to argue that continuing treatment is not the best course for the patient, although showing why it is contrary to the boy's interest to continue treatment when he is unconscious and cannot suffer from the interventions is a difficult task. Some clinicians have attempted to claim that it is a "moral affront" to continue treatment in such cases, but against that claim one would have to consider whether it would also be a "moral affront" to rely on the medical establishment or the state to cause the child to die against the parents' wishes.

What happens when the family makes what in the eyes of clinicians appears to be less than the best choice? The family may be the legally designated surrogate decision maker, but surrogates do not have unlimited discretion in making medical choices for their incompetent wards. There seem to be two options. First, society could insist that the surrogate choose what most reasonably is the single best course—as determined by a court or some other authority. Determining what is the best course may be difficult, but it is a standard often advocated. At first, this seems like the appropriate policy. Otherwise family is held to a lower standard than the court in the cases involving never-competent patients without family.

However, if the family must choose the best possible course, it has no choice at all (because some other authority will determine what that single course is and force the family to pursue it). Moreover, every case would have to go to a court or some other authority to determine exactly what is best.

This suggests a second course that may be preferable. In the case in which a family member or some other pre-existing surrogate is making the choice, we could give this person some limited range of discretion among plausible choices. In the case of Karen Quinlan, when Mr. Quinlan was appointed her guardian, he was never told he must turn off the respirator. He and other families are given some discretion as are other families. With this option something less than the best choice will be tolerable.

What Is the Standard Underlying This Family Discretion?

What standard would support granting this discretion to the family or other relevant surrogate? It cannot be literally the best interest standard. That would require overriding parents whenever they were even slightly wrong. The answer seems to be that the standard is some version of the *principle of limited familial autonomy*. That is what moral theorists are saying. Although the courts have never formally articulated such a principle, their decisions reflect this idea. The family is a fundamental institution in our society. It has limited authority to choose the values of its incompetent members. It has the right and duty to inculcate a value system into its incompetent members. It need not choose the best value system, but some plausible set of values should be transmitted. It has been suggested that the family has autonomy analogous to the individual. However, autonomy for the family cannot be unlimited as it is in the case of the individual.

Consider the analogy with what we tell parents about the education of their children. We require that they provide them an education. We expect that it be a good education. We as a society, however, do not monitor every choice, insisting that it be the best possible education. Parents are permitted to choose parochial schools, military schools, or aggressive achievement-oriented schools. As long as the family is within reason, the state will not second-guess it.

But at some point the society must be willing to say that the family deviates too radically. If the family chooses no formal education at all for its children, the state will intervene *parens patriae* and take custody. The autonomy of the family is vitally important, but it is limited.

What are the foundations of limited familial autonomy? Some find it in religious traditions, the divine ordination of the family as a fundamental social unit; others in pragmatic considerations such as the probability that the family is more committed to the welfare of the child than any other social group or the need to reward families for their service by allowing some limited discretion. Whatever the foundation, it is widely agreed it exists. The President's Commission, for example, says:

> This society has traditionally been very reluctant to intrude upon the functioning of families, both because doing so would be difficult and because it would also destroy some of the value of the family which seems to need a fair degree of privacy and discretion to maintain its significance. (President's Commission, 1983, p. 215)

The nuance of the notion of limited familial autonomy within the limits of reason is suggested by the following case:

CASE 14

Chad Green: The Case of Limited Familial Discretion about Chemotherapy

A two-and-a-half-year-old boy named Chad Green developed leukemia that, according to physicians, needed chemotherapy if the boy was to have a chance at survival. The family, however, believed in an alternative diet as a treatment. They felt that the chemotherapy would be too toxic and harmful for their son and that it would fail. They preferred treating his leukemia with a special diet of macrobiotic rice and Laetrile, an extract from apricot pits that is believed to be a therapy for cancer by many committed to alternative therapies.

When the family refused the recommended orthodox chemotherapy, the physician, Dr. John Truman of Harvard Medical School, felt obliged to seek judicial review. He eventually won a court order taking custody of the child for purposes of providing the recommenced therapy. The claim was, in effect, that the parents had exceeded the limits of reason in pursuing what was in the child's best interest.

The boy's parents protested vigorously, at one point taking the boy to Mexico to obtain the Laetrile. While theoretically they could have been prosecuted, wiser heads determined that no purpose would be served.

Dr. Truman continued to pursue the case. He realized that he might be able to work out a compromise that would respect the parents' views, at least to some extent, and still accomplish the ends he was seeking. He offered to treat the child with the special diet and Laetrile, obtaining safe and clean supplies, if the parents would agree to let him simultaneously administer the chemotherapy. While this did not completely satisfy either party, and neither was convinced that this compromise was the best possible course for the boy, they each realized that it accomplished much of what they were seeking. The court eventually accepted this compromise. The court, in effect, found that even if this was not the best possible course, it was within reason and should be allowed to proceed.[1]

The notion of limited familial discretion gives us a basis for further analysis of the case of Yusef presented in Chapter 1. As the boy lay permanently unconscious on a ventilator, the physicians were convinced that the best course would be to stop the ventilator and let him die. They could not persuade the parents, however, that this was best. Several strategies were available, none of which seemed to offer a satisfactory solution.

First, they could have tried to argue that Yusef was already deceased based on brain criteria for death. Of course, physicians are not normally required to treat a corpse. If the boy were already dead, then treatment could cease even against the parents' wishes. As we saw in Chapter 3, brain-based definitions of death are replacing the more traditional cardiac-based ones. In this case, however, limited brain activity remained, at least in the opinion of one of the neurologists who examined the patient. Moreover, in the District of Columbia at the time no law authorized death pronouncement based on brain function. Thus the strategy of declaring the boy dead would not work.

Second, the medical team could go to court to attempt to have the parents overruled on the grounds that their judgment was not best for the patient. We have seen that this approach can work in cases such as that of Chad Green. But in Yusef Camp's case, showing that the continuation of life support is contrary to the boy's interest would be difficult. We have just seen that parents are given limited discretion in deciding what is in their ward's interest. In this case, the boy is permanently unconscious, so it is hard for the physicians to show that the boy is being harmed in any way by continuing treatment. The medical team would likely fail if it went to court on the grounds that the parental judgment was contrary to the boy's interest.

There is still a third possible basis for seeking to override these parents. It could be claimed that the continuation of life support jeopardizes not the boy's interests, but the interests of third parties: of the other patients on that ward, of the nurses who have to deliver care, or of the citizens of the District of Columbia, who were funding the treatment through their Medicaid program.

Is it possible that the time has come to begin to set limits on patient care not on the basis of patient well-being or even patient rights, but on the basis of the interests of third parties? Seeing how third-party interests might justifiably enter these and other medical decisions is the focus of the next chapter.

Key Concepts

Advance Directive   A written expression of a person's wishes about medical care, especially care during a terminal or critical illness.

Best Interest Standard   The standard used by a proxy for medical decision making in cases in which it is impossible to know what the incompetent person's beliefs and values are. Such judgments are based on what are taken to be objective beliefs about what is good for the patient.

Principle of Autonomy Extended   The moral principle that is sometimes cited as supporting the duty to respect the autonomous choices of persons even after they have ceased to be competent.

Proxy Directive   An advance directive that specifies a person to serve as the surrogate decision maker in the event the writer is unable to speak for himself or herself.

Substantive Directive   An advance directive that records the patient's substantive wishes about medical treatment, specifying treatments that are desired or refused and/or criteria for making judgments. Usually, but not always, they are designed to apply when the patient is terminally ill or in a permanent vegetative state. Ventilators, chemotherapy, medically supplied nutrition and hydration, and other means of aggressive life support are often mentioned.

Substituted Judgment   The standard used by a proxy for medical decision making based on an incompetent person's beliefs and values as they were expressed while the person was capable of expressing them.

Bibliography

Areen, Judith. "The Legal Status of Consent Obtained from Families of Adult Patients to Withhold or Withdraw Treatment." *Journal of the American Medical Association* 258, No. 2 (July 10, 1987): 229–235.

Bok, Sissela. "Personal Directions for Care at the End of Life." *The New England Journal of Medicine* 295 (1976): 367–369.

Buchanan, Allen E., and Dan W. Brock. *Deciding for Others: The Ethics of Surrogate Decision Making.* Cambridge: Cambridge University Press, 1989.

Cantor, Norman L. *Advance Directives and the Pursuit of Death with Dignity.* Bloomington, IN: Indiana University Press, 1993.

Doukas, David J., and Laurence B. McCullough. "The Values History: The Evaluation of the Patient's Values and Advance Directives." *Journal of Family Practice* 32, No. 2 (1991): 145–153.

Dresser, Rebecca S., and John A. Robertson. "Quality of Life and Non-Treatment Decisions for Incompetent Patients: A Critique of the Orthodox Approach." *Law, Medicine, & Health Care* 17 (1989): 234–244.

Emanuel, Linda L., and Ezekiel J. Emanuel. "The Medical Directive: A New Comprehensive Advance Care Document." *Journal of the American Medical Association* 261 (June 9, 1989): 3288–3293.

Kielstein, Rita, and Hans-Martin Sass. "Using Stories to Assess Values and Establish Medical Directives." *Kennedy Institute of Ethics Journal* 3 (September 1993): 303–318.

President's Commission for the Study of Ethical Problems in Medicine and Biomedical and Behavioral Research. *Deciding to Forego Life-Sustaining Treatment: Ethical, Medical, and Legal Issues in Treatment Decisions.* Washington, DC: U.S. Government Printing Office, 1983.

United States Catholic Conference. *Advance Directives: A Guide To Help You Express Your Health Care Wishes.* Washington, DC: U.S. Catholic Conference, n.d. [current 2010].

Veatch, Robert M. *Death, Dying, and the Biological Revolution.* New Haven, CT: Yale University Press, 1976. [See also revised edition, 1989.]

Notes

1. Based on Custody of a Minor Mass., 379 N.E. 2d 1053 (1978) and other published reports of the case.

Social Ethics of Medicine: Allocating Resources, Health Insurance, Transplantation, and Human Subjects Research

Thus far the issues addressed in this volume have focused on the level of the individual patient/physician relationship. The Hippocratic ethic committed the physician to benefiting the patient. The principles clustered under the idea of respect for persons add duties to the agenda that do not necessarily end up benefiting the patient, but nevertheless still focus on the individual receiving medical services. There were at least two points at which hints of a more social concern emerged. In Chapter 4 we noted that modern discussions of confidentiality permit or even require disclosure of confidential information if necessary to provide significant benefit to third parties. In Chapter 6 we noted that Pope Pius XII considered medical treatments extraordinary if they involved a grave burden to other people. In both cases we delayed exploration of these third-party interests. This chapter opens medical ethical considerations to a more social dimension, asking when, if ever, our duties should include promoting the welfare of others or fulfilling duties to others.

THE NEED FOR A SOCIAL ETHIC FOR MEDICINE

The Limits of the Ethics of Individual Relations

The Hippocratic formula calls for benefiting the patient (in the singular). Ancient Hippocratic medicine was not oriented toward the health or welfare of the community or of other individuals. Modern medicine and modern interpretations of the oath have often continued this individualism. For example, the Declaration of Geneva states that "The health of my patient will be my first consideration." *Patient* is in the singular. Even those codes and oaths that express commitment to patients in the plural still only focus on the single physician's patients. There is no concept of moral community in the Hippocratic tradition. It focuses on patient welfare rather than more inclusive welfare of other persons or of society as a whole.

When modern ethics began to shift from a Hippocratic ethic of benefit to a more deontological ethic of rights and duties, drawing on the notion of respect for persons and the underlying principles of fidelity, autonomy, veracity, and avoiding killing, the new ethic was still addressing problems of the individual patient/physician relation—problems of confidentiality, informed consent, disclosure of diagnoses, and the care of the dying patient. It was as if in all the world there were only one physician and one patient. Similarly, ethics for nurses and other health professionals zeroed in on the individual patient. The moral problem was figuring out how the patient ought to be treated. The dispute between the consequentialist Hippocratic ethic and non-consequentialist ethic of respect for persons was inside the tradition of individualism. If respect for persons seemed to be winning the day, defeating the more traditional Hippocratic paternalism, it was because the controversies of the day posed questions of how to treat the individual patient. In that world, autonomy and the related respect-for-persons principles seemed to carry the day.

But autonomy's triumph was only temporary (Veatch, 1984). By the turn of the century, moral problems moved to a more social model. This shift required confronting the problems of ethical individualism. Both Hippocratic beneficence and respect for persons ignore duties to third parties. In the contemporary world ignoring society increasingly becomes impossible. Medicine must confront the issues of allocating scarce medical resources, providing health insurance, distributing transplantable organs, and conducting research on human subjects. In each of these areas the goal is not improving the welfare of the individual patient but benefiting members of a community of people who often have conflicting interests. Before examining these issues we need to examine what ethical principles can be brought to bear on them.

The Social Ethical Principles for Medical Ethics

SOCIAL UTILITY   It seems, at first, as if the principle for a social ethic ought to be what can be called **social utility**. In Chapter 4 we saw that the principles of beneficence and nonmaleficence can be combined into an overall measure of consequences called *utility.* In that chapter we were examining Hippocratic utility (benefits and harms to the individual patient). In Figure 17 we provide a final version of the diagram that has previously appeared in preliminary form in Chapters 4 and 5. In Figure 17 social utility takes its place as a consequence-maximizing principle at the social level.

The Nature of the Principle of Social Utility   Beneficence and nonmaleficence applied at the social level take into account all benefits and harms to all parties affected, not just the individual patient. Here the goal is the greatest aggregate good. This is the ethical principle of the classical social utilitarians, people like Jeremy Bentham (1996 [1789]) and John Stuart Mill (2001 [1863]). This is the ethical principle underlying standard cost-benefit analysis and many other strategies for health planning. In such analyses, planners attempt to determine the potential benefits and the potential costs (economic, social, and medical) of alternative uses of resources. Then they follow the course that will produce the most net benefit (often expressed per unit of cost). Their principle is social utility—that is, beneficence and nonmaleficence applied socially—to all parties potentially affected. This is just like Hippocratic utility maximizing, except that it is not limited to the individual patient.

	Consequentialist Principles	Duty-Based Principles
Individual	Subjective 1. Beneficence 2. Nonmaleficence —**Hippocratic Utility**— Objective 1. Beneficence 2. Nonmaleficence	**The Ethic of Respect for Persons** 1. Fidelity 2. Autonomy 3. Veracity 4. Avoidance of Killing
Social	Subjective 1. Beneficence 2. Nonmaleficence —**Social Utility**— Objective 1. Beneficence 2. Nonmaleficence	**Justice**

FIGURE 17   Ethical Principles—Final Form Including Social Principles

Critics raise questions about the social utility principle. Two kinds of problems arise, problems of quantification and problems of equity.

Quantification Problems   First, problems exist in determining what maximizes the net good. This is particularly severe in health care, where the benefits include such nebulous and subjective goods as relief of pain, keeping a patient alive until some important family event occurs, or relieving mental anguish. Critics claim that these are almost impossible to quantify and that efforts to do so expose the planners to the risk of incorporating biases in assigning weights to certain outcomes.

While the quantification problems are severe, social scientists have become very sophisticated in providing such quantifications. For example, considerable work has been done in developing scales that permit comparison of different disease states. Robert Kaplan's (Kaplan and Bush, 1982) Quality of Well-Being Scales were used by the Oregon Health Services Commission (1991) in the initial ranking of diagnosis–treatment pairs for its experiment in allocating Medicaid funds. This project attempted to decide which of several hundred possible medical interventions deserve priority. The commission asked people to rank various conditions on a scale from 0 to 1, with 0 being comparable to death and 1 being normal health. From this information, together with scientific data on the possible effects of the intervention and their costs, the commission staff could calculate the cost per unit of expected benefit. These studies have been developed with great care and sophistication. Others have attempted to develop a single unit that integrates both the number of years of survival from an intervention and the quality of life that survival brings. The unit, called the quality-adjusted life-year (QALY), permits comparison on a single scale of interventions that primarily extend life with those that primarily improve the quality of life. These sophisticated health planning measurements can be used in calculations of benefit/harm ratios so that alternative interventions can be ranked in terms of the amount of well-being or the number of QALYs bought per unit of resource invested.

Problems of Inequity   The real controversy in the use of aggregate net benefits for comparing different treatments is that it does not consider how benefits are distributed. According to the principle of social utility, the morally correct course is the one that will maximize the aggregate net benefit per unit of resources. This may hide the fact that the benefits are very unevenly distributed. It is the nature of medicine that some conditions and some patients are much harder and less efficient to treat than others. Patients with multiple chronic illnesses are less efficient to treat than those with acute, treatable conditions. People living in rural areas or inner cities may be harder to reach with medical services than suburbanites. A cost-benefit analysis comparing a health care investment for upper-middle-class suburbanites with one for rural area or inner city patients will show that the suburban health plan produced more benefit (lives saved or QALYs) per unit of investment.

The moral issue is whether giving such priorities would be ethical. It may turn out that the health care system that is the most efficient is not the most fair or just or equitable. If the most efficient system is not the most fair, what is the proper relationship between these two ethical concerns?

JUSTICE AS AN ALTERNATIVE SOCIAL ETHICAL PRINCIPLE   If we are not satisfied morally with the allocation of medical resources solely on the basis of maximizing the aggregate (net) good, we need a principle that pays attention to the distribution of the good. The principle of **justice** plays this role. It is a way of showing respect for persons at the social level; hence, it appears in Figure 17 in the lower right quadrant as a duty-based principle at the social level. Justice is the principle that people in similar situations should be treated equally. The key is determining when people are considered to be in morally similar situations. Different theories of justice identify different characteristics. In Greek culture, noble or aristocratic birth was considered relevant in deciding what constituted a fair allocation. In modern cultures, especially those influenced historically by Judeo-Christian thought, justice is interpreted in a more egalitarian manner. Justice is seen as requiring that people have opportunities for equality of well-being. In health care, this often leads to distributing health services on the basis of need. While need could be determined in terms of relative overall well-being, health care is often allocated on the basis of *medical* need.

We saw in Chapter 4 that medical well-being is a complex concept, including considerations of preventing death, curing disease, relieving suffering, and promoting health. Determining who is worst off medically requires some agreement on the value judgments to be made. These are the same problems that would be faced, however, by those who would strive to allocate medical resources on the basis of maximizing overall social utility. In either case, we need a metric for comparing medical well-being. While the social utilitarian might use units of QALYs to determine how to maximize their number in the aggregate, a proponent of the principle of justice would strive to make the distribution of QALYs as equal as possible.

Many ways might be used for conceptualizing opportunities for equality of well-being. If all that is called for is an *opportunity* for well-being, some would hold that, if people have had opportunities to be healthy, they do not have the same claim as others, even though they may be in equal medical need. A person needing a liver transplant as a result of a history of alcoholism might, according to this view, not be given the same claim as one with other causes of liver failure. If a health-risky behavior is voluntary (a controversial assumption), some would claim that those needing medical care as a result of these behaviors have a lesser claim (Moss and Siegler, 1991; Veatch, 1980).

In determining who is in the greatest need, controversy also exists over whether we should consider people's well-being in a "moment-in-time" or over a lifetime. A moment-in-time perspective would compare people at a particular time, focusing medical resources on those who were the worst off at that time. An "over-a-lifetime" perspective would compare entire lives. A frail 90-year-old with chronic illnesses could be seen as better off than a healthy 20-year-old with the genes for Huntington's disease, which will render him bedridden in another decade or so.

Triage based on treating the sickest among those who can benefit is a way of allocating according to egalitarian justice from the moment-in-time perspective (Baker and Strosberg, 1992). Some medical services such as relief of acute pain, treatment for acute, curable illness, and provision of preventive medical service such as immunizations seem to many to be distributed fairly on the basis of who has the greatest need at the moment. Other health care services are seen as fairly distributed on the basis of who are the worst off over their lifetimes. The key to the principle of justice is that spreading resources according to need is a duty of ethics even if it does not maximize the total good done.

Those who accept a principle of justice see it as a consideration in a social ethic of health care—for deciding how health care resources should be allocated. It would, for them, be a factor in how health insurance benefits should be structured, how a transplant program should operate, or how human subjects research should be conducted. Whether justice also survives as a duty after all other moral principles are taken into account depends on how one ends up ranking and balancing the claims of the competing moral principles. That is a matter that will be considered in Chapter 10. A pure egalitarian basis for distributing health care resources seems implausible because that could lead to reducing all patients to the lot of the worst off. All people equally dead would be purely egalitarian. A defender of egalitarian justice would have to explain how other principles might come into play to avoid this outcome.

ALLOCATION OF HEALTH CARE RESOURCES

The area of medical ethics that poses social ethical questions most dramatically is the allocation of health care resources. In the era of escalating health care costs, managed care, and global budgets for health care, the most controversial ethical issue is how scarce resources should be allocated (American Medical Association, Council on Ethical and Judicial Affairs, 1995; Anderlik, 2001; Daniels and Sabin, 2008; Menzel, 2007; Newdick, 2005; President's Commission, 1983; Ubel, 2000).

The Demand for Health Care Services

In the United States in 2008 we spent about 3.2 trillion dollars on health care.[1] That is over $7600 per person and 16.2 percent of the gross domestic product. In spite of the fact that this is almost three times the world median (and more than any country except Kiribati and Niue),[2] the health of Americans is in a sorry state. It ranks 49th in the world in life expectancy at birth[3] and 65th in infant mortality.[4] What is not recognized is that the continual recitation of aggregate social indicators such as life expectancy and infant mortality implies that maximizing aggregate health is the morally legitimate goal. In 2009 over 50 million Americans had no health insurance.[5] Still others were covered only part of the year or were woefully underinsured. There are dreadful differences in health based on income, education, and race. Enormous international differences exist as well.

The Inevitability of Rationing

Some people argue that we do not need to ration health care. If we just diverted resources from foolishness and waste elsewhere, enough would be available for health care. At this point, one can plug in his or her favorite budget target: the defense department, junkets for members of Congress, tobacco subsidies, highway construction, and the like. This may be a good argument when we talk to people outside of health care, but still it is not realistic. The cost of doing everything we would like to do in medicine for everyone who would like to receive it exceeds the gross domestic product. And that is without considering obligations to others in less wealthy parts of the world. Rationing is inevitable. There will always be more demands for health care services (some of which are quite marginal) than there are resources. In such a world rationing is morally necessary. Even if we recognize that there are enough funds to provide a decent minimum for everyone (and then some), every health plan must exclude some services—not only luxuries and useless treatments, but also marginal tests and procedures for some patients who have high-priority needs.[6] Let's try to get at the moral logic of this rationing, what is often expressed as a movement for cost containment.

CASE 15

DRG Limits and Myocardial Infarction

DRG 282 is the Medicare diagnosis-related group for AMI (acute myocardial infarction) without complications or comorbidities, patient discharged alive. All Medicare patients with this diagnosis in a given hospital generate a flat Medicare reimbursement to the hospital. Other hospitals would get the same reimbursement adjusted for regional and other variables. If the physicians at the hospital treat a patient for less than the cost of the reimbursement, the hospital keeps the difference—sometimes sharing the surplus with the physicians as an incentive to treat economically. If the cost exceeds the reimbursement, the hospital must cover the difference.

If the hospital has other services with surpluses, it can "cost-shift" to cover any such losses. That raises ethical issues, however. Either the services generating surpluses are getting reimbursed at too high a rate or the patients in the services generating surpluses are being undertreated. Too high a rate should lead to "ratcheting down" the reimbursement to a more appropriate amount, so ideally, there should be no surpluses in other services to make up any shortfalls.

In a study of three hospitals conducted some years ago, it was found that the average cost per patient was slightly over $10,000 for patients in DRG 282 (Veatch, 1986a). (Since the time of the study the length of stay in the hospital has decreased, but the costs have increased.) Of course, this is not the cost for each patient. Some who were difficult to treat will cost much more; other, easier cases, cost less. But this was the cost on average. The scheduled reimbursement was $7100 per patient. Thus, if those hospitals treated one hundred patients in a given time period, the cost would be over $1,000,000, but while they would have a global budget[7] it would be only one hundred times $7100, or $710,000, to pay the costs of the care for the group. It does not take a degree in accounting to realize that the cardiology service cannot survive on this basis without some subsidy. Assuming no other services are generating surpluses—and they should not be in a well-adjusted system—ethically, how should cardiologists respond?

The medical records of this group of hospitals showed that the average length of stay in the hospital for a myocardial infarction was thirteen days.[8] This was the average time that clinicians in these institutions believed that their patients needed to stay to obtain ideal medical benefit.[9] Further analysis of the individual medical records revealed that one of the cardiologists consistently had lengths of stay well beyond the average. His patients averaged eighteen days of stay, with an average cost of about $14,000. It was at first suspected that he might be a particularly skilled cardiologist who, therefore, assumed responsibility for particular difficult patients. This, however, proved not to be the case. There was no evidence that his patients had any different degree of severity than the other patients at these institutions. What is the proper response of the cardiologists to the economic pressure from the Medicare DRG system?

Ethical Responses to the Pressures for Cost Containment

The different ethical principles discussed in this volume offer very different ethical responses to the dilemma of pressures for cost containment. Taking various principles from Figure 17, we can see their implications. Examining those implications will provide a summary of the alternative ethics available in health care.

ETHICAL PRINCIPLES AT THE LEVEL OF THE INDIVIDUAL

The Subjective Form of Hippocratic (Patient-Benefiting) Utility   The Hippocratic Oath would have each physician treat for myocardial infarction (MI) by striving to benefit the patient according to the physician's judgment. That, of course, is exactly what these physicians, including the atypical physician who insisted on unusually long lengths of stay for his patient, were trying to do. The outlier physician's long hospital stays were what was called for by subjective Hippocratic utility. That physician believed the long hospital stays were best, even though colleagues would disagree.

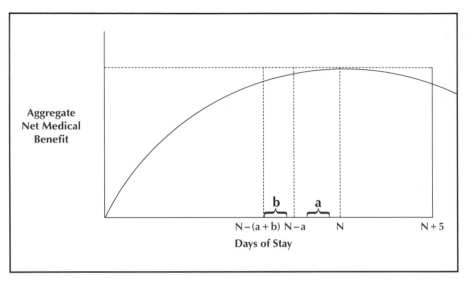

FIGURE 18   Schematic Representation of Aggregate Benefit Per Day of Stay in the Hospital

The graph in Figure 18 is a schematic representation of the cardiology resource problem. It can function as a general model of clinician investment of resources in patient care. The length of stay, which is represented on the horizontal axis, is an approximation of resources invested.[10] On the vertical axis, the aggregate (i.e., accumulated) net medical good done is represented. The curve shows that early units of investment are more efficient than later ones. They do more good than later units, which is another way of saying the early days in the hospital do more good than the later ones. If one keeps investing in more and more days, eventually no more good will be done; the curve becomes flat. A patient who is kept in the hospital even longer may actually begin to experience a net harm. Iatrogenic infection and other hospital-caused harms lead the curve to turn down, indicating that the aggregate good done for the patient may actually decrease.

The Objective Form of Hippocratic (Patient-Benefiting) Utility   Shifting from the goal of patient welfare assessed subjectively by the individual clinician to a more objective measure of effects through peer review and outcomes research may, by eliminating useless medical treatment, actually increase the net good done for the patient while as a side effect conserving resources. Imposing peer review constraints on the outlier intensive utilizer of days of stay will drive days of stay back to the consensus of colleagues.

This length of stay, symbolized by point N in Figure 18, approximates objective net medical benefit. Driving care back to this level by peer review is primarily motivated out of the modified Hippocratic concern of objectively promoting the patient's welfare, but resources are saved as a side effect. (Of course, peer review may also identify some underutilizers of treatment resources. Aggressive, patient-welfare-oriented peer review will increase expense in those cases. The net savings will be the reductions in overtreatment minus adjustments for undertreatment.) The concern is still patient-centered; it focuses on patient welfare. With Hippocratic utility, cost containment is a fringe benefit.

The Principle of Autonomy   Patients' estimates of their welfare may not be the same as the consensus of the peer review. Patients may rationally differ from their physicians on what counts as a medical benefit. They may consider nonmedical goods as well. The patient may contemplate going home (consider the desire for home cooking or seeing the grandchildren). Patients may decline what peer reviewers would determine to be real medical benefit because they evaluate medical and nonmedical benefits differently.

Rational persons do not want resources spent on treatments they are trying to refuse. Patients are saying no to last ditch cancer surgery when the face is half eaten away by cancer, to artificial hearts that leave one half comatose, and to respirators pumping oxygen into unconscious, decaying bodies. When patients say no, it is foolish to spend valuable resources forcing care on them even when consensus of medical expertise favors intervention.

If we add the principle of autonomy to the calculus, we reach the conclusion that it is morally wrong to benefit a patient who does not want to be benefited.

The result of the shift to an objective form of Hippocratic utility and adding the principle of autonomy is a modified Hippocratic principle: Benefit patient according to some objective standard of medical benefit rather than subjective judgments of benefit unless the patient (or surrogate) rejects the care being offered.

This modified Hippocratic formula is still patient-centered, but it now focuses on the rights as well as the welfare of the patient. It is based on autonomy as well as modified Hippocratic utility. We get another fringe benefit. If some of the hundred MI patients decline some marginal hospitalization, the average days of stay drops further. An amount of additional care would be refused that can be symbolized by the interval a in Figure 18. Average length of stay would be driven back to point labeled $(N - a)$. Costs would drop further.[11]

The resource allocation question could be addressed by simply letting the principle of autonomy have free reign. Some propose a free-market solution to the problem of health care resource allocation. Instead of worrying about the shortfall in the Medicare funding, we could go entirely to a privately funded system in which people self-pay for their health care either by paying out of pocket with whatever resources they consume or by buying private insurance in advance that defines the extent of the coverage available. Of course, some would get very inadequate health care by this free-market approach. Pure libertarians would, however, be willing to take these consequences. They claim that the fact that some would have to go without would be *unfortunate*, but not, they say, unfair (Engelhardt, 1996). Individuals might be moved by charity to provide assistance, but there would be no right, no entitlement, to any health care services. This would be a purely autonomy-driven health care system.

The moral reality, however, is that almost no one completely holds this approach to resource allocation based solely on the principle of autonomy. Every nation in the world recognizes some entitlement to some health care services. Even the United States recognizes entitlements through Medicare, Medicaid, CHAMPUS (the military insurance system), and the right of access to hospitals for emergency care. The question is on the basis of what ethical principle these entitlements will rest. Based on what was said earlier in this chapter, two alternative social ethical principles are candidates.

ETHICAL PRINCIPLES AT THE SOCIAL LEVEL   We have now cut the fat out of the system. What if lowering the outlier physician's level of care in the name of patient welfare and granting autonomy still leaves costs above reimbursement levels? Neither Hippocratic utility nor autonomy can help any more. Clinicians who stay focused on the level of individual responsibility would say that the cuts have gone as far as they should. They believe DRG reimbursement should rise to this level ($N - a$ in Figure 18).

The principles considered thus far focus on the individual patient: his or her medical welfare (assessed either by the individual clinician or by more objective standards) and his or her autonomy. Physicians today are quite comfortable with this approach. These operate on the top half of Figure 18, the principles that deal with the individual. Most clinicians now accept both the shift to objective standards for assessing outcomes and respect for patient autonomy. Still, resources may not be adequate to pay for all objectively beneficial and desired care. In fact, in a world of scarce resources, some medical services will almost certainly be considered too trivial, too marginal, or too expensive to be covered in basic insurance plans. If insurance in such a world of scarcity paid for literally every possible benefit, no matter how marginal, it would have to come at the expense of using those valuable resources for something else outside of health care that could easily be more important. In other words, a rational health insurance would set coverage so that not every marginal, inefficient benefit would be covered.

In the case of the DRG for MI, if treatments are eliminated for which there is no objective evidence of real benefit and those that are not desired by the patient are also eliminated, some savings will accrue. In the group of hospitals that provided the data, it was estimated that about $1000 in costs per patient would be eliminated by these reductions. That would have reduced costs to an average of about $9000 by eliminating only procedures for which there is no evidence of positive effects and those that patients do not want. But that still leaves a gap of $1900 per patient between reimbursement and what clinicians and patients would agree is useful and desirable.

The ethical question raised is what should be done with regard to marginally beneficial but expensive care. In the graph in Figure 18, consider care in the range marked by small *b*. By definition these services are beneficial. They do not offer great benefit, but peer review and objective outcomes measures lead both patients and peer reviewers to consider them on balance to be slightly beneficial after both the risks of side effects and the hoped-for benefits have been considered. They are, however, expensive in comparison to benefit. From the physician's point of view they are beneficial; from the patient's point of view they are desirable. Yet, from society's point of view these services constitute marginal, inefficient care. The resources could be used much more effectively somewhere else. Perhaps they could also be used more fairly elsewhere. To address the ethical principles underlying decisions of this sort, we need to move to the lower level of Figure 17, to the ethical principles labeled *social.*

Consider the choices that need to be made from point of view of people planning their own insurance system. Would they want insurance to cover marginally beneficial care? Would they, for example, want a new drug for lowering cholesterol that costs a thousand dollars a year covered when an older drug is almost as effective and costs only a few dollars a year?

We do not insist on ideal care in any other sphere of life. We do not fund ideal levels of housing, food, or education. Almost certainly we should not fund as part of any basic insurance coverage (public or private) all possible beneficial and desired health care no matter how marginal the benefit. In basic health care plans we almost certainly will not fund cosmetic surgery, private psychoanalysis, or exotic infertility treatments, even though we should acknowledge that for some people they offer some benefits that are desired. Likewise, we probably should not fund every imaginable diagnostic test or therapy, including those that produce very low probability of beneficial information or results. Funding all health care that is beneficial and desired will have to come at the expense of moving even further away from the ideal in these other spheres of life. Insurance premiums and reimbursement should take all this into account. If we want resources left for other goods in life, we do not want to reimburse for all possible beneficial care. We do not even want to reimburse for all beneficial and desired care. The only question left is what social ethical principle we ought to use for setting the limits.

In the case of Medicare reimbursement for MI, funding will require "backing down the curve," moving somewhat to the left of the point $(N - a)$ to eliminate care in the range designated as b. It is apparent, however, that there is no obvious point that would be the right amount of this marginally beneficial, desired care to be eliminated. Moreover, social utility and justice provide different answers.

Social Utility   Both those committed to social utility and those committed to justice would back down the curve in Figure 18, moving to the left from the maximal amount of good that could be done (point "N") for the MI patients. They would even move to the left of all the beneficial care that the patient desired (point "$N - a$"). They would do so in different ways, however. Social utilitarians would eliminate expenditures as long as the marginal resource would do as much or more good spent somewhere else. Backing down the curve, they would stop at the point at which the marginal resource spent on MI patients would do more good than if it were spent in any other way. Mathematically, if the highest point on the vertical axis (point N) is designated as B_{MAX}, they would move from that point to the left until the slope of the curve for MI patients was as steep or steeper than what the slope would be on any other curve representing expenditures for any other purpose. This is the driving idea behind cost-benefit analyses. Social utilitarians strive to identify alternative benefits that could have been obtained from each dollar spent on marginal health resources.

The Oregon Health Services Commission was doing precisely this when it did an initial ranking of possible uses of its Medicaid dollars. It attempted to identify the most efficient uses and ranked them highest. Inefficient uses tended to be of two kinds: services for patients who would very likely do well even without them (e.g., the later days of stay for MI patients) and services for patients who were so ill that the services had almost no chance of helping (such as end-stage AIDS patients). When the commissioners and others looked at the list, however, they found the initial results morally unacceptable. Some patients who were, according to their data, inefficient to treat nevertheless seemed to have moral claims, claims that are best characterized as claims of justice.

Justice   In the case of the allocation of limited funds for MI patients, those committed to the principle of justice—at least those who interpret justice to require allocating on the basis of need—would back down the curve in Figure 18 to the point at which the MI patients would be as poorly off or worse off than any other patients. As long as there were other patients in the system worse off, they would divert the funds. If the DRG system were properly designed and its goal were to target resources for the worst off, the reimbursement would be arranged precisely to accomplish that goal. A perfect reimbursement would exist, according to one who would give justice the first priority, if the $7100 was exactly the amount needed to keep the MI patients from being worse off than anyone else.

If the cardiology department operates on a global budget (i.e., if it allocates its total income among its total group of patients), this would still leave the problem of how to allocate among its patients. If the department allocated its resources solely on the basis of the principle of justice, it would pay attention only to who is the worst off. It would not consider how the funds could be used most efficiently, which would be the concern of the social utilitarians.

Many people believe that both justice and social utility are relevant to the allocation decision, so that some reconciling of social utility and justice is called for. How this might be done is the topic of Chapter 10.

The Role of the Clinician in Allocation Decisions

There is one final question that must be addressed in the general discussion of allocating scarce resources before turning to some specific examples. Should saving resources be a goal of the clinician at the bedside? There is a real split among clinicians as well as lay people on this issue. Two options are available, neither of which is terribly attractive.

MAKE THE CLINICIAN THE ONE WHO DECIDES WHERE TO CUT COSTS   Making the clinician society's cost-containment agent has advantages. Clinicians may know where there is some fat in the system, where cuts can be made. This option also has the advantage of keeping bureaucrats out of decisions. However, if clinicians take on this role, they would abandon their traditional commitment to be exclusively agents for their patients. Those who advocate this role for clinicians are, in effect, lobbying for abandoning the exclusive commitment of clinicians to the individual ethical principles and incorporating the social ones into their moral mandate. There are also serious objections to asking clinicians to take on this role. These problems are both practical and principled.

Practical Problems in Calculating   There are practical problems in expecting the clinician at the bedside to be society's gatekeeper. We saw in Chapter 4 that deciding what counts as a benefit and a harm is a complex, subjective task. Acting as a rationing agent inevitably involves trade-offs of competing goods. Clinicians may make value trade-offs in systematically atypical ways. For example, some trade-offs will require comparing the value of the medical care being contemplated with other medical goods. An extra day in the hospital for the MI patient must be compared with an extra day in the nursing home for the Alzheimer's patient, funding a well-baby clinic, or providing pain relief for cancer patients. It could be argued that cardiologists should be expected to make these trade-offs atypically. They probably will (and perhaps ought to) give too much priority to cardiology just as other specialists would see special value in the services they provide. Recall that we are speaking of eliminating real, if marginal, benefits. The specialist who has devoted his or her life to one particular medical service is in a poor position to decide how much value that service offers in comparison to other medical services.

It can be expected that clinicians will be biased in these tasks. They are not malicious; this kind of bias is simply the nature of specialization. People grow to place unusual values on the services they provide. Surgeons are likely to prefer to cut; radiologists prefer radiation; medical oncologists prefer chemotherapy. None of them should be placed in a position of deciding when to sacrifice their services for those of other practitioners.

Likewise, clinicians will have to compare medical goods with nonmedical goods if they are societal gatekeepers. They must decide whether funds are better spent on medicine or on education, housing, or food stamps. Once again, they cannot be expected to be in a position to make these trade-offs. All experts ought to be biased. At least that is the claim of the critics of using the clinician as cost-containment agent.

Finally, the gatekeeper role will require making choices between completing ethical principles and theories. There is increasing evidence that various professional groups have predictable preferences for various ethical principles. Physicians, having historically been consequentialists, tend to prefer the consequentialist principles. When they are forced to make resource allocation decisions, they give special priority to social utility over justice. Other professions may have other orientations. There is some evidence, for instance, that clergy and lawyers tend to emphasize duty-based ethical principles. They are likely to give more weight to justice. The choice of ethical principles, clearly, is not based on any medical expertise.

Clinicians simply have no basis for making choices among competing medical goods, between medical goods and competing goods from outside medicine, or among competing ethical principles. Even the clinician with the most noble intentions can be expected to make these trade-offs in an atypical fashion.

Problems in Principle with Abandoning the Patient-Centered Ethic   There is a second objection to using the clinician as a cost-containment agent. Traditionally, the clinician role has been one of being an advocate for the patient. Traditionally, the role of the clinician was Hippocratic and paternalistic. As that ethic was replaced with a more duty-based respect for persons ethic, the clinician's role still remained patient-centered. The clinician would now serve the rights as well as the welfare of patients, but the patient was still the focus. Should clinicians also take responsibility for social ethical issues such as resource allocation?

Do we really want to ask clinicians to abandon their role of patient advocates? Especially if it can be shown that they might make the trade-offs incorrectly in the first place, would it not be better to keep the clinician in the patient advocate role? Asking the clinician to take on resource allocation tasks is in effect asking him or her to remove the Hippocratic Oath from the waiting room wall and replace it with a sign that reads:

> Warning all ye who enter here. I will generally serve your interests, but in the case of marginally beneficial expensive care I will abandon you in order to serve society as their cost-containment agent.

AN EXEMPTION FROM SOCIAL ETHICS FOR CLINICIANS   The alternative is to give the clinician an exemption from social ethics, at least for the typical case. (Clinicians may still face choices that must include social ethical principles in special situations and when they realize that two or more of their patients are competing for the clinician's attention.) This will still not mean a retreat to the Hippocratic ethic. It could still require objective assessment of medical effects. It could still require respect for autonomy and rights of patients. But it would exempt the physician from having to decide to abandon the patient at the margin, freeing him or her to remain loyal as an advocate for the patient. It would raise the clinician to the same high moral calling of the defense attorney, who is obliged ethically to remain loyal to the client even if the attorney believes the client is guilty.

In law, the system relies on other actors—prosecutors and judges and jury members—to see that the system as a whole is fair. The corollary to exempting the physician from social ethical responsibilities is that also in medicine someone else must take on this responsibility. If it is correct that not all desired and beneficial health services can be funded through basic health insurance programs—that some will be so minimally beneficial and so expensive that other services have moral priority—then society as a whole through the planning of the limits on its insurance coverage and through its delegated representatives will have to decide which services are morally of such low priority that they cannot be funded. Someone must take on the onerous moral responsibility of incorporating social ethical principles into health care programs. If the clinician can be expected to do the job in the wrong way and perhaps should have a special moral duty of serving the patient that is incompatible with taking on the duties of social ethical resource allocation, then the members of the society will have to find others to take on this responsibility. This task may fall to government officials, insurance company employees, hospital administrators, or the patients themselves, but someone will have to decide to place limits on what health insurance will cover.

HEALTH INSURANCE

The Affordable Care Act of 2010

In March 2010 the U.S. government made a historic decision to expand greatly the citizen's right of access to affordable health insurance. In response to decades of debate about universal access to health care, it passed the Patient Protection and Affordability Act of 2010 (U.S. House of Representatives, 2010). The legislation is projected to provide access to insurance for many more (but not all) citizens and legal residents, some 32 million of the currently uninsured. Among the most important provisions of this complex law, health insurance exchanges will be created to permit uninsured and self-employed people to purchase insurance and permit small businesses to get insurance for their employees at competitive prices. Low-income people will receive subsidies for purchasing their insurance. Medicare payroll taxes will be expanded for high-income earners and a tax will be added on the most expensive plans. Medicare recipients will be provided expanded drug coverage. Medicaid will be expanded to cover those up to 133 percent of the poverty level. Starting almost immediately, insurance companies will not be able to exclude children with pre-existing conditions and in 2014, this provision will be expanded to everyone else. Children are allowed to stay on their parents' plan until age 26. In one of the more controversial provisions, by 2014 everyone (with some exceptions for low-income people) will be required to buy insurance or pay a $695 annual fine. Meanwhile, employers with more than fifty employees will have to provide health insurance or, if a worker receives a federal subsidy to buy insurance, the employer will have to pay a $2000 fee per worker.

Ethical Issues

The legislation is designed to increase greatly the number of people insured while making people pay their fair share of the costs. The ethical controversy starts in the disputes about what counts as one's fair share (Annas, 2010; Brody, 2010; Murray, 2010). The private free market in insurance would be one in which insurers can exclude those who are ill or predictably will have high expected health costs and young, healthy people with very low health care costs would either be charged very low amounts for their insurance or opt out entirely from insurance posing serious issues. Those born with serious, expensive genetic illness would never be able to pay for their insurance at market rates and the healthy would be uninsured or pay very small amounts.

THE RIGHT TO HEALTH CARE   This raises the moral issue of whether all humans can, in some sense, be said to have a "right" to health care. Certainly, they cannot have a right to all the health care they could possibly desire. This would include luxury services (cosmetic surgery) and procedures so expensive that the system could not survive. Likewise, it seems they could not have a right to services not proven effective or at least to services demonstrated not to accomplish the outcome they seek (gold spikes for cancer).

The issue is whether humans have any basic right to obtain certain health care services and, if so, who has the correlative obligation to provide them. The services would have to meet criteria that are related to the ability of a society to provide resources and would surely be limited to a core of services that meet criteria of effectiveness and cost-effectiveness. Some would argue against a right to even these basic services on the grounds that society simply has no such responsibility (Sade, 1971). Others, however, offer at least three grounds upon which everyone would have a right to such services and that a society has an obligation to provide them.

(1) Health Care and Society's Interest   First, at least some health care, including some basic health services, may be in the interests of the members of society. Treatment of infectious diseases may benefit others as well as the patient. Not only will society save money; the health of others may require that infectious diseases be treated to avoid illness and death of others. Other services may benefit society in the long run by reducing social costs and eliminating the need for more complex medical services. It may simply be good, self-interested action to provide these services to everyone.

(2) Health Care as a Social Good   Second, some may view health care as a "social good" that has been made possible by society and that therefore everyone has a right of access. The knowledge that makes medicine possible is produced socially. Public funds and private charities generate knowledge in such a way that it would be impossible to say that only those who choose to have insurance have a right to them. Everyone who pays taxes or otherwise contributes to the functioning of social institutions is in some sense partly responsible for the production of medical knowledge. Likewise, physicians and other health professionals receive education that, even in private schools, is heavily subsidized by the government and charities. No physician can claim he or she created the skills of the professional without public support. If citizens are part of the creation of medical knowledge, they have some right to access to the benefits it produces.

(3) Health Care as a Matter of Justice   A third ground on which people might be said to have a right to a basic level of health care services is more fundamental. The principle of justice, interpreted as most modern commentators would interpret it, requires that social practices be arranged so as to benefit everyone and especially the worst off among us. Thus, according to advocates for social justice, a basic social institution such as health care that limited its benefits to those who can afford to pay will have failed to respond to a fundamental moral claim of the members of the society least able to protect themselves. That is probably the fundamental moral basis for the overwhelming majority of more developed countries and many less developed ones committing to some form of near-universal access to basic health care. Albeit limited by the resources available to the society, almost all societies provide that access.

MANDATORY COVERAGE   The single most controversial element of the Affordable Care Act has been the requirement that almost everyone have insurance or pay a penalty. For individuals the charge is less than the cost of insurance ($695), but this offends some with libertarian inclinations. For employers the risk is a fee if employees avail themselves of the subsidy to buy insurance they need because of the absence of the employer's coverage. The principle of autonomy, some would say, is violated by this quasi-mandatory participation.

Those who reject mandatory participation need to face the fact that many other forms of social insurance are mandatory in American society: Everyone is taxed to provide "mandatory" fire protection; everyone with an automobile is required to buy insurance. Other social goods such as education, the armed forces, public transportation, and the social security system include mandatory participation in funding. Even those who have moral objections (say to the military) must pay their share of taxes. To the extent that health care is a social good like highways and fire protection, everyone must pay a fair share in order for the society to function.

Even if health care is not social in these ways, as a practical matter it would be very difficult for society to restrict access to those who have proper insurance. Consider someone picked up unconscious on the street by emergency medical personnel. If insurance is optional and only those with insurance or ability to pay get hospital services, it would be almost impossible for EMTs and emergency room (ER) personnel to know whom to treat. As a practical matter, society should have a rule that everyone gets treated and should pay their fair share for such services. Likewise, children and mentally incompetent adults should receive basic medical services. In fact, the law requires that parents provide such services and pay appropriately for them. Without mandatory coverage (or some sort of bond to cover costs), those incompetent to decide about their own care could not get treatments that the law has determined they deserve. As a practical matter incompetent persons must be covered and society needs to make arrangements to cover those competent to choose to reject insurance, at least for infectious diseases, emergency services, and services needed to keep people healthy enough to fulfill their duties to family members and others upon whom they are dependent and their duties as citizens.

THE MULTIPLE LISTS PROBLEM   This raises a final problem with universal or nearly universal health insurance, what can be called the "multiple-lists" problem. It seems clear that, if there is to be near-universal coverage, it has to be limited to some list of covered services. Luxury services, very expensive services that produce only marginal benefits, and experimental services surely will not be included in the basic tier. Many assume that this means there should be a standard list of "medically necessary" services to which everyone should be entitled.

The problem with this is that no medical service is "medically necessary" if one is willing to bear the cost of omitting it. Moreover, different medical services are considered critical to different people. For some, abortion or aggressive attempts at life preservation are crucial. For others, these interventions may be useless or even immoral. Less well understood is the fact that literally every medical intervention decision requires an evaluation of whether the expected benefits are worth the burdens, side effects, and other costs. The necessity of an intervention is a function of how much the expected outcome is valued in comparison with the negatives it brings.

Thus, different people would choose quite different lists of services as part of the "basic tier" of insured health services. If everyone gets the same standard package of services, the ones who design the list will benefit most; those culturally most distant from the designers (those who have different beliefs and values) will get less. They may not see any value in a covered service and therefore reject it even if it is fully covered, or they may see only slight value, but be forced into a position in which their insurance premiums are used for relatively unattractive services while those they really want (such as alternative medicine) are excluded.

This suggests that any single package of health services connected to universal or near-universal insurance will benefit some more than others. If everyone must pay but some are expected to get more benefits than others because of their unique values, something is unfair. The alternative would be to let groups supporting a range of alternative values design insurance packages that could compete in the market place. Each would have to cover certain services (ER treatments, infectious disease treatments, and care for children and other incompetents). Each would also have to cover conditions for which risk is well known in advance in order to avoid those who know they are low risk choosing plans without that item being covered thus leaving those known to be a risk as the only ones choosing the packages with the covered service. (Consider that only young blacks and others of child-bearing age with sickle-cell trait would be the ones selecting insurance plans that cover sickle-cell disease because others would know they never would need that coverage.) It may be that, even with universal or near-universal insurance such as is promised with the Affordable Health Care Act, multiple plans will have to be offered, each with its own unique bundle of health care services provided that all of those offered would cover conditions requiring treatment to protect the public as well as those to which the risk is well known and predictable in advance. Giving everyone an entitlement to a fixed dollar premium with which they could shop from a list of plans with different coverages might be the only fair way to make sure that all cultural tastes are served. Unfortunately, continuing to link health insurance primarily to employment means that, at most, a small number of choices will be available.

It is very early in the U.S. development of nearly universal health insurance (even if systems in other countries are more mature). There will surely be many ethical controversies as well as practical problems as the plan is rolled out over the next decade.

ORGAN TRANSPLANTATION

A third area in which medical ethics is necessarily social is organ transplantation. (For more detailed discussions, see Task Force on Organ Transplantation, 1986; Veatch, 2000; Shelton and Balint, 2001; Swazey and Fox, 2009; World Health Organization, 2010.) The ethics of transplantation generally involves three issues: the fundamental morality of transplanting body parts, the ethics of organ procurement, and the ethics of allocation. All of these involve social moral controversies.

Is Performing Transplants "Playing God"?

The first moral issue is whether transplanting human body parts from one being to another is tampering with the human's basic nature in ways that go beyond what is acceptable human conduct. The controversy is exacerbated when the organs come from non-human animals. Some people consider organ transplant not only psychologically repulsive, but morally and religiously questionable as well. Nevertheless, the major Western religious traditions are all supportive of organ transplant, even transplants involving the heart—the traditional, romantic "seat of the soul." The problem of whether modern medical interventions go beyond what is morally acceptable for humans is the subject of Chapter 9.

Procurement of Organs

Procuring organs for transplant has been a more mundane, but no less controversial, issue. Procurement raises even more directly the question of the relation of the individual to society. Some commentators have held that human organs of the deceased cannot possibly be of any use to the dead person and should automatically become the property of the state to be used for good social purposes, including not only transplant, but research, education, and other medical therapies as well. Some countries have now legislated that organs can be taken without consent provided the individual or family have not registered an explicit objection. This has been called "routine salvaging" (Dukeminier and Sanders, 1968). It is the law in some Latin, Scandinavian, and Asian countries. The United States, Britain, and other Anglophone and Germanic countries, however, have remained committed to the model of donation of organs. They rely on the belief that the individual has rights against the state, and these rights extend to control of the corpse. Organs may, therefore, be procured only with the consent of the person from which they are taken (or that person's surrogate). This view reflects the individualism of liberal Western political philosophy. The principles of informed consent, and the related respect-for-persons principles of fidelity to commitments and truth telling, control the procurement of organs in these countries.

Because there is a chronic, severe shortage of transplantable organs from suitable deceased donors, more and more organs are being procured from living donors. Although in theory unpaired, life-preserving organs such as the heart or liver could be procured, such procurement would amount to killing the donor and is not seriously contemplated by most people. Procuring a single kidney, however, is feasible and increasingly common. Also, a part of a liver (a liver lobe) can be procured and transplanted. Since liver tissue regenerates, the long-term consequences are normally manageable.

Living donors of kidneys and liver lobes are almost always close family members or friends capable of consenting to the procurement. Occasionally, an altruistic person volunteers to donate to a stranger, in which case the organ is usually allocated using the algorithm for distributing organs to those on the waiting list for deceased donor organs. These donors (sometimes called "non-directed" donors) must be screened for mental and physical issues and, at least in the United States, by law no money or other valuable consideration can be exchanged. Ethical controversy has arisen over whether unrelated donors (either friends or strangers) are morally acceptable and, more recently, over whether donor–recipient pairs could exchange organs to make the system more efficient.

For example, because kidneys must be blood-compatible, people of O-blood type can only receive organs from an O-blood organ donor. A family member with O-blood could give a kidney to a loved one with some other blood type, but those who are not O-blood type normally cannot give a kidney to an O. One option would be for the non-O family member to give a kidney to the waiting list to be allocated according to the normal protocol in exchange for which the next suitable O-kidney from a deceased donor could go to the person in the family of the living donor.

This adds a kidney and shortens the overall waiting time of those on the list because two people (one extra person) are removed from the list. The problem, however, is that the people of O-blood type higher on the list than the one whose family contributed the kidney are passed over and actually have the waiting time increased. Since they were the hardest to transplant, they already had the longest waiting times. This means that the worst off (the ones with the predictably longest wait times) do even worse even though, on average the group on the wait list does better. A defender of maximizing social utility finds this outcome acceptable, but the defender of the moral principle of justice who interprets the principle as requiring fairness will have moral objection (Zenios, Woodle, and Ross, 2001).

The problem is even more complicated in the case of swaps or exchanges involving two or more living donors (Montgomery et al., 2006). A person of O-blood type willing to donate to a stranger could, instead of donating to the wait list, provide that kidney to someone with O-blood who has a family member or friend willing to donate, but who has an incompatible blood type, say, someone of type A. The A-blood kidney could then be given to a recipient with AB-blood who has a donor available who is incompatible for reasons other than blood type (e.g., a size difference). If that donor happened to be of O-blood, the chain could start all over. Otherwise the final kidney in the chain could go to someone on the waiting list who has no available donor.

Two ethical problems arise. First, some people find the exchange inherently offensive because it means receiving a stranger's kidney rather than a family member's. Presumably, such people would have the right to refuse to participate, waiting instead for a deceased donor even though it might take much longer. Second, without the exchange, the original donor's O-blood kidney would have gone to the waiting list, meeting the need of the hardest-to-treat group of patients. With an exchange such as the chain described, the final kidney will likely not be usable by the hardest-to-treat group on the waiting list. Thus, the fairness problem re-emerges.

Organ Allocation

Some of the most dramatic and contested social ethical issues arise today over the ethics of allocating scarce organs for transplant. In late 2010 there were over 109,000 people waiting for organs in the United States. The supply is inevitably scarce and will be at least until artificial organs or animal organ sources become more routine.

When there is an inevitably short supply of a resource, the social ethics of resource allocation becomes crucial. What has been said earlier in this chapter made clear that, if a libertarian, free-market allocation is unacceptable, two principles will govern allocation: social utility and justice.

CASE 16

Allocating Livers: Local vs. Regional Priority

The liver is an organ crucial for life. People with severe liver disease need a transplant to survive. There is no treatment alternative as there is with kidneys. About 16,000 people in the United States are on the waiting list for livers. In 2009 over 1500 people died waiting for a liver. Recently, a national public policy controversy over the allocation of livers has posed a stark choice. When a liver is procured from a recently deceased person, that liver can be used locally or can be transported to a more distant transplant center. Serious disagreement exists over whether livers should be kept locally or moved to patients who are further away but with more urgent need. For each patient needing a liver transplant, a statistic called a MELD (Model for End-stage Liver Disease) score can be calculated. It predicts patient death within three months and can be used to determine which patients on the waiting list have the greatest urgency for a transplant. After excluding those who are already too ill to be listed for a transplant, livers are generally given to the person with the most urgent need. The controversy is over whether this system should first be applied only to the patients in the area of the organ procurement organization that obtained the organ (usually a metropolitan area) or should go to patients with higher MELD scores nationally or regionally.

The federal government's Department of Health and Human Services was concerned that some local areas had more very sick candidates for liver transplant than others. This meant that the current policy of using livers first locally led to relatively well-off patients getting livers when much sicker patients in other areas did not get transplanted. The concern was that equally sick patients were getting treated differently in different areas. The government issued a rule requiring UNOS to develop a policy that would treat patients more fairly (U.S. Department of Health and Human Services, 1999).

UNOS (the United Network for Organ Sharing—the national body charged with obtaining and allocating organs) favored keeping livers locally. Defenders of a local priority pointed to several factors including the advantage of a shorter time before transplant so that organs would deteriorate less, a concern that transporting organs to treat sicker patients might produce worse outcomes, and a belief that people would be more willing to donate organs if they were used locally. The ethical issue was whether fairness requires transporting organs to those areas with the sickest patients or the added advantages of using organs locally justifies the unequal access.

SOCIAL UTILITY   An ethic of allocation driven solely by the principle of maximizing social utility would, in this case, favor a priority for local allocation of livers. At least three benefits support that conclusion: getting organs in better condition, treating patients with predicted better outcomes, and possibly getting more organs. Everyone would agree that it makes no sense to transport organs such a great distance that they become useless. Thus, most people oppose a national sharing of livers. The inequalities of access can be addressed adequately if livers are shared within each of the fifteen regions of the country created by UNOS. But regional sharing poses at least some risk of deterioration of the organs and good social utilitarians—those committed to maximizing the aggregate social benefit—would insist on the shortest possible time between procurement and transplant. They would also insist that the livers go to the patients who can get the most benefit. Often in medicine those might be the sickest patients, but in the case of liver transplant, the sickest—the patients closest to death based on the MELD scores—would not do as well as healthier patients. Finally, they would insist on using organs in such a way that people were most inclined to donate. If a local use would encourage donation (a point that some have doubted), then they would opt for local use even if it meant that the most needy patients did not get the organs. Many at UNOS, including many of the physicians in the UNOS leadership, favor utility maximizing, that is, using organs in such a way that the most possible good is done, even if that meant unequal access (Heiney, 2000).

JUSTICE   Those committed to the importance of the principle of justice in allocating scarce resources—including many of the nonphysicians involved in organ allocation—are not automatically swayed by the data showing that more years of graft survival could result from local allocation. They claim that, especially with a public program such as organ transplantation, all persons should have an equal right to the benefits of the program regardless of their geographical location. For kidney allocation, they tend to favor adjustments in the organ allocation formula to provide more equal access by adding weight to factors such as time on the waiting list, blood type, and a marker for previous exposure to foreign tissue that decreases the chance of finding a suitable organ. For livers they favor allocation to those most likely to die without transplant even if these patients may not do as well.

BALANCING SOCIAL UTILITY AND JUSTICE   The resolution of this dispute will depend on how we should resolve conflict among competing ethical principles, the topic of Chapter 10. The tensions between the public officials at the Department of Health and Human Services—the ones concerned about justice or fairness—and the UNOS officials—the ones concerned about maximizing social utility—reflect the underlying dispute about two very different ethical approaches. Not being able to resolve the question of which principle deserves priority, they reached a compromise. They negotiated a policy of giving some weight in the allocation to considerations of medical utility (such as an absolute priority in allocating livers to perfect HLA (human leukocyte antigen) matches and a priority to acute fulminating liver failure) and some weight to considerations of justice, measured mainly by MELD scores. Likewise, in allocating kidneys, some weight is given to predictors of good outcome (HLA match, patient age, and sensitivity to foreign tissue) and some is given to fairness and more equal access (expressed in terms of time on the waiting list). The UNOS Ethics Committee is formally committed to the importance of both ethical principles (UNOS, 2010).

RESEARCH INVOLVING HUMAN SUBJECTS

A fourth area in which medical ethics inevitably becomes social is research involving human subjects (Brody, 1998; Katz, 1972; Lederer, 2009; Levine, 1988; Veatch, 1987). It is striking that a physician committed whole-heartedly to the Hippocratic ethic of doing whatever will benefit the patient is logically committed to the view that all research involving human subjects, that is, all interventions for the purpose of producing generalizable knowledge rather than for the benefit of the patient, is unethical.

Distinguishing Research and Innovative Therapy

Here it is important to distinguish between true **research** and what is sometimes called **innovative therapy**. Throughout history when a patient has had a condition that did not respond to standard treatments, physicians have felt compelled to try something that can be called innovative therapy. Through most of history new treatments were attempted without any systematic scientific plan or intention. The goal was to try to help the patient. Risks were considered acceptable given the bleak alternatives. Medical research is a much more recent phenomenon, dating from only the nineteenth century. Its goal is not to benefit the patient, but to advance scientific knowledge. Research that involves randomization between two different treatments is ideal for isolating the critical variable being studied. It is morally justified only when researchers honestly do not know which of two treatments is preferable—when they are at or near what is called the **indifference point** or **equipoise**. In those situations, placing a patient in the randomized design cannot be to the patient's advantage compared to simply receiving the standard treatment since there is no basis at the inception of the study for believing anything other than that the standard treatment is superior.

Medical research involving human subjects must meet all the ethical criteria discussed in earlier chapters of this book. A potential subject must give an adequately informed consent meeting the standards discussed in Chapter 5. The subject's autonomy must be respected. If private information is collected about the subject, the rules of confidentiality grounded in the principle of fidelity must be followed. The principle of veracity must be followed as well. Hence, psychological studies built on the intentional deception of the subject have long been controversial. Based on traditional individually focused principles of beneficence and nonmaleficence, risks to the subject must be minimized. But here medical research departs from traditional clinical medicine. The obvious way to protect subjects from harm from procedures that cannot be known in advance to be beneficial to them is to avoid doing the research. If researchers have no reason in advance to believe the experimental treatment is better than the standard treatment, the subject would always be protected by simply not doing the study. This is true even more obviously in the case of research on normal subjects. If medical research is justified at all, it must be by appeal to some ethical principle of maximizing benefit to the individual patient or subject.

Social Ethics for Research Involving Human Subjects

SOCIAL UTILITY An examination of the standard guidelines for research involving human subjects will always reveal that the first, minimal condition for justifying studies on humans is that they are believed to offer hope of producing knowledge valuable to the society that cannot be obtained in any other manner. Thus, the study must be supported by the principle of social utility. Hippocratic utility—patient-centered concern about benefits and harms—will not do to justify research. It is generalizable, scientific knowledge that is being pursued, not patient welfare. At the same time, terrible abuses of human subjects have occurred in the name of promoting social utility. We have now learned that these occurred not only in the Nazi concentration camps, but also in other societies including the United States (Moreno, 2000).

RESPECT FOR PERSONS The Nuremberg code makes clear that social utility is not the only criterion for justifying medical research involving human subjects. As we saw in Chapter 4, it gives a strong commitment to self-determination or what is now in ethical theory normally called autonomy. Since the time of the writing of the Nuremberg Code, the most important document summarizing the ethics of human subjects research is the Belmont Report of the U.S. National Commission for the Protection of Human Subjects of Biomedical and Behavior Research (1978). It is built on three ethical principles: beneficence (which it treats as if it were social utility—including duties to avoid harm as well as benefit), respect for persons, and justice. From respect for persons it builds a consent doctrine and could as well have developed commitment to confidentiality and honesty.

JUSTICE   From the principle of justice, the Belmont Report recognizes a duty to ensure fairness in recruiting subjects. No study can recruit subjects solely from wards serving low-income patients or from prisons, mental hospitals, or other institutions that would produce inequity in subject selection (unless the nature of the study required that only these subjects participate). More recently, the principle of justice has been understood to require adequate recruitment of subjects to apply the findings across racial and gender differences.

Other advocates of the principle of justice have claimed that the requirements of justice must go further. Consider the following case:

CASE 17

Justice in Design of Research

Some years ago, researchers at a major medical center wanted to test several chemotherapeutic agents for toxicity and make an initial estimate of the effectiveness of the combination of drugs. One of the agents, methotrexate, can have serious side effects, but the protocol called for giving it in the high dose followed the next day with a dose of leucovorin, which would neutralize the methotrexate. The methotrexate would be administered every 21 days at the hospital, the leucovorin for three days. The controversy was over whether the leucovorin could be prescribed for the subjects to take at home, which would pose the risk of patients accidentally or intentionally omitting a dose—a mistake that could prove fatal.

Those who favored administering the leucovorin in the hospital argued that it would be safer for the patients if they were hospitalized for three days out of every twenty-one, while they take their medication. They pointed out it would also provide for more carefully controlled science. Researchers would maintain better control over the amount of medication and timing of its administration. They also were concerned that researchers not inadvertently be a party to a suicide by means of refusing to take the leucovorin.

On the other hand, defenders of permitting the leucovorin to be taken at home emphasized the burden of making sick patients come to the hospital for three days out of every twenty-one of their remaining time. Some suggested that because they were particularly sick, they had a special claim to have the research design as convenient and pleasant for them as possible. As long as they knew the risks of taking the medication at home they should be permitted to do so or given a choice to come to the hospital. It seemed that the safest course was also the best science, but that advantage would come at what some subjects would take as an additional burden of an already very difficult life.[12]

If the only ethical principle guiding this study were social utility, it seems obvious which research design should be chosen. Hospitalizing the patients for three days out of every twenty-one ensures better control and closer monitoring of the subjects. Moreover, it seems to provide better protection for patients against the risk that they will not take the rescue agent. If the alternative is to send a professional staff person from the study to the patient's home to administer the leucovorin, hospital administration might even be cheaper. From a utilitarian perspective, hospitalization seems the clear choice.

But these are very sick patients. Asking them to spend three out of twenty-one of the few days they have remaining seems a considerable burden for them. Many patients might legitimately prefer to stay at home and take their leucovorin without having to be in the hospital or under the watch of the researchers. If these subjects are among the worst off—as they well might be—then those who subscribe to a needs-based theory of justice could conclude that they have a special claim to have their interests served even if doing so does not maximize social utility. Especially, if these advocates of the principle of justice also minimized concern about the risk of the patients committing suicide and held a strong commitment to self-determination, they may well conclude that the morally correct protocol was at-home administration. Although at-home administration would sacrifice social utility, it would promote the well-being of these particularly needy persons.

The choice of the proper research design will depend on how we resolve the conflict between social utility and justice, a subject we shall address in Chapter 10. Before turning to the question of resolving conflict among principles, however, the next chapter considers problems of genetics and new birth technologies as a way of understanding how basic attitudes about control of human life shape judgments in bioethics.

Key Concepts

Indifference Point   In research involving randomized clinical trials, the state in which researchers honestly do not have reason to believe that one treatment is preferable to the others. Randomized clinical trials are normally believed to be ethical only if investigators are at the indifference point (sometimes also called clinical equipoise).

Innovative Therapy   Therapy sometimes used by clinicians and lay people in cases in which standard therapy is believed to be ineffective. The purpose is to try whatever is plausible for the benefit of the patient, not the production of generalizable, scientific knowledge (cf. Research).

Justice   The principle that an action is morally right insofar as it treats people in similar situations equally. Different theories of justice provide different bases for allocating resources justly. For example, egalitarian justice would distribute health care on the basis of need (cf. Social Utility).

Research   The systematic pursuit of scientific knowledge for the purpose of advancing science. In medicine, research interventions using human subjects may turn out to benefit the subject, but that is not the purpose, and in ethically acceptable research using human subjects the benefit from the research interventions cannot be known in advance.

Social Utility   The principle that an action or rule is morally right insofar as it produces as much or more net good consequences as any alternative, taking into account the benefits and harms for all parties affected.

Bibliography

SOCIAL ETHICAL THEORY

Bentham, Jeremy. *An Introduction to the Principles of Morals and Legislation* Edited by J. H. Burns, and H. L. A. Hart; with a new introduction by F. Rosen; and an interpretive essay by H. L. A. Hart. New York: Oxford University Press, 1996 [1789].

Engelhardt, H. Tristram. *The Foundations of Bioethics*, 2nd ed. New York: Oxford University Press, 1996.

Lebacqz, Karen. *Six Theories of Justice: Perspectives from Philosophical and Theological Ethics.* Minneapolis, MN: Augsburg, 1986.

Mill, John Stuart. *Utilitarianism.* Indianapolis, IN: Hackett Pub., 2001 [1863].

Rawls, John. *A Theory of Justice.* Cambridge, MA: Harvard University Press, 1971.

Veatch, Robert M. *The Foundations of Justice: Why the Retarded and the Rest of Us Have Claims to Equality.* New York: Oxford University Press, 1986b.

ALLOCATION OF SCARCE MEDICAL RESOURCES

American Medical Association, Council on Ethical and Judicial Affairs. "Ethical Considerations in the Allocation of Organs and Other Scarce Medical Resources Among Patients." *Archives of Internal Medicine* 155, No. 1 (January 9, 1995): 29–40.

Anderlik, Mary R. *The Ethics of Managed Care: A Pragmatic Approach.* Bloomington, IN: Indiana University Press, 2001.

Baker, Robert, and Martin Strosberg. "Triage and Equality: An Historical Reassessment of Utilitarian Analyses of Triage." *Kennedy Institute of Ethics Journal* 2 (June 1992): 103–123.

Daniels, Norman, and James E. Sabin. *Setting Limits Fairly: Learning to Share Resources for Health*, 2nd ed. Oxford/New York: Oxford University Press, 2008.

Kaplan, R. M., and J. W. Bush. "Health-Related Quality of Life Measurement for Evaluation Research and Policy Analysis." *Health Psychology* 11 (1982): 61–80.

Menzel, Paul. "Allocation of Scarce Resources." In *The Blackwell Guide to Medical Ethics,* ed. Rosamond Rhodes, Leslie P. Francis, and Anita Silvers. Malden, MA: Blackwell Pub., 2007, pp. 305–322.

Newdick, Christopher. *Who Should We Treat? Rights, Rationing, and Resources in the NHS,* 2nd ed. Oxford/New York: Oxford University Press, 2005.

Oregon Health Services Commission. *Prioritization of Health Services: A Report to the Governor and Legislature.* n.p.: Oregon Health Services Commission, 1991.

President's Commission for the Study of Ethical Problems in Medicine and Biomedical and Behavioral Research. *Securing Access to Health Care,* Vol. 1. Washington, DC: U.S. Government Printing Office, 1983.

Strosberg, Martin A., Joshua M. Weiner, and Robert Baker, with I. Alan Fein. *Rationing America's Medical Care: The Oregon Plan and Beyond.* Washington, DC: The Brookings Institution, 1992.

Ubel, Peter. *Pricing Life: Why It's Time for Health Care Rationing.* Cambridge, MA: The MIT Press, 2000.

Veatch, Robert M. "Voluntary Risks to Health: The Ethical Issues." *Journal of the American Medical Association* 243 (January 4, 1980): 50–55.

Veatch, Robert M. "Autonomy's Temporary Triumph." *The Hastings Center Report* 14, No. 5 (October 1984): 38–40.

Veatch, Robert M. "DRGs and the Ethical Reallocation of Resources." *Hastings Center Report* 16, No. 3 (June 1986a): 32–40.

HEALTH INSURANCE

Annas, George J. "The Real Pro-life Stance—Health Care Reform and Abortion Funding." *New England Journal of Medicine* 362, No. 16 (2010): e56.

Brody, Howard. "Medicine's Ethical Responsibility for Health Care Reform—the Top Five List." *New England Journal of Medicine* 362, No. 4 (2010): 283–285.

Murray, Thomas H. "American Values and Health Care Reform." *New England Journal of Medicine* 362, No. 4 (2010): 285–287.

Sade, Robert M. "Medical Care as a Right: A Refutation." *New England Journal of Medicine* 285 (1971): 1288–1292.

U.S. House of Representatives. Compilation of Patient Protection and Affordable Care Act [As Amended Through May 1, 2010] Including Patient Protection and Affordable Care Act Health-related Portions of the Health Care and Education Reconciliation Act of 2010. [Washington, DC: U.S. Government], 2010. Available at: http://docs.house.gov/energy-commerce/ppacacon.pdf, accessed October 7, 2010. A government summary of provisions is available at: http://www.healthcare.gov/law/about/order/byyear.html, accessed October 7, 2010.

ORGAN TRANSPLANTATION

Dukeminier, Jesse, and David Sanders. "Organ Transplantation: A Proposal for Routine Salvaging of Cadaver Organs." *New England Journal of Medicine* 279 (1968): 413–419.

Heiney, Douglas A. *Memorandum: Proposed Liver Allocation Policy Development Plan for Public Comment.* Richmond, VA: UNOS, February 15, 2000.

Montgomery, Robert A., Sommer E. Gentry, William H. Marks, Daniel S. Warren, Janet Hiller, Julie Houp, Andrea A. Zachary, J. Keith Melancon, Warren R. Maley, Hamid Rabb, Christopher Simpkins, and Dorry L. Segev. "Domino Paired Kidney Donation: a Strategy to Make Best Use of Live Non-directed Donation." *Lancet* 368, No. 9533 (2006): 419–421.

Moss, Alvin H., and Mark Siegler. "Should Alcoholics Compete Equally for Liver Transplantation?" *Journal of the American Medical Association* 265 (1991): 1295–1298.

Shelton, Wayne, and John Balint. *The Ethics of Organ Transplantation.* New York: JAI, 2001.

Swazey, Judith P., and Renée C. Fox. "Ethical Issues in Organ Transplantation in the United States." In *The Cambridge World History of Medical Ethics*, ed. Robert B. Baker and Laurence B. McCullough. New York: Cambridge University Press, 2009, pp. 678–683.

Task Force on Organ Transplantation. *Organ Transplantation: Issues and Recommendations.* Washington, DC: United States Department of Health and Human Services, 1986.

UNOS, "Ethical Principles to be Considered in the Allocation of Human Organs" (Approved by the OPTN/UNOS Board of Directors on June 22, 2010).

U.S. Department of Health and Human Services, Health Resources and Services Administration. "Organ Procurement and Transplantation Network; Final Rule." *Federal Register* 42, CFR Part 121 (October 20, 1999): 5650–5661.

Veatch, Robert M. *Transplantation Ethics.* Washington, DC: Georgetown University Press, 2000.

World Health Organization. *WHO Guiding Principles on Human Cell, Tissue and Organ Transplantation.* Geneva, Switzerland: World Health Organization, 2010.

RESEARCH INVOLVING HUMAN SUBJECTS

Brody, Baruch. *The Ethics of Biomedical Research: An International Perspective.* New York: Oxford University Press, 1998.

Katz, Jay. *Experimentation with Human Beings.* New York: Russell Sage Foundation, 1972.

Lederer, Susan E. "The Ethics of Experimenting on Human Subjects." In *The Cambridge World History of Medical Ethics*, ed. Robert B. Baker and Laurence B. McCullough. New York: Cambridge University Press, 2009, pp. 558–565.

Levine, Robert J. *Ethics and Regulation of Clinical Research*, 2nd ed. New Haven, CT: Yale University Press, 1988.

Moreno, Jonathan D. *Undue Risk: Secret State Experiments on Humans.* New York: W. H. Freeman and Company, 2000.

National Commission for the Protection of Human Subjects of Biomedical and Behavioral Research. *The Belmont Report: Ethical Principles and Guidelines for the Protection of Human Subjects of Research.* Washington, DC: U.S. Government Printing Office, 1978.

Price, David, ed. *Organ and Tissue Transplantation.* Aldershot, Hampshire/Burlington, VT: Ashgate, 2006.

Veatch, Robert M. *The Patient as Partner—A Theory of Human-Experimentation Ethics.* Bloomington, IN: Indiana University Press, 1987.

Zenios, Stefanos A., E. Steve Woodle, and Lainie Friedman Ross. "Primum non Nocere: Avoiding Harm to Vulnerable Wait List Candidates in an Indirect Kidney Exchange." *Transplantation* 72, No. 4 (August 27, 2001): 648–654.

Notes

1. U.S. Department of Health and Human Services, Centers for Medicare and Medicaid Services http://www.cms.gov/NationalHealthExpendData/25_NHE_Fact_Sheet.asp#TopOfPage, accessed October 5, 2010.

2. World Health Organization, *World Health Statistics: 2010. Part II: Global Health Indicators.* Geneva: World Health Organization, 2010, p. 96. http://www.who.int/whosis/whostat/EN_WHS10_Part2.pdf, accessed October 5, 2010.

3. CIA—The World Factbook. "Country Comparison: Life Expectancy at Birth." http://www.cia.gov/library/publications/the-world-factbook/rankorder/2102rank.html, accessed October 5, 2010.

4. CIA—The World Factbook. "Country Comparison: Infant mortality Rate." http://www.cia.gov/library/publications/the-world-factbook/rankorder/2091rank.html, accessed October 5, 2010.

5. DeNavas-Walt, Carmen, Bernadette D. Proctor, and Jessica C. Smith. *U.S. Census Bureau, Current Population Reports, P60–238, Income, Poverty, and Health Insurance Coverage in the United States: 2009*, Washington, DC: U.S. Government Printing Office, Washington, DC, 2010, p. 23.

6. The classic illustration of this is the test for occult blood in the stool used as an indicator of possible cancer. Everyone agrees that this test is worthwhile. The famous paper by Duncan Neuhauser and Ann M. Lewicki ("What Do We Gain from the Sixth Stool Guaiac?" *New England Journal of Medicine* 293, No. 5 (July 31, 1975): 226–228) showed that it cost

(in 1975 dollars) $1175 to find a positive result, a wise investment. But when the test is performed, some 9 percent of the positives will be missed. The test can be repeated, finding most of those that were missed the first time, but still missing a few. The second time around, it costs $5492 to find a case, still what many would consider a good investment. (The cost per case found goes up because, since there are fewer positives left in the population, more tests have to be performed to find a person who is positive.) If the test is repeated a third time, it will cost $49,150 to find a positive; the fourth time, $469,534, and still not quite all the positives will be located. The test can be repeated indefinitely, each time being more expensive because there are fewer and fewer positives left to be found. The sixth test would cost $47,107,214 to find a case. By the time we get to the sixth test, the cost seems unreasonable, yet from the point of view of the patient whose case was found, it would be valuable. The problem is that there is no clear principle upon which to say we have gone far enough. The test is simple, virtually risk-free, and could be repeated over and over. At some point every insurance plan will say the cost is too great for the expected benefit given the other uses to which the funds could be put.

7. A global budget is an overall financial funding resource supplied to a hospital department, a managed care organization, a health system, or a national health care plan from which those responsible must provide all the care for all the patients in their system. Global budgets are often set by governments or by the collective funding received from insurers or subscribers in such a way that the total funding is not sufficient for health care providers to deliver all the services they would like to provide for each patient. The ethical task is to determine, first, whether the overall size of the budget is morally justified and, second, how the inevitably deficient resources should be allocated among the patients.

8. Since these data were gathered, the average length of stay has been reduced considerably. It is now closer to seven days. The ethical problem of having an ideal length of stay that would generate more costs than reimbursements would cover remains the same.

9. Technically, the average length of stay may represent something less than the ideal length, since physicians may already have been motivated by their cost consciousness to send patients home when they had received almost all the benefit that could be expected, rather than keeping them to the point when medical benefit was fully maximized.

10. It is only an approximation because clearly the early days of hospitalization for a myocardial infarction consume resources more intensely. Still, the graph represents the economist's notion of decreasing marginal utility of units of resources. The more invested, the lesser the incremental addition to the good that is done.

11. Some might be concerned that, if we include the principle of autonomy, we would also have to add services that patients desire even though they are not endorsed by peer review as beneficial. If, however, autonomy only generates "negative rights," that is, the right to refuse treatments, it does not require providing services, only omitting them.

12. The case is based on Veatch, Robert M. "Case Study: Risk-Taking in Cancer Chemotherapy." *IRB* (August–September 1979): 4–6.

Human Control of Life: Genetics, Birth Technologies, and Modifying Human Nature

Many of the themes already discussed in this book are also relevant to new developments in genetics and reproductive technologies. Issues of autonomy and consent, veracity, fidelity in the patient/physician relation, and the allocation of scarce resources arise when these technologies are used. We now have the power not only to diagnose genetic disease and advise potential parents about the characteristics of offspring, but also to insert new genetic material into human beings to correct for defective genes and even to improve on the nature of the species. We are beginning to develop the capacity to use human stem cells to create genetically matched body chemicals and, potentially, even body parts (Hinxton Group, 2008; National Institutes of Health, 2007; The National Academies (U.S.), 2006; United Kingdom, Medical Research Council, 2008). A moratorium on much federal government–funded stem cell research that existed through much of the first decade of the twenty-first century was lifted by the Obama administration in 2009 (National Institutes of Health, 2009). In theory, we could someday soon be able to use these technologies to create a genetically identical copy (a clone) of a human being, raising many controversial questions (President's Council on Bioethics, 2002). This first suggests science fiction scenarios of creating copies of the best soldiers or scientists; however, the more plausible first attempts at producing a clone might be in the somewhat more sympathetic and tragic case. For example, consider the case of a couple with an infant dying from an accident. That couple might want to replace their lost child by creating a genetically identical new child. Even though most people might find this ethically repulsive, it would not be exceptionally difficult to try and would probably be legal if attempted entirely with private funds. It might even succeed or, of course, produce a terribly damaged new human being. Even more likely will be the use of stem cells to generate "replacement parts" such as damaged cells or tissues as in the recent developments described in Case 18:

CASE 18

Using Stem Cells to Re-Grow Spinal Cord Nerve Cells

In the fall of 2010, the Geron Corporation gained federal approval to launch a truly world-changing experiment: the first-in-human attempt to use embryonic stem cells to cure (or at least ameliorate) a serious medical problem in a human. A patient at the Shepherd Center, a spinal cord injury rehabilitation center in Atlanta, had recently suffered a life-changing spinal cord injury and was left paralyzed from the chest down. The patient, whose name was not made public, had control of arms and bladder and could breathe spontaneously but had no control of leg muscles.

The experimental technique, called GRNOPC1, involved injecting cells obtained from human embryos. An injection involved 2 million cells stimulated to develop into myelinated glial cells. The goal is to have the cells insulate the nerve cells of the spinal cord. This would allow restoration of impulse transmission that would, in turn, permit movement and sensations.

The embryos were obtained from a fertility clinic—embryos held in reserve for couples seeking pregnancy by in vitro fertilization. The use of such embryos, with the permission of the couples from whom the sperm and egg cells were obtained, has now become standard practice in stem cell research, but remains controversial. Obtaining the pluripotential cells (cells that have the capacity to develop into various bodily cell types) requires the destruction of the embryo. Ten subjects are planned for this initial trial, which is likely to be the first of many such experiments ushering in a new era in human medicine.[1]

When any of these and other manipulations of reproductive cells are attempted in humans, the consent of the patient or surrogate for the patient is needed just as in any other medical experiment or treatment, but these and other reproductive and stem cell technologies also raise other questions. We also have the ability to create new human life in a test tube and implant the newly created embryo into the uterus of the woman who supplied the egg cell, or even into another woman (President's Council on Bioethics, 2004). Implantation can be done with the recipient promising to return the newborn infant to the woman who supplied the egg—a process called **surrogate motherhood**—or with the understanding that the woman who gestates the pregnancy is to keep the newborn and raise the child whose genetic makeup is unrelated to her own. The process of offering an egg in this way is sometimes called egg donation. In theory, **in vitro fertilization**, as this process has come to be called, could even be undertaken for the purpose of providing the newborn to yet a third woman. To the extent that promises of confidentiality or promises about relinquishing the newborn are made, the ethics of promise keeping arises just as in any other medical relation. The development of pre-implantation and in utero diagnosis with the possibility of aborting embryos with unacceptable genetic makeup raise the same issues that arise in other abortions: When, if ever, is it ethical to terminate embryonic and fetal life? They will force us to deal again with the meaning of the principle of avoidance of killing.

Since some of the more useful stem cells are obtained from aborted fetuses, those who have moral reservations about abortion must face the question of whether they can condone the use of the stem cells obtained without appearing to support abortion. All of these new technologies of birth can be extremely expensive. In vitro fertilization, for example, typically costs $12,400 for the initial cycle and may require several additional cycles.[2] Thus, using these technologies raises the same issues of justice in resource allocation that arise in any other health care rationing controversy.

Yet, there is an additional dimension of medical ethics that arises with particular vigor in these contexts of genetics and birth technologies: Should human beings manipulate the very nature of the species? Is it the appropriate role of humans to be active controllers of human nature or should they only enjoy it more passively? Is it the proper role of the human to tamper with the creation in ways depicted in the Frankenstein myth or to take charge of nature and shape it for the human's own ends? This chapter focuses on these more basic philosophical issues while exploring the ethics of the new genetic, stem cell, and birth technologies. These broader issues cut across the more traditional normative disputes in medical ethics about ethical principles discussed in earlier chapters.

THE HUMAN AS CREATED AND AS CREATOR

Medical Manipulation as Playing God

When Mary Wollstonecraft Shelley created the story of Frankenstein in 1817, she provided an alternative title, *The Modern Prometheus*.[3] Thus, she harkened back to the legend of the Greek god who not only molded the clay figures that became humans, but also stole fire from heaven to make it available to human beings, giving them powers they had never before possessed. The metaphor of "playing God" has become common in the era of the biological revolution.[4] It is often used by those who fear that humans are going beyond appropriate limits in remolding or "recreating" the human's nature. These critics suggest that genetic engineering and the "manufacture" or "fabrication" of new human beings take us beyond the normal mission of medicine—to save life, cure disease, and relieve suffering.[5] They believe that we are on the verge of changing the species so radically that we can be said to be changing its fundamental nature.

The critical underlying question is whether it is moral to make these radical changes. Some commentators, often influenced by conservative religious traditions, hold that the human is a finite creature prone to make mistakes. Thus, they tend to be pessimists, fearing that changes initiated by humans will ultimately be for the worse. They point to the dangers of atomic energy, environmental disasters, and medical experiments that have gone horribly wrong. Their premise is that basic changes in the human species will lead to sinister biological effects that, on balance, are bound to be terribly harmful. For others the objection goes beyond the seriousness of the consequences to a more fundamental issue: moral limits on how far humans should go in using their knowledge of science to change their nature. They point to the religious symbolism of a Biblical creation story in which the human sins by eating of the forbidden fruit of knowledge.

Having Dominion over the Earth

Others have quite a different set of moral intuitions. They claim that, on balance, humans' use of science has dramatically improved the human situation and, drawing on another religious metaphor, speak of humans as "co-creators" having a moral duty to use knowledge of science not only to combat disease, but also to improve on nature. They opt to make human reproduction and human existence more progressive, rational, and planned.[6] These more optimistic and interventionistic advocates have appropriated a different religious symbol, pointing to the other Biblical creation story in which the human is to have dominion over the earth and "subdue it." In this chapter our primary concern is whether interventions in genetics and birth technologies push the limits of human authority to manipulate or rationalize (depending on one's perspective) the basics of human nature.

GENETICS AND THE CONTROL OF HUMAN REPRODUCTION

Genetics

For centuries humans have had a vague idea that parents somehow influence the characteristics of their offspring. The science of genetics, which the nineteenth-century Austrian botanist and priest Johann Gregor Mendel is credited with founding, provided a basis for beginning to understand the biological influence of parents on their children.

Early in the twentieth century, vague notions of inheritance of disease and mental incapacities provided a basis of a eugenics movement leading not only to extermination campaigns in Nazi Germany but also compulsory sterilization laws in thirty U.S. states. In the famous 1927 U.S. Supreme Court decision *Buck v. Bell* (274 U.S. 200), Justice Holmes, heavily influenced by the eugenics movement, misleadingly declared that "three generations of imbeciles is enough."[7]

GENETIC COUNSELING AND TESTING   These naive, often confused understandings of the science of genetics combined with a moral subordination of the rights of the individual to purported societal interests produced a sorry chapter in early medical ethics. However, by the end of the 1960s, the complexities of genetics were beginning to become clearer. Moreover, the focus on societal interests was gradually replaced with a more traditional medical perspective in which the motivation for intervention was the prevention of human suffering. This shift gave parents, for the first time, a scientific basis for making reproductive choices in light of their interests and those of their offspring. Legal abortion in the United States in the 1960s was limited to so-called hard cases, those that threatened the life and health of the pregnant woman and those that involved rape, incest, and "fetal deformity." Thus, we had not only more complete scientific information and a more rights-oriented ethic, but also a law that would permit at least modest choices about whether to carry pregnancies through to delivery.

Since then, genetic counseling has gradually emerged as a field that makes information available to individuals and couples potentially at risk of genetic disease or whose offspring might be affected. Moreover, specific, scientific genetic tests have permitted more precise identification of genetic anomalies in fetuses as well as postnatal human beings.

This has led to testing to identify both potential carriers of genetic disease and those who actually have the diseases. In the process, serious ethical issues are raised (Clarke, 2007; Devettere, 2010; Human Genetics Commission, 2006; Monsen, 2009). In the case of autosomal recessive genetic diseases such as Tay-Sachs syndrome, sickle-cell anemia, or cystic fibrosis, each parent must contribute a copy of the defective gene for the disease to manifest itself. This means that, even before marriage, people who have these diseases in their family can be tested to learn whether they have a copy of the disease-causing gene. If both prospective parents have the gene, they can be counseled about remaining childless (through contraception, sterilization, or other strategies) or, if the genetic status of the fetus can be tested in utero, whether to terminate the pregnancy.

Genetic counseling can also be used for other conditions. Autosomal dominant conditions such as Huntington's disease, retinoblastoma, and neurofibromatosis express themselves if only a single copy of the gene is present. Thus, a single affected parent can transmit them. In the case of retinoblastoma, a tumor of the eye that will be fatal if untreated, surgical removal of at least one eye may prevent death, but will leave the patient with compromised vision or no sight at all.

Huntington's disease does not manifest itself until the affected person is in his or her thirties or later, but then leaves the person with progressive muscular paralysis that eventually leads to early death. It was the disease of folk singer Woody Guthrie. Each child of an affected person has a 50 percent chance of having the defective gene. Because symptoms do not occur until adulthood, affected persons in the past often reproduced and passed the gene along to their offspring before they knew whether they were affected. Now it is possible to test persons at risk of Huntington's disease so they can make choices about reproduction. However, in the process they will learn, perhaps years in advance, whether they themselves have the disease. Some claim that healthy people should not know in advance how they will die; others insist that those at risk should have this information, perhaps even when they are still children, so that they can plan marriage, career, and other life choices in light of it.

We can also test for such chromosome conditions as trisomy-21 or Down syndrome, which leads to varying degrees of mental retardation and perhaps accompanying physical problems with the heart and digestive track, and trisomy-18, a rapidly debilitating and fatal disease. These often result from abnormalities in the process by which chromosomes combine during fertilization so they are not passed from parents. In other cases parents may also have the condition (as in some cases of Down syndrome). When the parent has the chromosomal abnormality, he or she can be tested and the condition identified. Even if the parent does not have the abnormality, fetal chromosomes can be screened, making possible choices about abortion of affected fetuses or preparation if the fetus is carried to term.

Some chromosomal abnormalities are sex-linked, meaning that normally only males will be affected. Some of these conditions, such as Duchenne muscular dystrophy, are quite serious, while others, such as color blindness, can be quite minimal. Often the only prenatal screening possible is determination of the sex of the fetus. Since normally only males are affected, aborting all male fetuses of those with a family history of the condition will prevent births of affected infants. However, this will also mean aborting normal males half of the time.

Making choices in the context of genetic counseling poses not only traditional ethical problems of deciding about abortion, fertility regulation, informed consent, confidentiality, forgoing life support, and allocation of resources, but also whether humans should be choosing the genetic makeup of their children. Some people—for example, those who reject advance knowledge of their Huntington's disease status— believe that it is more "natural" and appropriate to let the disease evolve without knowing whether their children have a 50–50 chance of inheriting the gene. Others insist that it is irresponsible to make reproductive choices in ignorance of one's genetic status. Similar controversy exists about whether individuals should learn the sex and genetic status of the fetus or should adopt the traditional approach and wait until birth to gain this information.

Genetic counselors and others who advise prospective parents professionally, such as clergy and physicians, also face moral choices in the context of genetic counseling. A basic question for them is how they should interact with their clients. Many now take the position that they should be "nondirective"; that is, they should not attempt to transmit their own moral views to their clients. Instead, they maintain, they should provide them with scientific, social, and psychological information and leave the evaluative choices up to them. These genetic counselors are aware of the issues raised in Chapter 4 about how difficult and subjective it is to determine what counts as a good outcome. They give priority to client autonomy, trying to let the client control the value judgments, including the ethical choices.

However, this value-neutral position is increasingly being called into question. Contemporary philosophy of science now suggests that value neutrality is impossible, that counselor values will inevitably seep into the information they transmit, and that deciding which information is *important enough* to provide will necessarily require some value judgments on the counselor's part. Moreover, some evaluations seem to pose such clear-cut choices that many would consider it unethical to fail to voice an opinion about them. For example, parents can now decide to abort a fetus simply because it is not the preferred gender or because it has a minor medical condition such as color blindness. They can also choose to bear children in spite of horrendous, painful, and fatal conditions such as trisomy-18. Many genetic counselors consider either of these sorts of choices so obviously wrong that it would call for more directive counseling. Deciding whether to be directive in these situations will depend not only on one's views about abortion and autonomy, but also about how one feels about intervening into life's most mysterious and important processes.

This suggests a serious problem for the future of genetic counseling. If counselors cannot be completely neutral and feel that some choices are so obviously immoral that they cannot in good conscience refrain from conveying their disapproval, how can prospective parents and others being counseled protect themselves from undue and distorting influences from their counselors? The moral beliefs of genetic counselors should not determine decisions made by counselees who are regarded as autonomous and self-determining moral agents, and yet these people cannot make their decisions without the assistance of such counseling.

One approach would be to strive to have counselors try to be as fair and unbiased as possible while still realizing that their communications will inevitably contain value perspectives. If those being counseled understood that all counseling conveys value judgments, and if counselors openly expressed their points of view, clients could pick their counselors and the institutions in which the counselors work on the basis of compatibility of values as well as availability of factual information. For important decisions they might seek out other counselors for second opinions, intentionally pursuing counselors whose values are quite different. For example, a traditional Catholic might first get counseling from someone from within that religion's tradition and then seek out a counselor whose values and beliefs are different. Even if these counselors try to present "just the facts" and present them as fairly as possible, in at least some cases, the messages are bound to be quite different.

GENETIC SCREENING   Genetic screening carries the process of genetic counseling to a new and more systemic level (Baily and Murray, 2009; Tong, 2007). For many genetic conditions, one can test for the presence of a gene that predisposes the individual or that person's offspring to genetic disease by using a blood test or some other simple, inexpensive procedure. This makes it feasible to screen whole groups of people. The earliest population screening was carried out on African Americans for the sickle-cell disease gene and those in the Ashkenazi Jewish community for Tay-Sachs genes. With screening, prospective parents would know prior to marriage or prior to conceiving children whether each carried a gene for the disease. If they did, in the simplest recessive conditions, then one in four of their children would have the disease and two in four would carry a single copy of the gene, meaning that they would not have the disease but could pass a gene on to their children.

Since screening is targeted at whole communities, it is difficult for counselors who propose testing to be value-neutral. One would not advocate the expense and effort of a communitywide program unless one were committed to the position that the disease in question was quite serious and worth preventing. Moreover, many of the earlier conditions for which screening was done involved ethnic minority communities and often led to the recommendation that couples limit child-bearing or abort affected fetuses. These proposals smacked of a campaign designed to eliminate significant numbers of the future generation of the group involved (often Blacks and Jews). Some radical commentators termed this a form of genocide. Later, screening became available for such diseases as cystic fibrosis and phenylketonuria (PKU), which affect nonminority Caucasians. However, suspicions about screening have continued and a concern about eugenics still lingers.

Within the past few years evidence has become available that specific genetic tests can identify people who are at risk of serious diseases such as breast cancer and certain forms of colon cancer. It is believed that specific genes, such as the BRCA1 gene for breast cancer, predispose individuals for disease that in some cases can only be treated by radical procedures such as bilateral preventative mastectomy. Genes for other conditions, such as familial polyposis colon cancer, can be detected in children before the disease manifests itself in adulthood. Regular monitoring can be undertaken for those with the predisposing gene to identify early appearance of the disease.

Both genetic testing and screening pose serious social problems for those who are identified as having the predisposing genes or even the carrier state. There is increasing concern that insurance companies may discriminate against those with such genes or that employers may resist hiring them for fear that their health insurance costs will increase. (Some of these issues may be addressed by the new Affordable Health Care Act, but concern still exists.) Even more subtle is the question of whether knowing one carries such a gene will be stigmatizing or lead to lower self-image. Some maintain that it is better not to know one's genetic makeup and thus avoid the risk of discrimination and social-psychological sequelae. Others believe that it would be distressing to those at risk of disease to know the tests were available and yet not to know whether they were affected. The risks of genetic discrimination would not deter them from being tested.

THE HUMAN GENOME PROJECT   The potential for genetic testing and intervention escalated in 1990 when the United States Congress formally committed to the **Human Genome Project**. Part of an international genetic research initiative, the project, costing $2.7 billion, mapped 25,000 genes and was completed in 2003. More than 1800 disease genes have been identified leading to over a thousand tests for human genetic conditions.[8] The goal is eventually to identify the position of every gene in the human body and to be able to intervene in order to diagnose and modify any of those genes. Work in both governmental and private labs is progressing rapidly toward this objective.

Because we are likely to be able to diagnose problematic genes before we can remove and replace them or provide other therapy to respond to their impact, the Human Genome Project is viewed with great suspicion by those who believe that abortion is ethically unacceptable. On the other hand, those who are technological optimists see the possibility of heading off medical problems at their genetic source one by one, thereby leading to a healthier population and great reductions in suffering and medical costs.

The more realistic understand that many diseases are not genetic in their origin and, of those that are, many are *polygenic*; that is, they involve many genes. This means that medical scientists will still have to determine how genes interact in order to address such major chronic diseases as many cancers, heart disease, stroke, and diseases of senescence. It is likely that we will find that the same genes that increase risk of some undesirable conditions also are essential for preventing other equally unattractive outcomes.

The crucial question from the point of view of ethics is whether the goal—full knowledge of the human genetically—is an ideal worthy of pursuit or a malicious, Promethean quest that takes humans beyond the knowledge that is appropriate for them and opens up possibilities for intervention that are best left untouched.

GENETIC ENGINEERING   What many of the "dominion and subdue" school take as their ultimate goal is subsumed under what is sometimes called **genetic engineering**. Whereas genetic counseling and screening are devoted primarily to identifying problematic genes and avoiding their transmission, genetic engineering is more direct and aggressive. It strives to overcome the effects of the bad genes by inserting the proper genetic information and eventually removing those genes causing problems. To date clinical uses have included attempts to treat a type of inherited childhood blindness, myeloid blood diseases, severe combined immunodeficiency, and various cancers including melanoma, lung cancer, and torpedo cancer.[9]

Therapy vs. Enhancement   The ultimate goal is to learn to identify and remove harmful genes as well as to add missing ones. A distinction can be made that some consider morally significant between **gene therapy** and **gene enhancement**. Some people have conditions clearly identified as diseases, as bodily conditions that people evaluate negatively and that are deviations from some imagined normal state. The first attempts at gene therapy in humans, such as the case that follows, attempted to insert missing genes. They were thus "therapeutic" rather than enhancement attempts.

CASE 19

Experimenting with Gene Therapy: The Case of Jesse Gelsinger

Eighteen-year-old Jesse Gelsinger suffered from ornithine transcarbamylase (OTC) deficiency, a rare genetic disorder that blocks the body's ability to break down ammonia.[10] His disease had been controlled by drugs and by maintaining a strict and unpleasant non-protein diet all his life.

In the fall of 1999, Jesse agreed to participate in an experiment at the University of Pennsylvania's Institute for Human Gene Therapy. Like any more-traditional research, this experiment had to meet the usual requirements of adequately informed consent and review by an institutional review board to ensure that there were no undue risks. (Later review questioned whether this review was adequate.[11]) This experiment was different, however, in that it would attempt to change the genetic makeup of the patient. Researchers would administer a modified cold virus (called an adenovirus) hoping that the virus would carry the genetic material Jesse was missing and cure his OTC by permitting him to produce the enzyme he needed to metabolize ammonia. Gene therapy, first attempted in the early 1990s, has now been tried in thousands of patients with various genetic anomalies, with the hope of introducing missing genes into the body. Seventeen previous subjects had participated in the University of Pennsylvania experiment without serious problems and a few had even shown improvement. Jesse Gelsinger, however, was the first patient to receive the virus with the genetic material directly into the liver's blood supply. Moreover, Jesse's liver functioned at a particularly low level.

After receiving the injection of the virus, Jesse's liver began to fail rapidly. Over the next three days, other organs began to fail and he suffered massive brain damage. He died four days later.

In contrast to therapy, enhancement involves and attempts to improve on a normal healthy body. Some people would like to be able to add to the normal lifespan or improve on what are considered normal human characteristics. Perhaps they would like to have a more pleasant personality or less of a desire to eat. These are likely to turn out to be polygenic characteristics that do not lend themselves to gene modification.

It is possible, however, that some of these could be controlled by a single gene responsible for a simple enzyme. We have recently seen that drugs changing metabolism of a single body chemical such as serotonin can have major effects on personality and weight.

This distinction between therapy and enhancement rests on some hypothetical point that can be called "normal health." Bringing people up to that point could be considered therapy while taking them beyond that point might be considered enhancement. Providing "therapy" generates considerable support, but enhancement is considered much more controversial (Mehlman, 2003; Savulescu and Bostrom, 2009; Zylinska, 2010). Moreover, the dividing point between them is very hard to define. For example, would someone who comes from a long line of very short people who is himself short be considered normal (compared to his ancestors) or abnormally short (compared to the rest of the population)? Would a female who is short be considered as "abnormal" as a male of similar height? Would parents who wanted their daughter to grow to be as tall as her brother (who happens to be tall enough to have a lucrative basketball career) be considered pursuing therapy or enhancement?

The simple cases of therapy for serious genetic diseases generate the most sympathy. Even those reluctant to tamper with genes cannot help feeling sympathy for Jesse Gelsinger and others like him who are missing genes necessary for normal bodily functions. On the other hand, enhancement generates nervousness even among the "dominion and subdue" people. They may worry, for example, that if some people in a population engaged in enhancement, others would be forced to copy them just to stay competitive.

Somatic vs. Reproductive Cell Changes   A second moral distinction in the genetic engineering debate is also considered important. To date, attempts to add genes to people with genetic diseases have involved inserting new genetic material into somatic cells. This **somatic cell gene therapy** means that the effort, if successful, will affect only the individual treated, not that person's offspring. The reproductive cells of that person will still contain the genetic defect. That person's offspring will be similarly affected. In the case of some autosomal recessive conditions, in which a second gene is needed from the mate before the disease can occur, leaving the reproductive cells unchanged may not pose an immediate problem. However, for dominant conditions it could. The more aggressively interventionistic camp advocates eliminating the problematic gene permanently so that it is not passed from one generation to the next. This is sometimes called *germ-line* or *reproductive cell gene therapy* because an attempt is made to fix the egg or sperm cells, not just the somatic cells (Cole-Turner, 2008).

Such reproductive cell gene therapy is potentially riskier than somatic cell therapy. If inserting a new gene or replacing a defective one is done somatically and the effect is unexpectedly deleterious, the problem has been created for only one generation. In the case of reproductive cell therapy, by contrast, the problem would be perpetuated in future generations unless some additional gene therapy were invented to reverse the changes. Reproductive cell genetic changes have already been carried out in animal studies. For example, a strain of "shiverer" mice has been bred so the animals' nervous system lacks myelin, a basic protein. Shiverer mice are missing a gene responsible for production of this protein. Researchers have microinjected the necessary gene into zygotes of shiverer mice. In at least one case, the gene was success-fully incorporated into offspring that went on to transmit the gene to successive generations (Walters and Gage, 1997, pp. 60–61). Researchers, ethicists, and social commentators are now beginning to take seriously the possibility of attempting similar germ-line genetic changes in humans, but moral and legal limits constrain the intentional effort to modify human germ-line modification.[12]

New Reproductive Technologies

Closely related to the controversy over genetics is the newly emerging tension over new reproductive technologies. Here the conflict between those who fear tampering with nature and those who favor human rational control reaches new heights.

ARTIFICIAL INSEMINATION AND CONTRACEPTION   Contemporary controversies over human control of reproduction have their roots in some older techniques. For centuries it has been known that male infertility and male-transmitted genetic disease could be addressed by relying on sperm cells other than the husband's. This has been done through AID (artificial insemination by donor) or, in cases in which the husband's sperm is viable but other problems arise, AIH (artificial insemination by the husband). Undoubtedly, sperm has also been obtained by NID (natural insemination by donor) either with or without the husband's knowledge.

All of these have been rejected by some traditional ethics as being "unnatural." Their concern is partly over the involvement of a third party, meaning the conception is, in some sense, out of wedlock. However, some people object even to AIH. This is the view of the Catholic Church, which maintains that all sexual relations must be "natural," that is, consistent with the *natural moral law*. Sexual relations must be reserved for fulfilling the natural or proper ends of marriage, which involve both pro-creation and a unitive function. (The latter is sometimes referred to as "the bond that holds man and woman together" [Ashley and O'Rourke, 1997, p. 210]). According to this view, every sexual act must be open to both of these functions (and hence artifi-cial birth control is forbidden as "unnatural"). More recent interpretations recognize the acceptability of sexual acts in which procreation is not possible. Holders of this view accept as moral the rhythm method of controlling fertility, and some also accept oral contraceptives, holding these pose no artificial or morally unacceptable barriers to sexual relations. Nevertheless, those within this tradition still insist that any method must be within the context of a marriage relation in which at least some sexual relations take place when the reproductive function can be fulfilled. Moreover, intentional manipulations that place artificial barriers or involve artificial separation of the procreative and unitive functions are still unacceptable (Sacred Congregation for the Doctrine of the Faith, 1987). This means that not only artificial birth control but any reproductive acts, including artificial insemination, that do not involve natural coitus are unacceptable.

Of course, many outside this tradition do not share the view that the morality of reproduction is determined by assessing whether these so-called natural ends or pur-poses have been met. In varying degrees, they have grown to accept various techniques that have been labeled "artificial": barrier methods of contraception, sterilization, artificial insemination using a husband's or even a donor's sperm. The moral choices involved in deciding about artificial insemination were replicated in subsequent decades as previously undreamed-of manipulations of reproductive processes began to emerge.

IN VITRO FERTILIZATION   The change can be dated. On July 25, 1978, Louise Brown, the world's first so-called test-tube baby, was born.[13] Drs. Patrick Steptoe and Robert Edwards developed the technique of removing eggs from a woman's ovary and fertilizing them with semen in a Petri dish.[14] **In vitro fertilization**, as the procedure is called, was to be used exclusively for treating infertility in married couples.

In the early days of in vitro fertilization, one of the moral issues involved what amounts to controversy over doing research on human subjects without consent. It seemed that these babies who had been brought into existence in such a novel way were at risk of trauma. We could not be sure that they would not have terrible malformations. Critics argued that the procedure could not be said to be for the benefit of the babies that would not otherwise have been alive.

Now that millions of infants have been born using these techniques, this concern has lessened, but a more fundamental concern remains. Is there something about in vitro fertilization that pushes human manipulation of the beginnings of life too far? The generation of human life has traditionally been thought to be a mystery, something largely out of human hands. Some believe that that is the way it ought to be. They consider it hubris to put control of fertilization into human hands, literally bringing it out into the open and placing the process under glass.

In vitro fertilization not only divorces reproduction from sexual relations, but it also permits a substantial opportunity for human control. Now it is standard practice to fertilize several eggs, permitting physicians to select the most desirable ones for implantation. Pre-implantation genetic testing is on the horizon. Excess embryos are discarded, frozen for later use, consigned to research, donated to other infertile couples. They are emerging as a major source of stem cells. The metaphors of manufacture, (re)production, and fabrication are used by critics to suggest manipulation and tampering in a process that has an almost sacred quality to it. In the meantime, the group that supports such endeavors points to the values symbolized by the image of having dominion and subduing. They see human control of the generation of life itself to be the ultimate triumph in the rationalization of planning, selecting, and improving the chances of eliminating disease as well as infertility.

SURROGATE MOTHERHOOD   Once the technology of in vitro fertilization is developed, there is no technical reason why the people utilizing it must be limited to married couples. The same techniques could be used for unmarried partners and, with the help of sperm donors, lesbian couples. Even more controversial is the fact that there would be no technical reason for the fertilized egg to be implanted in the same woman from which it was taken. Surrogates can be used to gestate the embryo; they would agree to return the newborn to the woman who contributed the egg and her partner. This method could be used either for medical reasons—for a woman whose uterus would not support a pregnancy or for those who would be endangered by pregnancy—or for reasons of convenience—for women who preferred not to be pregnant.

A woman who lacked ovaries but wanted to become pregnant could receive a "donated" egg that would be fertilized by her partner and implanted in her. Thus, she could become pregnant and gestate a fetus that, while not genetically hers, is hers to gestate and raise. All these procedures have now become commonplace. In fact, it is now possible that there can be at least five "parents" involved in the creation and birth of a child: the man who is the source of the sperm, the woman who is the source of the egg, the one who gestates the fertilized egg, and the two who take responsibility for nurturing the postnatal child.

CASE 20

The Mary Beth Whitehead Case

William and Betsy Stern wanted to have a child, but Mrs. Stern had chosen not to bear one herself because of a medical condition which she believed would have been dangerously aggravated by a pregnancy. In February 1985, Mr. Stern signed a surrogacy agreement with Mary Beth Whitehead in which Ms. Whitehead agreed for a $10,000 fee to be artificially inseminated with Mr. Stern's sperm and to carry the offspring to term. She agreed that after delivering the baby she would turn the child over to the Sterns and that they would become the legal parents.

A baby girl was born on March 27, 1986. Ms. Whitehead called her Sara; the Sterns called her Melissa; and eventually the courts called her Baby M. After the birth, Ms. Whitehead refused to relinquish parental rights. In her book, *A Mother's Story,* Mary Beth Whitehead recalls one of many confrontations she had with the Sterns after the birth.

> I looked at Betsy Stern and thought to myself, "Betsy, I'm not selling this child. I started this when I actually believed it wasn't my child. Everyone convinced me that it was your child, but going through the pregnancy and the pain of labor, and then seeing the baby has made me realize that this is my baby, not yours."[15]

In the following months, Ms. Whitehead and her husband at the time, Rick, disputed the case with the Sterns. The infant was in the Sterns' possession only for a short while after her birth before Ms. Whitehead took her and fled from her home in New Jersey to Florida, where she led a life on the run for several weeks. Eventually, the police seized the child, and she was returned to the Sterns.

But the battle was far from over. Although the baby remained in the Sterns' care, a lengthy legal custody battle occurred. On March 31, 1987, the New Jersey Superior Court ruled Baby M would remain in the sole custody of her father, William Stern. Mary Beth Whitehead's parental rights were terminated.

Mr. Stern had filed suit claiming his rights had been violated. He claimed he was being denied equal protection under the Fourteenth Amendment of the Constitution. He argued that since men who provide sperm for artificial insemination legally surrender their parental rights, women should be treated similarly. The debate centered on whether women are bound by contractual commitments signed prior to conceiving as surrogate mothers to surrender parental rights.

The Supreme Court of the State of New Jersey, which eventually reviewed the lower court opinion, ultimately awarded custody to the Sterns, but denied the equal protection argument, thus apparently undermining binding surrogacy contracts. Mary Beth Whitehead's parental rights were restored, and she was later allowed (in a separate court decision) unsupervised, uninterrupted "liberal" visitation privileges. In future cases, the possibility remains that a surrogate mother who changed her mind about a commitment to surrender parental rights could nevertheless gain custody.[16]

As the complexity of these relations increases, the moral issues also increase. When only two people contribute to the process, their motivation is more clear. As soon as a third party becomes involved, even in AID, the question of compensation to motivate their assistance arises. Sperm donors have always been paid, raising the issue of why women who provide an egg cell or a womb for gestation should not also be compensated. Some argue that there are significant differences in the time, burden, and risk involved, but it is not clear whether that implies that payment would be more or less justified. Presently, markets to pay surrogates who provide a womb (or a womb plus an egg, as Mary Beth Whitehead did) are considered highly suspect and actually prohibited in some jurisdictions. Excluding compensation is believed to make the decision to participate, particularly by poor women, less coercive, but it also raises questions about fairness for women who accept a considerable burden for the benefit of others.

The central issue in the controversy over surrogacy contracts is whether women who agree to serve as surrogates are bound morally or legally to follow through on their commitment to hand over the child to the people who originally were to become the postnatal parents. Those committed to the right of competent persons to form binding contracts consider policies permitting surrogates to cancel their commitment unfair. They ask, in the terms of Chapter 5, Is there a duty of fidelity to promises? These defenders of surrogacy contracts hold that people should be screened to ensure that they are mentally competent and stable before they make such commitments, but that, once a commitment is made, they have a moral duty to keep it. To do otherwise is unfair to both the man and the woman who were promised that the child would be theirs to nurture and who made emotional, social, and psychological commitments based on that promise.

Critics are not satisfied with this defense. They point out that those who agree to become surrogates are often of lower socioeconomic and educational status. Payment for surrogacy is sometimes considered de facto irresistible for such persons. Moreover, pregnancy is not a mere business transaction, for bearing a child is an enormous, emotional undertaking. Bonds are created between the pregnant woman and the fetus she is carrying that may not be predictable. They claim that women need a period of time after pregnancy to reassess and determine whether they can continue to commit to relinquishing the child they have borne. One problem with this argument, however, is that it seems to suggest that women, in at least this one respect, are unique in that, even if they are adults deemed mentally competent, they cannot make autonomous, rational commitments that are free from nonrational, emotional factors beyond their control. Defenders of autonomy and the right and duty to contract insist that women as a group cannot be held hostage to those who cannot predict the emotional impact of their pregnancy. That argument, in turn, has reinforced opposition from those who doubt the legitimacy of extracorporeal manipulations of life's beginnings.

CLONING   The newest birth technology to capture the public fascination is **cloning** (Haugen, Musser, and Lovelace, 2009; Lauritzen, 2001; President's Council on Bioethics, 2002; United Nations, 2009). Cloning is the asexual reproduction of an organism by taking the nucleus along with its chromosomal material from a cell of an existing creature and implanting it into an enucleated egg cell or other cell of another creature. Although currently cloning is limited to research and possible generation of new tissues and organs (such as in the case of spinal cord injury), the modified cell, once charged by an electric shock, has the potential to grow and develop into a new being. The resulting creature, barring mutations, will be a genetically identical copy of the original one, a being who has pre-existed it by a significant amount of time. It is like an identical twin, but with the critical difference that the clone can observe its biological future insofar as it is genetically determined.

Of course, there is more to a creature, especially a human, than genes. A being is shaped by environment, time and place, and nurturing. Therefore, even a genetic clone will not be truly identical to its genetic parent. But this asexual reproduction is controversial in part because of the concerns we are tracing in this chapter: concerns about tampering with human nature and its rational control. Seeing even the genetic future is a radical change from the mysterious unknown of more traditional organic development.

Cloning also raises the specter of producing multiple copies of people who are particularly suited for certain roles—warrior, intellectual, sex object. In reality, the chance of such a Brave New World enterprise seems remote. Far more likely are the agricultural and live stock applications of cloning and, among humans, some unusual, if sympathetic needs. One imagined scenario is of a couple who, perhaps after a long period of attempting to bear a child, finally conceives and has a baby. Then, after one or the other is incapable of reproducing, the baby is critically injured in an accident. As the child is dying the couple realizes that their only opportunity to bear another child that is genetically their own would be to clone the dying baby. The technology involved is relatively simple, at least compared with research in space or nuclear physics. They might persuade some reproductive medicine specialist, perhaps motivated out of scientific curiosity and ego as well as sympathy for the couple, to attempt to clone another child. In fact, scientists are already stepping forward to make the attempt to clone a human and some men and women are apparently eager to cooperate. Efforts are under way in several countries to make such attempts illegal.

The real controversy clearly is not scientific or legal. It is ethical. Cloning involves decisions about what constitutes benefit and harm, whether parents should have the autonomy to choose to pursue creating a clone, whether the risks to the clone can be justified when there is no being, no patient, to benefit prior to the act of cloning, and whether resources are justly and fairly devoted to such reproductive technologies. Cloning is an ethical controversy that raises the questions of ethical principles that have dominated most of this book and most of the recent medical ethics debate. Cloning, as well as the other technologies in this chapter, has captured the public imagination because it forces us to decide whether some medical technologies go beyond what is morally tolerable human manipulation of the very processes of life.

Making moral choices about birth technologies and the other medical matters discussed in this book requires integrating considerations of these basic questions of willingness to intervene into the very nature of the human with the ethical principles considered in earlier chapters. We must combine a judgment about our basic willingness to intervene with our decisions about who has moral standing, which ethical principles apply, and how to resolve conflicts among ethical principles. Only then can we be confident that an ethically examined choice has been made. The next chapter looks at the problem of resolving conflict among ethical principles.

Key Concepts

Cloning   The asexual reproduction of an organism by taking the nucleus along with its chromosomal material from a cell of an existing creature and implanting it into an enucleated egg cell or other cell of another creature.

Gene Enhancement   Genetic engineering designed to improve on the normal genetic constitution of an individual.

Gene Therapy   Genetic engineering designed to correct a genetically caused medical problem.

Genetic Engineering   Genetic intervention that strives to overcome the effects of bad genes or to improve the genetic constitution of an individual by removing unacceptable genes or inserting more acceptable ones.

Genetic Screening   The testing of groups at risk of genetic disease for the purposes of identifying those who possess certain genes that make individuals susceptible to genetic disease or carrier status.

Germ-line or Reproductive Cell Gene Therapy   Gene therapy or enhancement targeted on the germ cells, that is, those cells that are involved in reproduction. The intention is that the effects will be transmitted to future generations.

In Vitro Fertilization   The medical procedure whereby an egg is fertilized by sperm outside the woman's body, normally followed by implantation into the uterus. "In vitro" is the Latin for "in glass." Hence, the popular expression "test tube baby." In fact, other pieces of laboratory equipment are usually used.

Somatic Cell Gene Therapy or Enhancement   Gene therapy or enhancement targeted on the somatic cells, that is, those that are not involved in reproduction. The intention is that the effects will not be transmitted to future generations.

Surrogate Motherhood   An arrangement whereby a woman bears a child for another woman with the intention that the other woman become the nurturing parent. This can involve implantation of the embryo following in vitro fertilization of the other woman's egg cell or artificial insemination of the surrogate mother.

The Human Genome Project   An international genetic research initiative that has as its goal the identification of the position of all of the 50,000–100,000 genes in the human body. The United States Congress formally committed to the support of this project in 1990, when it was expected to take fifteen years to complete.

Bibliography

Alpern, Kenneth D., ed. *The Ethics of Reproductive Technology.* New York: Oxford University Press, 1992.

Ashley, Benedict M., and Kevin D. O'Rourke. *Health Care Ethics: A Theological Analysis,* 4th ed. Washington, DC: Georgetown University Press, 1997.

Baily, Mary Ann, and Thomas H. Murray, eds. *Ethics and Newborn Genetic Screening: New Technologies, New Challenges.* Baltimore, MD: Johns Hopkins University Press, 2009.

Clarke, Angus. "Genetic Counseling." In *Principles of Health Care Ethics,* ed. Richard E. Ashcroft, Angus Dawson, Heather Draper, and John R. McMillan. Chichester, England: Wiley, 2007, pp. 427–434.

Coady, C. A. J. "Playing God." In *Human Enhancement,* ed. Julian Savulescu and Nick Bostrom. Oxford/New York: Oxford University Press, 2009, pp. 155–180.

Cohen, Cynthia B., ed. *New Ways of Making Babies: The Case of Egg Donation.* Bloomington, IN: Indiana University Press, 1996.

Cole-Turner, Ronald, ed. *Design and Destiny: Jewish and Christian Perspectives on Human Germline Modification.* Cambridge, MA: MIT Press, 2008, pp. 119–143.

Davis, Dena S. *Genetic Dilemmas: Reproductive Technologies, Parental Choices and Children's Futures.* New York: Routledge, 2001.

Devettere, Raymond J. "Medical Genetics." In his: *Practical Decision Making in Health Care Ethics: Cases and Concepts,* 3rd ed. Washington, DC: Georgetown University Press, 2010, pp. 420–457.

Evans, John Hyde. *Playing God?: Human Genetic Engineering and the Rationalization of Public Bioethical Debate.* Chicago, IL: University of Chicago Press, 2002.

Fletcher, Joseph. *The Ethics of Genetic Control: Ending Reproductive Roulette.* Garden City, NY: Anchor Books, 1974.

Goodfield, June. *Playing God: Genetic Engineering and the Manipulation of Life.* London: Sphere Books, 1977.

Gostin, Larry, ed. *Surrogate Motherhood: Politics and Privacy.* Bloomington, IN: Indiana University Press, 1990.

Green, Ronald M. *Babies by Design: The Ethics of Genetic Choice.* New Haven, CT: Yale University Press, 2007.

Haugen, David M., Susan Musser, and Kacy Lovelace, eds. *The Ethics of Cloning.* Detroit, MI: Greenhaven Press, 2009.

Hinxton Group: An International Consortium on Stem Cells, Ethics & Law. *Consensus Statement: Science, Ethics and Policy Challenges of Pluripotent Stem Cell-Derived Gametes.* Baltimore, MD: The Hinxton Group 2008.

Hull, Richard T., ed. *Ethical Issues in the New Reproductive Technologies.* Amherst, NY: Prometheus Books, 2007.

Human Genetics Commission (United Kingdom). *Making Babies: Reproductive Decisions and Genetic Technologies.* London: Human Genetics Commission, 2006.

Kass, Leon R. "Forbidding Science: Some Beginning Reflections." *Science and Engineering Ethics* 15, No. 3 (September 2009): 271–282.

Kass, Leon R., and James Q. Wilson. *The Ethics of Human Cloning.* Washington, DC: AEI Press, 1998.

Larue, Gerald A. *Playing God: Fifty Religions' Views on Your Right to Die.* Wakefield, RI: Moyer Bell, 1996.

Lauritzen, Paul. *Pursuing Parenthood: Ethical Issues in Assisted Reproduction.* Bloomington, IN: Indiana University Press, 1993.

Lauritzen, Paul, ed. *Cloning and the Future of Human Embryo Research.* New York: Oxford University Press, 2001.

Lombardo, Paul A. "Three Generations, No Imbeciles: New Light on *Buck v. Bell.*" *New York University Law Review* 60 (1985): 30–62.

McGee, Glenn, ed. *The Human Cloning Debate*, 2nd ed. Berkeley, CA: Berkeley Hills Books, 2000.

Mehlman, Maxwell J. *Wondergenes: Genetic Enhancement and the Future of Society.* Bloomington, IN: Indiana University Press, 2003.

Monsen, Rita Black, ed. *Genetics and Ethics in Health Care: New Questions in the Age of Genomic Health.* Silver Spring, MD: American Nurses Association, 2009.

Murray, Thomas H., Mark A. Rothstein, and Robert F. Murray, Jr. *The Human Genome Project and the Future of Health Care.* Bloomington, IN: Indiana University Press, 1996.

The National Academies (U.S.). *Understanding Stem Cells: An Overview of the Science and Issues from the National Academies.* Washington, DC: National Academies Press, October 2006.

National Institutes of Health [NIH] (United States). *Implementation of Executive Order on Removing Barriers to Responsible Scientific Research Involving Human Stem Cells.* [notice] Bethesda, MD: National Institutes of Health [NIH], 2009.

National Institutes of Health [NIH] (United States). *Stem Cell Information.* Bethesda, MD: National Institutes of Health [NIH], 2007.

New Jersey Commission on Legal and Ethical Problems in the Delivery of Health Care. *After Baby M: The Legal, Ethical and Social Dimensions of Surrogacy.* Trenton, NJ: New Jersey Commission on Legal and Ethical Problems in the Delivery of Health Care, 1992.

Parens, Erik, and Eric Juengst. "Inadvertently Crossing the Germ Line." *Science* 292, No. 5516 (April 20, 2001): 397.

Peters, Ted. *Playing God?: Genetic Determinism and Human Freedom.* New York and London: Routledge, 1997.

President's Council on Bioethics. *Human Cloning and Human Dignity.* New York: Public Affairs, 2002.

President's Council on Bioethics. *Reproduction & Responsibility: The Regulation of New Biotechnologies.* Washington, DC: The Council, 2004.

Ramsey, Paul. *Fabricated Man.* New Haven: Yale University Press, 1970.

Robertson, John A. *Children of Choice: Freedom and the New Reproductive Technologies.* Princeton, NJ: Princeton University Press, 1994.

Sacred Congregation for the Doctrine of the Faith. "Instruction on Respect for Human Life in Its Origin and on the Dignity of Procreation." *Origins* 16, No. 40 (March 19, 1987): 698–711.

Savulescu, Julian, and Nick Bostrom, eds. *Human Enhancement.* Oxford; New York: Oxford University Press, 2009.

Scully, Thomas J., and Celia Scully. *Playing God: The New World of Medical Choices.* New York: Simon & Schuster, 1987.

Shelley, Mary Wollstonecraft. *Frankenstein or the Modern Prometheus.* New York: Collier Books, 1961 [1817].

Sproul, R. C., ed. *Playing God: Dissecting Biomedical Ethics and Manipulating the Body.* Grand Rapids, MI: Baker Books, 1997.

Steptoe, Patrick C, and Robert G. Edwards. "Birth after the Reimplantation of a Human Embryo." *Lancet* 2, No. 8085 (1978): 366.

Stolberg, S. G. "The Biotech Death of Jesse Gelsinger." *New York Times Magazine,* November 28, 1999, pp. 136–140, 149–150.

Tong, Rosemarie. "Genetic Screening, Counseling, and Therapy." In her: *New Perspectives in Health Care Ethics: an Interdisciplinary and Crosscultural Approach.* Upper Saddle River, NJ: Pearson/Prentice Hall, 2007, pp. 177–215.

UNESCO, International Bioethics Committee. *Proceedings 1995.* Paris: UNESCO, 1995.

UNESCO, International Bioethics Committee. *Report of the IBC on Human Cloning and International Governance.* United Nations, 2009.

United Kingdom, Medical Research Council; United Kingdom. Biotechnology and Biological Sciences Research Council. *Stem Cell Dialogue.* United Kingdom: British Market Research Bureau, 2008.

van den Belt, Henk. "Playing God in Frankenstein's Footsteps: Synthetic Biology and the Meaning of Life." *Nanoethics* 3, No. 3 (December 2009): 257–268

Walter, James J. "Human Germline Therapy: Proper Human Responsibility or Playing God?" In *Design and Destiny: Jewish and Christian Perspectives on Human Germline Modification,* ed. Ronald Cole-Turner. Cambridge, MA: MIT Press, 2008, pp. 119–143.

Walters, LeRoy, and Julie Gage Palmer. *The Ethics of Human Gene Therapy.* New York: Oxford University Press, 1997.

Weiss, Rick, and Deborah Nelson. "Teen Dies Undergoing Experimental Gene Therapy." *The Washington Post,* September 21, 1999, pp. A1, A21.

Weiss, Rick, and Deborah Nelson. "FDA Lists Violations by Gene Therapy Director at U-Penn." *The Washington Post,* March 4, 2000, p. A4.

Whitehead, Mary Beth, and with Loretta Schwartz-Nobel. *A Mother's Story: The Truth About the Baby M Case.* New York: St. Martin's Press, 1989.

Zylinska, Joanna. "Playing God, Playing Adam: The Politics and Ethics of Enhancement." *Journal of Bioethical Inquiry* 7, No. 2 (June, 2010): 149–161.

Notes

1. This case was constructed from news accounts of the events. See http://pagingdrgupta. blogs.cnn.com/2010/10/11/first-human-injected-in-human-embryonic-stem-cell-trial/?iref= allsearch; http://www.nytimes.com/2010/10/12/health/research/12brfs-AFIRSTFORSTE_ BRF.html?_r=1&scp=1&sq=stem%20cells%20atlanta&st=cse (all accessed October 14, 2010).

2. The cost comes from the American Society of Reproductive Medicine. http://www. asrm.org/awards/index.aspx?id=3012, accessed November 3, 2010.

3. The brief story is well worth reading. See Shelley (1961).

4. According to the Bioethics Research Library database, no fewer than 69 books and articles exploring these themes have appropriated the metaphor in their titles. See, for example, Zylinska (2010), van den Belt (2009), Coady (2009), Walter (2008), Evans (2002), Sproul (1997), Larue (1996), Peters (1997), Goodfield (1977), and Scully and Scully (1987).

5. For a forceful early statement of this perspective, see Ramsey (1970); for a more recent example, see Kass (2009).

6. For a dramatic example of this pro-interventionist commitment, see Fletcher (1974).

7. For an analysis of how the court erroneously interpreted the facts of this case, see Lombardo (1985).

8. See http://www.nih.gov/about/researchresultsforthepublic/HumanGenomeProject.pdf. Also see http://www.genome.gov/11006943, accessed November 3, 2010.

9. See http://www.ornl.gov/sci/techresources/Human_Genome/medicine/genetherapy. shtml#status, accessed November 2, 2010.

10. See Weiss and Nelson (1999) and Stolberg (1999).

11. See Weiss and Nelson (2000).
12. For an early example of genetic intervention that unintentionally changed mitochondrial DNA, see Parens and Juengst (2001).
13. Louise Brown, now an adult, married Wesley Mullinder in 2004 and gave birth to her own child, a son, in 2006. In 2010, Robert G. Edwards, the physician who with colleague Patrick Steptoe developed the in vitro fertilization technique and performed the procedure on Louise Brown's mother, won the Nobel Prize in medicine for the feat. As of 2010 over 4 million babies had been born worldwide through in vitro fertilization.
14. See Steptoe and Edwards (1978).
15. See Whitehead and Schwartz-Nobel (1989).
16. This summary is based on In re Baby M. 109 N.J. 396, 537 A.2d 1277 (1988), Lauritzen (1993), and Whitehead (1989, p. 22).

10 Resolving Conflicts Among Principles

The chapters up to this point have introduced the concept of moral standing and a group of possible ethical principles. Some of these principles involve maximizing good consequences and minimizing bad ones—beneficence and nonmaleficence. Taken together they are sometimes simply referred to as the principle of utility. In bioethics, utility comes in two forms. The traditional medical ethic maximized utility for the individual patient. It paid no attention to the benefits and harms for other parties or to principles other than beneficence and nonmaleficence. In the modern period, bioethics has been influenced by classical social policy discussion to consider the consequences for all parties affected by a possible action. This would include the consequences not only for the patient, but also for everyone else who is affected, directly or indirectly: other patients, their families and friends, the relations of the physician and other health care providers, the insurance company paying the bill, and society at large.

Contemporary biomedical ethics also supplements the principles. In Chapter 5 we discovered that sometimes physicians and patients were expected to refuse to maximize good consequences. They were constrained in doing good by principles that require certain actions regardless of the consequences—principles of fidelity, autonomy, and veracity. Collectively they are sometimes referred to as the principles that require "respect for persons." Then in Chapter 6, we considered the possibility of an additional principle under the heading of respect for persons—the principle of avoiding killing. After considering how surrogates might make some medical decisions in Chapter 7, we turned to the social ethics of medicine to consider whether the principles of social utility and justice were relevant to allocation of scarce resources, health insurance, transplantation, and research on human subjects.

We have noted from time to time that some of these principles could conflict with one another. Telling the truth to the patient might cause harm; benefitting the patient might require breaching the promise of confidentiality. Allocating resources so as to maximize good consequences might produce an unjust distribution of the benefits. The health provider or patient who tried to live by all these principles all the time would find himself or herself paralyzed, unable to act because fulfilling the requirements of one principle would require breaking those of another.

The task of this chapter is to examine how different ethical theories attempt to resolve this potential conflict among ethical principles. In order to understand how such conflicts can be avoided, we need first to distinguish between different kinds of moral duty (**exceptionless duty**, *prima facie* **duty**, and **duty proper**). After that we will explore four strategies for resolving the conflict among principles. Then we will illustrate how these strategies work by considering ways to reconcile social utility and justice in allocating scarce medical resources. Finally, we will need to understand something about the way the principles are translated into more specific ethical rules and rights—the kinds of maxims that tend to show up in codes of ethics and hospital policies designed to provide moral guidance to providers of health care.

DIFFERENT CONCEPTS OF DUTY

Duty, according to Kant and deontologists generally, is independent of consequences. For example, the duty of promise keeping does not hold just in those cases where the consequences will be best if the promise is kept. It is also, in some sense, a duty even if the consequences are worse if we keep the promise. Here, however, we need to talk about several different kinds of duties in medical ethics.

Absolute, Exceptionless Duties

Sometimes we talk about *absolute, exceptionless duties.* In a mature, adult world, very few people believe there are very many exceptionless, absolutely binding, rules. Parents may have said, "It is your duty to keep a promise no matter what." That got across the point that keeping promises was important. Parents and teachers may have at first conveyed the idea that never under any circumstances should one break a promise. Immanuel Kant is often believed to hold something like that view. He believed that every single time one breaks a promise one has done something that is morally incorrect. Most don't quite hold to that view, however.

CASE 21

Conflicting Promises: A Physician in A Bind

Dr. Lewis Hammonds has a patient, Florence Yasmin, who is suffering from a serious malignancy. Ms. Yasmin, after months of pain and increasing incapacity, says to Dr. Hammonds, "Doctor, if this pain gets so unbearable I can't stand it anymore, promise me you'll put me out of my misery and kill me."

This is a weak moment for Dr. Hammonds, who responds, saying, "All right, I promise you I will end your life if you are that miserable. I will inject enough phenobarbital to mercifully kill you."

Normally, he would not have made such a promise, but in this instance for some reason he did. Two months later, the disease progresses to the point that Ms. Yasmin is in constant misery, and she says, "This is that moment, Doctor. I really need your help now. Will you mercifully put me out of my misery?"

It happens that Dr. Hammonds, like many people, also believes that it is morally wrong for a physician to kill, even for mercy. Moreover, he believes that, even if it were not wrong in principle, it would be wrong to violate the law that prohibits physician mercy killings. So now Dr. Hammonds has gotten himself into a bind. He has made a promise, which he believes is his duty to keep, but he also holds that it is his duty as a physician not to engage in mercy killing even when the patient is mentally competent and voluntarily requests such help. He has made two commitments, not to kill and to keep promises. As long as he believes these duties are exceptionless, he has no way out of his bind.

Prima Facie Duties

In a case like this one, ethical theorists contrast absolute or exceptionless duties with what are called *prima facie* duties. *Prima facie* duties are duties that are morally binding, other things being equal. So, generally, if one makes a promise, it is one's *prima facie* duty to keep the promise. At least the promise should be kept unless there is some other conflicting moral duty. But generally it is also a *prima facie* duty not to kill people. That is to say that if nothing else were at stake, no exceptional circumstances, it is one's duty not to kill, at least not to kill human beings.

One can analyze the promise made to kill this patient into two moral components. There is the component of the promise made and there is the component of the act of killing. Much as in physics a physicist might analyze a force into two or more vectors, so in ethics we can separate a moral action into two or more analytically distinguishable components. Looking at only one of those dimensions, say the act of promising, we would say it is one's *prima facie* duty to keep promises. That is, looking only at the dimension of promise keeping, the physician has a duty to do what he said he would do. If there were no other moral dimension involved, he should keep his promise.

On the other hand, looking at the situation only from the dimension of killing, we might conclude it is his duty not to kill. If there were no other moral dimension involved, he should not kill. We could then say there are two *prima facie* duties and that, in this case, they conflict with each other. Just as in physics two vectors of force may pull in opposite directions, so in ethics two *prima facie* duties may "pull" in opposite directions.

When someone feels in a moral bind the way Dr. Hammonds did, it may be because he or she feels two *prima facie* moral principles pulling him or her in different directions. Two moral elements clash, and each of them conveys a *prima facie* duty. In such cases, we need a method of resolving conflict among conflicting principles or duties.

Duty Proper

The distinction between *prima facie* duties and *duty proper* may help clarify such situations. W. D. Ross (1939) was a philosopher who proposed the strategy of balancing two conflicting *prima facie* duties. Ross said that, when there are two conflicting *prima facie* duties, one of them will be more weighty and become one's *duty proper*.

Somehow Dr. Hammonds needs to come to some answer, some course of action. That calls for a theory of resolution of conflict among principles, an area of great controversy and importance in contemporary medical ethics. Whichever course of action is determined to have priority is labeled the *duty proper*. Thus, Dr. Hammonds can be said to have two *prima facie* duties (to keep promises and avoid killing), but only one duty proper.

THEORIES OF CONFLICT RESOLUTION

Different ethical theories of conflict resolution lead to the conclusion that one or another principle wins out. Four general approaches are available.

Single-Principle Theories

One solution is to deny that there are two *prima facie* principles in conflict. The Hippocratic principle that the physician's only duty is to do what he or she thinks will benefit the patient is a good example. If Dr. Hammonds held such a view, he would feel bound neither to keep promises nor to avoid killing in all cases; he would only be bound to try to benefit the patient. If keeping his promise and euthanizing the patient would be most beneficial for her, then that would be his duty proper. If breaking the promise would be more beneficial to the patient, then that would be the duty proper. If there is only one principle, whatever it may be, then there can be no conflict, at least at this level.

Radical libertarians are another example of **single-principle theorists**. They escalate the principle of respect for autonomy to the level of the overarching principle. It is, for radical libertarians, the only morally governing principle. Hence, if autonomy were the only principle, Dr. Hammonds could do whatever respected Ms. Yasmin's autonomy. If she agreed to be killed for mercy, he could do so. On the other hand, his autonomy would have to be respected as well, so he could not be compelled to kill her, only permitted to do so if he agreed. The physician Robert Sade (1971) and the physician philosopher H. Tristram Engelhardt (especially in his early 1986 work) are often interpreted as giving autonomy this central position.[1] The philosopher Robert Nozick (1974) has been seen in this way as well. Anyone who does not like the result of permitting consenting adults to kill one another probably will be uncomfortable with elevating autonomy to the position of the single dominating principle in health care ethics. This view considers irrelevant the maximizing of good consequences or any of the other principles such as fidelity or veracity (the duties to keep promises and tell the truth).

Ranking (Lexically Ordering) Principles

The problem with the single-principle approach is that it seems to many people to be too simplistic. It would mean, in the case of Dr. Hammands, that there is nothing intrinsically wrong with either breaking a promise or killing. In the case of allocating scarce resources, it would mean nothing is morally wrong if some people, through no fault of their own, simply do not have the resources to get the basic health care needed to live a normal life. Many people believe there is more than one right-making characteristic of actions. For example, we may have a duty both to avoid killing people and to keep promises. In such cases we might be able to rank the principles in order of priority. If the choice is between the principle of fidelity with its derivative duty to keep promises on the one hand and the principle of avoiding killing on the other, perhaps we can rank one categorically above the other. Perhaps the notion of never killing takes precedence over the duty of fidelity to promises, for example. If so, then the conflict between the two *prima facie* duties is resolved; avoidance of killing is the duty proper.

This attempt to rank principles is sometimes called **lexical ordering**, referring to ordering as in a dictionary or lexicon, that is, all instances of one principle before any of the next just as in a dictionary all words starting with *a* come before any words starting with *b*. The term was introduced by the philosopher John Rawls (1971), who argued that among his two principles of justice, the first must be satisfied before the second.[2]

Lexically ranking principles would solve the problem of finding a duty proper without reducing all ethics to a single principle. The difficulty, however, is that most people find it about as implausible to rank any one principle in first priority in all possible cases as it is to identify a single, all-purpose principle. In our example, some people may believe that in all circumstances either fidelity or avoidance of killing should always take priority, but most would probably find that implausible.

Balancing

The approach that has particularly wide appeal at the present time is one that denies that a single principle can be found to resolve all conflict and also denies the possibility of an exceptionless ranking. Instead it relies on the metaphor of *balancing* competing *prima facie* principles (see, for example, Beauchamp and Childress, 2009).[3] Just as with vectors in physics, sometimes one *prima facie* principle may be perceived as the most "weighty," sometimes another. This permits either fidelity to promises or avoidance of killing to win out depending on the circumstances.

The problem with balancing approaches is that they seem to rely on the intuition of the decision maker, and just about any pre-existing intuition can be claimed to be more "weighty."[4] Opponents in a moral dispute may each discern that his or her principle is more weighty. Balancing may end up providing very little help in resolving moral disputes. It leaves an ethical controversy unresolved. Gert, Culver, and Clouser (2006, pp. 99–129) criticize intuitive balancing of principles on these grounds. In the real world of ethics, most of us feel that often there really is more of a clear answer to the ethical dispute than a balancing approach to resolving conflict among principles would suggest.

If we accepted an approach of balancing conflicting principles, we would face a second problem: We would always have to hold open the possibility that some sufficiently strong counterweight could be envisioned so that even our most firmly held moral convictions could be placed in doubt. Slavery is generally considered immoral because it violates the principle of autonomy. If, however, someone believed that autonomy had to be balanced against the principle of beneficence, one would have to hold out the possibility that in some (perhaps hypothetical) situation, so much good would come from slavery that "on balance" it might be justified in some case. If one is prepared to say that slavery is *always* wrong even if great extra benefit to society came from it, one probably cannot believe in a balancing method of resolving conflict among conflicting principles. If we had to balance conflicting principles, we would have to admit that in some case there might be enough good resulting from the majority enslaving the minority that, in that case, the slavery would "outweigh" the violation of autonomy.

Combining Ranking and Balancing

One other possible solution has been proposed to the problem of how to resolve conflict among principles in medical ethics. This attempts to combine both ranking and balancing strategies. Perhaps some principles can be grouped into clusters. Within the clusters, individual principles might be considered co-equal in importance so that they can only be balanced against one another. Even if that is the case, however, it is possible that one cluster might, when taken together, be more weighty, more significant, than another (Veatch, 1981, 1995).

Such an approach might, for example, treat the consequentialist principles— beneficence and nonmaleficence—as a cluster that cannot be ranked one over the other. According to this view, beneficence and nonmaleficence must be balanced against each other rather than, for example, giving nonmaleficence priority as the slogan *primum non nocere* (first, do no harm) suggests. Thus, the principles on the left half of Figure 18 in Chapter 8 would be balanced against each other.

Likewise, the principles that give rise to duties that are not based on consequence maximizing, those on the right half of Figure 18, could be treated as co-equal and balanced against one another. Thus, if there is a conflict between respecting a physician's autonomy to choose where to practice medicine and arranging physicians so that justice is served by giving everyone a fair opportunity to receive medical care, neither principle would automatically and in all cases win out. Autonomy and justice would be balanced against one another. But, in contrast to more straightforward balancing approaches, perhaps either the consequence-maximizing principles or the duty-based ones could be ranked above the other group. For example, the nonconsequentialist or duty-based cluster of principles—including fidelity, autonomy, and veracity as well as avoidance of killing and justice—in aggregate, might be ranked above the consequence-maximizing cluster. Thus, balancing within clusters is combined with lexical ordering between the two clusters. The mere amount of good consequences would not justify violating autonomy or justice.

Following this combined ranking-and-balancing approach seems to square with many of our considered moral judgments. For example, it is very widely held that it is not acceptable to treat a competent[5] patient without the patient's consent, at least if the treatment is offered for the patient's own good. In fact, in American law, no competent patient has ever been forced by a court of law to undergo medical treatment for his or her own good against his or her will. This holds even if the physician who wants to treat the patient can persuasively show that it is in the patient's overwhelming interest to be treated against his or her will. Expressed in terms of ranking-and-balancing, the principle of autonomy (one of the duty-based principles) always is ranked above Hippocratic utility (a consequence-maximizing principle).

On the other hand, the case of Dr. Hammonds appears more ambivalent because the primary conflict is between two of the duty-based principles—fidelity and avoiding killing. Neither is automatically given priority. It may be in this case that other, more subtle, moral considerations come into play. For example, in addition to promise keeping and avoiding killing, some people might see Dr. Hammonds as having a third duty: to benefit the patient. Even if Hippocratic patient benefit does not ever rise to the level of outweighing one of the duty-based principles, it might come into play as a "tie-breaker" between two of the duty-based considerations. This could lead some people—those more sympathetic to Dr. Hammonds' duty to keep his promise to kill for mercy—to conclude that the combined force of the promise made and the Hippocratic duty outweighs the moral obligation to avoid killing. On the other hand, those who think Dr. Hammonds should not kill, even when he has promised, might believe that, as a citizen, he has also promised to obey the laws of the land, including the law prohibiting mercy killing. They might view this as a case in which a *prima facie* duty to keep a promise to kill for mercy is outweighed by the combined force of the *prima facie* duty to avoid killing and the *prima facie* duty to keep the promise to obey the law. Thus, both liberals and conservatives on mercy killing could explain their positions in this case.

The discussion thus far assumes that all the principles we have discussed should be part of a general theory in bioethics. Some, however, might not include all the principles. They might, for example, accept the "ranking-and-balancing" approach to conflict resolution, but not accept the suggestion that avoiding killing should be among the duty-based principles. They would be left with a *prima facie* duty to keep the promise to kill combined with a Hippocratic (consequence-maximizing) principle that requires doing what will benefit the patient. Even though someone who ranked the duty-based principles above the consequence-maximizing ones would give Hippocratic utility only secondary importance, in this case, if one excluded the principle of avoiding killing, the promise to kill would be unimpeded by the principle of avoiding killing and would be re-enforced by Hippocratic utility (assuming that the physician perceived that the patient would be better off if spared the terminal suffering). This would lead to a strong, unimpeded sense that Dr. Hammond has a duty to kill Ms. Yasmin. Some more militant defenders of mercy killing and assisted suicide probably reason in this manner.

The ranking-and-balancing approach suggests that there is likely to be great controversy in society over merciful killing, especially if the patient is competent and has requested the killing and if the physician has made a previous promise to commit the mercy killing. Those who give Hippocratic utility priority as a single principle will agree with those who rank promise keeping as the highest consideration that Dr. Hammonds should kill. Those who subordinate Hippocratic utility to avoiding killing will reach the opposite conclusion, while those who include both a principle of fidelity and a principle of avoiding killing, giving them equal weight, will be ambivalent.

Many people now accept the suggestion that autonomy always takes precedence over Hippocratic utility and may well also accept the claim that either previous promises made to patients or Hippocratic utility could conflict with the duty to avoid killing, leaving a society divided over cases such as Dr. Hammonds'. They might be more skeptical, however, over the suggestion that the various principles grouped under the heading of respect for persons can take precedence over social utility as well. After all, we routinely constrain autonomy in the name of public health. As we have seen in Chapter 5, some non-Hippocratic codes actually require a health provider to breach the promise of confidentiality made to the patient in order to protect the interests of third parties from credible threats of serious bodily harm. We also accept compulsory immunizations and quarantine for public health reasons. We thus need to understand how one might justify compromising autonomy in the name of social goods. In the next section we will see how different theories of conflict resolution go about doing this.

Ways of Reconciling Social Utility and Justice

When conflicts among principles involve social ethical questions, both social utility and justice are at stake. We need to know how they are related to each other. In some cases, doing what maximizes social utility will turn out also to produce a just distribution. Thus, if an antibiotic is in scarce supply, providing doses to those who have the most serious infections may also produce the most medical good. The difficult case is the one in which the two principles conflict. Sometimes giving a scarce drug to the sickest may mean giving it to someone who has relatively small chance to benefit while giving it to patients in somewhat better shape may predictably do much more good.

TREATING SOCIAL UTILITY AND JUSTICE AS EQUALLY IMPORTANT   Those who favor balancing of competing principles as a method for resolving conflict accept the view that neither social utility nor justice nor any other principle can always be considered to prevail. If each principle tells us what is *prima facie* morally required, then, according to this view, when principles conflict they must be balanced off against one another. As we saw in Chapter 8, the current formula for allocating kidneys for transplant follows this approach.

THE RAWLSIAN MAXIMIN RECONCILIATION OF JUSTICE AND UTILITY   Treating social utility and justice as equally weighty is not the only method of resolving the conflict between competing social ethical principles. One of the most important developments in twentieth-century ethics is the work of the philosopher John Rawls (1971), who we saw was a proponent of a lexical ranking strategy. Rawls examines the theory of how justice in distribution should be related to maximizing social utility. His view operates at a very abstract level, but some of his followers have attempted to determine the implications for a health care delivery system (Green, 1976; Daniels, 1985, 2008; Veatch, 1991; DeGrazia, 1991; cf. Powers and Faden, 2006; Segall, 2010). One interpretation relies on one of Rawls's principles, sometimes called the *difference principle*. It specifies that when basic goods are distributed they should be distributed equally unless the inequalities result in an advantage to the worst off compared to a more purely equal distribution. Theorists debate whether the difference principle can be applied to health care, but if it were, it could support a practice of paying high salaries to physicians, but only if it were necessary as an incentive to get physicians to expend effort to help the worst off. It could also justify shifting some resources to healthier patients if that were the only way to benefit the worst off. The general idea of the difference principle is that equality is the rule unless treating people unequally increases the benefit to the worst off.

While the Rawlsian difference principle is sometimes treated as a "principle of justice," it can better be understood as a justification for abandoning purely egalitarian justice when certain kinds of social utility are served, that is, when advantage is gained by the worst off.

THE PARTIAL LEXICAL ORDERING OF DUTY-BASED PRINCIPLES OVER CONSE-QUENCE-MAXIMIZING PRINCIPLES   As we saw earlier in this chapter, another approach to resolving the competing claims of social utility and justice would rely to some extent on what is sometimes called the *lexical ordering* of principles. Instead of simply balancing social utility and justice, we might balance beneficence and nonmaleficence and then balance the requirements of the various duty-based principles, but give priority to the combined duty-based principles over the combined consequence-maximizing ones.

At first, this would seem to lead to a counterintuitive result in the case of public health efforts to require immunization or quarantine. Respecting the autonomy of those with infectious disease would seem to risk great harm to others. Only the most radical libertarians would always give people complete freedom to act autonomously—even if it meant refusing immunizations and quarantine so that many other innocent people were put at risk.

One explanation of why we would compromise autonomy here could be that the social good (utility) of limiting personal freedom in this case is so great that, when balanced against autonomy, it wins out. That is how those following a balancing strategy might explain the sacrifice of autonomy in this case.

But permitting social utility to be balanced against autonomy poses some problems. Since countless millions of people could theoretically benefit from constraining the freedom of one person, it may turn out to be all too easy to justify constraints of freedom. It could support not only compulsory immunization, but also compulsory participation in medical research—even very dangerous medical research. In this case, one person's freedom would be lost and potentially great harm could be done to that person, but, if millions could benefit, the aggregate benefit might, according to a balancing approach, not only outweigh the harm to the conscripted research subject, but also outweigh the violation of his or her autonomy.

Perhaps a more limited justification for constraining freedom in public health cases can be found without invoking social utility. Some constraints of autonomy might serve the purposes of justice; they might not merely produce social utility, but also produce benefits for the worst-off people. Those at risk of polio or anthrax might be said to be among the worst off. Justice to the worst off could be used to justify limited constraints on the autonomy of individuals.

Other duty-based principles might also come into play. In certain cases the one whose autonomy is constrained might have promised to act in a certain way. Promises are routinely understood to constrain autonomy. In some cases, constraining autonomy might be needed to avoid killing of others. Avoiding killing is also routinely understood to constrain autonomy. Thus, several other duty-based principles could provide a more limited justification for compromising autonomy—even if the consequence-maximizing principles are *always* subordinated to the combined force of the duty-based ones.

THE BALANCING APPROACH Some people will probably be unpersuaded by a lexical ranking of duty-based principles over consequence-maximizing ones. They might, instead, balance all the principles, including those focused on producing benefits and avoiding harms. The United Network for Organ Sharing (UNOS) kidney allocation formula reflects concern for both doing good for patients (even if they are not the worst off) and invoking the principle of justice to make sure the worst off get special attention. The UNOS Ethics Committee formally endorsed the idea that social utility and justice should be given equal weight.[6] That was a political compromise between the social utilitarians and the justice theorists on the committee. This, however, raises the question of how to incorporate concerns for both social utility and justice into a single policy.

For allocating kidneys the recommendation was that some points would be given for factors that predict beneficial outcome (such as a good tissue match and the young age of the patient) and other points should be given for those who are worst off (those with hard-to-match blood types, those with antibodies that make only a small number of organs acceptable, and those on the waiting list a long time). Then in the 1990s UNOS Ethics Committee proposed that the maximum number of points included as predictors of good outcome should equal the maximum number of points included to make the system more just. Thus social utility and justice were given equal maximum weight.

Other areas of health resource allocation do not lend themselves to point-based formulas. Nevertheless, strategies are being proposed to incorporate both considerations of good outcome and fair allocation.

Holding Percentage of Ideal Costs Constant for Each Patient. One approach would be to first determine for any given health care service (a hospital, clinical department, or DRG) the costs of ideal care (point N in Figure 19 of Chapter 8). Then one could take the ratio of available budget to ideal budget. (For example, if the cost for ideal care were a $100 million but only $80 million were available, the ratio would be 80 percent.) Then one could deliver to each patient that fraction of his or her ideal resources. That would treat each person equally in the sense of giving each person the same fraction of the services he or she needs, while at the same time recognizing that concentrating all resources on the sickest would be very inefficient. Thus, if 80 percent of ideal funding were available, everyone would receive 80 percent of the services he or she could use. Of course, since there is declining marginal utility with health care resources, supplying 80 percent of the ideal resources should normally provide much more than 80 percent of the possible benefit one could receive with ideal levels of services.

Holding Percentage of Maximum Benefits Constant for Each Patient. There are refinements of this approach that may be even more satisfying. It is known, for instance, that if everyone is treated with the same percentage of his or her ideal resources, not everyone will achieve the same degree of success. Getting 80 percent of a heart transplant, for example, would produce no benefit at all. Therefore instead of giving everyone the same percentage of their maximum usable resources, we could give everyone the same percentage of his or her maximum benefit. As before, when we realize that the benefits from health resources tend to decrease as more resources are expended, a system that had only a tolerable fraction of its maximally useful resources

($7100/$9000 or 79 percent in the case of the myocardial infarction example in Chapter 8) would be able to provide a very high percentage of its maximal possible benefit, perhaps as high as 98 or 99 percent. The moral logic here is that justice is achieved by treating all patients equally in the sense that each gets the same percentage of his or her maximal possible benefit while utility is served by permitting some resources to be used for well-off people, who can nevertheless be helped efficiently by modest treatments.

Giving Worse-Off Patients a Proportionally Greater Percentage of Their Possible Benefits. This approach might still be seen by defenders of egalitarian justice as giving too much of the resources to the already well off. They would ask why should someone who is already quite healthy get the same percentage of the available medical benefit as someone who was medically very poorly off. This could lead to a further adjustment. For example, an administrator might strive to balance utility and justice by giving the worst-off patients the highest percentage of their maximum benefit and giving the best-off patient the smallest percentage.[7]

These are all examples of strategies for integrating consideration of social utility and egalitarian justice.

TRANSLATING PRINCIPLES TO RULES

However one resolves the problem of conflicting principles, one more critical step will be required before one can determine what is morally required in a particular case: The principles—which are very abstract—must be related to the specific case. One final disagreement in bioethical theory arises in deciding just how to go about relating principles and cases. In our map of the "levels of moral discourse" in Chapter 1 the second level dealt with rules and rights. This level was positioned between the individual case and the level of normative ethics (including the part dealing with the principles of morally right action). In Figure 2 of that chapter, we illustrated the continuum of views about how seriously various rules or rights claims should be taken in mediating between abstract principles and individual case judgments.

We saw that at one extreme we might, theoretically, derive moral rules from principles and then treat these rules as exceptionless in controlling individual decisions (a position sometimes called *legalism*). That turns out to be quite implausible, however. Only if the exceptions are built into the rule might this work at all. For example, we have discussed the rule, "Always get consent before medical treatment," but we built into that rule certain qualifiers such as that the patient must be mentally competent and the treatment must be offered for the patient's own good. Even then, some people might be able to imagine exceptions to the rule, at least in some cultures.

At the other extreme is the position known as *antinomianism* in which no moral rules apply. Every case would be confronted *de novo* by the decision maker. But that seems unnecessarily restrictive. Even those who are skeptical about moral rules probably should be willing to treat rules as "rules-of-thumb" or "guidelines." These might summarize previous thinking about similar situations and give the decision maker at least some idea of how others have thought about such cases. This view, sometimes also called the *summary rule* position, is favored by medical ethicists such as Joseph Fletcher (1966). He referred to this view as *situationalism,* since it concentrated on the specific situation. This view is also sometimes called *particularism* (Hooker and Little, 2000). This view is also attractive to many physicians and other clinicians who are partial to making decisions by focusing on the individual case. Situationalism takes the abstract principles of right action from the normative level and carries them to the bedside, using rules or bills of rights or codes of ethics as guides, but never permitting the rule to dominate individualized moral judgment about what the principles require in the case.

In many ways the most interesting position along the continuum is located between this situational view and a rigid legalism. In Figure 2 of Chapter 1, this is referred to as the *rules of practice* position. It emerged as a backlash against treating rules as mere guidelines or rules-of-thumb, particularly in the work of the philosopher John Rawls (1955) and the moral theologian Paul Ramsey (1967).

Their view is that one cannot jump back and forth directly between abstract principles and individual cases. Rather there exist in a society certain "practices" that are rule-bound and that rules (or correlative rights claims) must mediate between the abstract principles and the individual case. The principles, for them, determine the rules, and the rules, in turn, determine what constitutes morally appropriate conduct in the individual case.

There are both pragmatic and more principled reasons why some people support the rules of practice position. The pragmatic reason is that humans are fallible. Particularly in medical settings where tensions may be great and decision making rapid, some people may fear error if the principles are brought directly to each case rather than having the benefit of the wisdom of past decisions in similar situations. "Always get consent before surgery" may turn out to give the morally right conduct more reliably than telling surgeons to use their own judgment in each case. This pragmatic argument may be particularly appealing when patient and health professional do not know each other well.

The more principled argument rests on the claim that the moral life is simply more appropriately thought of as a life in which people "play by the rules." A sports analogy is sometimes used. Someone might imagine that in the game of baseball, the game would be better if we allowed the batter four strikes. No one, however, would think it reasonable to put forward that proposal while a batter is up with two strikes on him in the ninth inning of a game. While in the middle of the game, one simply plays by the rules. At annual meetings, there might be a special time to consider changes in the rules based on abstract considerations about whether the game would be improved, but those proposals are not appropriate in the middle of the game.

So, likewise, in the game of life some people believe that morality is a matter of playing by the rules. There may analogously be certain special moments when the moral rules are assessed by the principles. The World Medical Association or the United Nations may have special times when they consider whether to amend the codes of ethics for patient/professional relations, but, at least according to those who subscribe to the **rules-of-practice** view, that normally should not happen when an individual case decision is being made.

A view about the relation between principles and individual cases has been put forward called *specification.* Henry Richardson (1990) suggests that we can move from very abstract principles, particularly when two or more principles are in conflict, by "specifying" the implications of the principles for a particular "domain" of action. For those who believe it is too difficult to work out a general theory of how principles are ranked or balanced for the entire range of human conduct, they may believe that they can at least specify that relation for a more limited domain. For example, even if one is reluctant to claim that autonomy always wins out over utility, one might still specify that it does win out in the area of the rights of competent patients to consent and refuse consent to medical treatment offered for their own good. Specification may involve several principles. The specification that physicians in their role as licensed health professionals should not kill even for mercy might be an example of a specification of the implication of the principles of avoiding killing, promise keeping, beneficence, and nonmaleficence in the domain of the practice of medicine. One might reach this conclusion, even if one cannot completely work out these relations in other domains such as military action, police power, self-defense, and so forth. Alternatively, at least in the Netherlands, authorities have specified that physicians under certain limited circumstances can kill for mercy, suggesting a different specification of these abstract moral principles.

Theorists continue to argue among themselves whether specification is simply a reformulation of either the rules-of-thumb or rules-of-practice position. Defenders of this claim ask why it would be that one would specify the one relationship among principles in one domain and another relation in another domain when the same principles and the same weighting of the principles were at stake. On the other hand, the approach of specification permits one to move forward working in one domain—such as health care—without having to resolve endless controversies in other domains.

CONCLUSION

A complete analysis of moral problems in bioethics will require not only identifying what the proper principles of right action are, but also determining how to resolve conflicts among them and how to move from this level of principle to the level of the individual case. Even among those who can agree on the meaning and implications of certain principles, they may fail to reach agreement on what to do at the bedside because they disagree about how to rank or balance the principles. They may also disagree because they hold different positions on how to move from the level of principle to the level of the case and back again. A full and stable theory will be one that is in equilibrium, where the considered judgments about individual cases, the rules and notions of how to apply the rules, and the principles are consistent from one branch of bioethics to another. The working out of this equilibrium may require looking at both case judgments and principles as well as the mediating rules and fine-tuning them until a stable harmony is achieved. That harmony will also have to include the other branches of normative ethics—the theory of the good and the theory of the virtues. The theory of the good was discussed briefly in Chapter 4. A discussion of the virtues, which at certain points in the history of medical ethics have dominated the field, is the subject of Chapter 11.

Key Concepts

Duty Proper   One's duty taking into account all relevant *prima facie* duties and the relevant rules for assigning priority to these *prima facie* duties.

Exceptionless Duties   Duties that are binding in all circumstances. Logic tells us that there cannot be two exceptionless duties that could possibly conflict with one another (cf. *Prima facie* duties; Duty proper).

Lexical Ordering   Ordering potentially conflicting ethical principles as in a dictionary or lexicon, that is, all instances of one principle before any of the next just as in a dictionary all words beginning with *a* come before any words beginning with *b*.

***Prima facie* Duties**   Duties that are morally binding, other things being equal. Such duties may be overridden by other duties that are considered higher priority or more weighty (cf. Exceptionless duties; Duty proper).

Rules-of-Practice   The view that rules define moral practices. Such rules mediate between abstract ethical principles and individual case-by-case judgments by providing firm positions. The rules-of-practice view is not normally amenable to the application of ethical principles directly to case judgments.

Single-Principle Theories   Theories that determine rightness or wrongness of actions or rules in all circumstances on the basis of a single principle. The Hippocratic ethic (Key Concepts, Chapter 2) and social utilitarianism (Key Concepts, Chapter 8) are both examples of single-principle theories.

Situationalism   The view that moral rules mediate between abstract ethical principles and individual case-by-case judgments by providing "rules-of-thumb" or guidelines rather than more rigid exceptionless rules or rules-of-practice.

Specification   The practice of applying ethical principles to a domain (such as health care) so that the proper relation among principles is articulated for a range of decisions without necessarily implying that the same relation would apply to decisions outside that domain.

Bibliography

Beauchamp, Tom L., and James F. Childress, eds. *Principles of Biomedical Ethics*, 6th ed. New York: Oxford University Press, 2009.

Brody, Baruch. *Life and Death Decision Making*. New York: Oxford University Press, 1988.

Burdick, James F., Jeremiah G. Turcotte, and Robert M. Veatch. "General Principles for Allocating Human Organs and Tissues." *Transplantation Proceedings* 24, No. 5 (October 1992): 2226–2235.

Daniels, Norman. *Just Health Care*. Cambridge University Press: Cambridge, England, 1985.

Daniels, Norman. *Just Health: Meeting Health Needs Fairly*. New York: Cambridge University Press, 2008.

DeGrazia, David. "Grounding a Right to Health Care in Self-Respect and Self-Esteem." *Public Affairs Quarterly* 5 (October 1991): 301–318.

DeGrazia, David. "Moving Forward in Bioethical Theory: Theories, Cases, and Specified Principlism." *Journal of Medicine and Philosophy* 17 (1992): 511–539.

Engelhardt, H. Tristram. *The Foundations of Bioethics.* New York: Oxford University Press, 1986.

OPTN/UNOS Ethics Committee. *Ethical Principles to be Considered in the Allocation of Human Organs,* June 22, 2010, available on the web at http://optn.transplant.hrsa.gov/resources/bioethics.asp?index=10, accessed June 18, 2011.

Fletcher, Joseph. *Situation Ethics: The New Morality.* Philadelphia, PA: Westminster Press, 1966.

Gert, Bernard, Charles M. Culver, and K. Danner Clouser. *Bioethics: A Systematic Approach.* New York: Oxford University Press, 2006.

Green, Ronald M. "Health Care and Justice in Contract theory Perspective." In *Ethics and Health Policy,* ed. Robert M. Veatch and Roy Branson. Cambridge: Ballinger, 1976, pp. 111–126.

Hooker, Brad, and Little, Margaret Olivia, eds. *Moral Particularism.* New York: Oxford University Press, 2000.

Powers, Madison, and Ruth Faden. *Social Justice: The Moral Foundations of Public Health and Health Policy.* New York: Oxford University Press, 2006.

Nozick, Robert. *Anarchy, State, and Utopia.* New York: Basic Books, 1974.

Ramsey, Paul. *Deeds and Rules in Christian Ethics.* New York: Charles Scribner's Sons, 1967.

Rawls, John. *A Theory of Justice.* Cambridge, MA: Harvard University Press, 1971.

Rawls, John. "Two Concepts of Rules." *The Philosophical Review* 44 (1955): 3–32.

Richardson, Henry S. "Specifying Norms as a Way to Resolve Concrete Ethical Problems." *Philosophy and Public Affairs* 19 (1990): 279–310.

Ross, W. D. *The Right and the Good.* Oxford: Oxford University Press, 1939.

Sade, Robert M. "Medical Care as a Right: A Refutation." *New England Journal of Medicine* 285 (1971): 1288–1292.

Segall, Schlomi. *Health, Luck, and Justice.* Princeton, NJ: Princeton University Press, 2010.

Shelp, Earl E., ed. *Justice and Health Care.* Dordrecht, Holland: Reidel, 1981.

Veatch, Robert M. *A Theory of Medical Ethics.* New York: Basic Books, 1981.

Veatch, Robert M. "Justice and the Right to Health Care: An Egalitarian Account." In *Rights to Health Care,* ed. Thomas J. Bole, III and William B. Bondeson. Dordrecht, Netherlands: Kluwer Academic Publishers, 1991, pp. 83–102.

Veatch, Robert M. "Egalitarian Justice and the Right to Health Care." In *Health Care Reform: A Human Rights Approach,* ed. Audrey R. Chapman. Washington, DC: Georgetown University Press, 1994, pp. 106–123.

Veatch, Robert M. "Resolving Conflict Among Principles: Ranking, Balancing, and Specifying." *Kennedy Institute of Ethics Journal* 5 (September 1995): 199–218.

Notes

1. Engelhardt's view is complex. He has put forward this view as his ethic for pluralistic societies where there is no agreement on some more specific religious or sectarian moral system. He also recognized a principle of beneficence, but it prevailed only in narrower communities or when individuals exercised their right to be charitable. In the second edition of *The Foundations of Bioethics* he calls the single, overarching principle for pluralistic, secular communities the *principle of permission*, but it functions in a way similar to what he had earlier called the principle of autonomy.

2. Rawls's second principle, in turn, is divided into two parts, and the second part of the second principle must be satisfied before the first part of it. Hence, some have said there is rally a rank- or lexical-ordering among three conditions.

3. Some, such as Baruch Brody (1988), object to the numerical quantification of the balancing image, claiming that ethics cannot be reduced to such quantification. Brody prefers, instead, the image of "conflicting appeals," but the result is similar—sometimes

one appeal will win out, sometimes another, depending on power or force of the appeal.

4. Efforts have been made to add more reason to the balancing by claiming that a process of *specification* of abstract principles so that for particular "domains" or sphere of action, one principle will take precedence without it having that principle ranked as prior for all types of actions (DeGrazia, 1992; Richardson, 1990). The problem with specification, however, is that, if a reason can be found for giving priority for one principle over another in one domain, it is hard to see why the same reason wouldn't give it lexical priority over the other in other domains as well. This would make balancing with specification look essentially like ranking approaches.

5. Note this applies only to competent patients who would have moral claims to have their autonomy respected. Incompetent persons cannot be said to be substantially autonomous, so there cannot be a conflict between autonomy and beneficence in their case.

6. The published version of the committee's position in the 1990s endorses the equal weight idea (Burdick, Turcotte, and Veatch, 1992). More recently, the UNOS Ethics Committee revisited the issue and endorsed once again the importance of both utility and justice as independent principles, but did not take a position on whether they were equally weighty ("Ethical Principles to be Considered, 2010").

7. See Veatch (1994), for a further exploration of this strategy.

11

The Virtues in Bioethics

In addition to the question of what things are intrinsically good and what principles identify right-making characteristics of actions, the third level of moral discourse (i.e., normative ethics) includes another question: What traits of human character are praiseworthy? This branch of normative ethics is usually referred to as *virtue theory*. Here the attention is placed not on the external features of behavior—whether it produces good consequences or involves telling a lie, for example—but rather on the internal disposition of the one carrying out the action.

Virtues are simply praiseworthy traits of human character. Although much of biomedical ethics in the past generation has focused on the principles of action rather than the character traits of the one doing the acting, traditional health professional ethics was concerned as much or more with the character of the health professional. Within the past thirty years a resurgence of interest has occurred in virtue ethics in health care (Campbell, 2005; de Raeve, 2006; Drane, 1988; Hauerwas, 1981, 2004; Lebacqz, 2004; Oakley, 2007, 2009; Pellegrino, 2006, 2007; Shelp, 1985; Veatch, 2006). Much of this interest can be traced back to the work of Alasdair MacIntyre (1981) and others, who rediscovered virtue theory in the early 1980s.

What is at stake is whether those discussing ethics in health care want to address the behavior itself or the disposition of the one carrying out the behavior. One view emphasizes the internal disposition of the one engaging in the behavior. Holders of this view believe that it is not so much the behavior that ethics is concerned about but rather the character of the actor. This was the concern of many moralists and clinicians historically. The alternative view, the view of most analysts in the last decades of the twentieth century, is that what we really should worry about is whether the behavior itself is morally right—regardless of the attitudinal disposition of the one carrying it out.

For example, one of the principles of right action is **beneficence**—the notion that an action is morally right insofar as it produces consequences that are as good or better than alternative actions. *Beneficence* means literally "doing good." By contrast, virtue theorists might advocate the virtue of **benevolence**—the idea that willing the good is a morally praiseworthy trait of character. *Benevolence* means literally "willing the good."

It is apparent that there can be a correspondence between principles and virtues. The virtue of benevolence corresponds to the principle of beneficence. One might expect that people with benevolent character are more likely to act in ways that produce good consequences, that is, those willing the good might be more likely to do the good. But it is critical that this correspondence is not necessarily perfect. One might will the good and end up bungling so that the consequences are actually not good. One might be a well-meaning do-gooder who ends up doing more harm than good. Such a person would be benevolent, but not beneficent. Or, alternatively, one might not be of benevolent character—not willing good outcomes—yet for various reasons, end up acting in a way that produces good consequences. This could happen if the one lacking in benevolence miscalculates or if he or she is selfishly promoting his or her own interests, yet is clever enough to know that the best strategy is to look good to others. Thus a rational, self-promoting physician who really cares not at all about a patient's welfare may, out of self-interest, do something good for a patient—especially if he knows others are watching or if he desires a good evaluation.

This raises important questions in ethics about the relation between virtues and principles of right action: whether promoting virtue in health professionals is a good way to increase the chance of right conduct and whether morally good character or right conduct is more important. One would think that encouraging a virtue would increase the odds of the corresponding behavior occurring—that encouraging benevolence increases the chance of beneficence—but that may not always be the case. It also raises questions about exactly which virtues are intrinsically praiseworthy.

Virtue Lists

While the list of principles of morally right action is fairly short and relatively consistent from one ethical theory to another—we considered only seven principles in the previous chapters of this book—lists of virtues reveal much more variation. Each ethical approach seems to have its own virtue list. This is true in professional ethics, in secular, philosophical ethics, and also in religious ethical systems. Moreover, while many people tend to think of the various virtues as noncontroversial—platitudes that are obviously worthy of praise even if they are hard to instill in people—some virtues in some ethical systems actually turn out to be rather controversial. Consider the various lists of professional, secular, and religious virtues in Figure 19.

PROFESSIONAL VIRTUES The Hippocratic Oath, reflecting its origins in a Greek mystery religion, affirms two virtues, both of which have unmistakable religious overtones: purity and holiness. The Hippocratic physician is to maintain purity and manifest a holy disposition. These virtues appear to be behind the injunction to avoid surgery. At least according to one interpretation, Hippocratic physicians should avoid contact with blood, since it would render one "impure." Thus, it is suggested that the Hippocratic physician should leave surgery to others (lay people) who do not have to maintain their ritually pure state.

Professional Virtues	Secular Virtues	Religious Virtues
Hippocratic: Purity Holiness	**General:** Benevolence Care	**Jewish:** Gemilut Hasadim (loving kindness) Tzedex (loyalty or obedience)
Percival: Tenderness Steadiness Condescension Authority	**Greek:** Wisdom Temperance Courage Justice	**Christian:** Faith Hope Love (Agape)
WMA (1948): Conscience Dignity	**Japanese:** Kindness Devotion	**Muslim:** Contentedness Gratitude
AMA (1957) Respect for dignity of man Devotion	**Homeric:** Skill Cunning Courage	Generosity Magnanimity
AMA (1980): Compassion Respect for human dignity	Self-reliance Loyalty Love of Friends Hatred of Enemies Courtesy Generosity Hospitality	**Hindu:** Care Attention Humility Constant reflection
Florence Nightingale Pledge: Purity Faithfulness		**Confucian:** Humaneness Compassion Filial Piety

FIGURE 19   Lists of Virtues

Of course, neither of these virtues is the first to come to mind in modern health care. When the nurses adopted a modified and updated version of the Hippocratic Oath that they called the Florence Nightingale Pledge (in honor of the world's most famous nurse), they kept the virtue of purity, but replaced "holiness" with "faithfulness"—still a virtue with religious overtones, but less explicitly religious than "holiness."

Other health professional codifications have chosen somewhat different virtues. Thomas Percival, in his 1803 *Medical Ethics* chose four virtues for his fellow physicians, some of which seem strange and controversial today: tenderness and steadiness along with condescension and authority. The latter two would particularly raise eyebrows today. When the AMA first adopted a code of ethics in 1847, it copied Percival's virtues word for word. When the World Medical Association adopted its code in 1948, it was essentially a rewrite of the Hippocratic Oath, but when it came to selecting virtues, its authors chose "conscience" and "dignity." The 1957 AMA code chose "respect for the dignity of man" and "devotion." When the AMA did its most recent substantial rewrite in 1980, it fixed the gender reference so that the first virtue was changed to "respect for human dignity" but devotion was also changed—to "compassion." What is striking with these lists is that they seem rather random and varied. While some, such as "condescension," are truly controversial, the others could be included in most people's lists, but often are omitted without much sense of loss.

SECULAR VIRTUES   The variation is even more pronounced when one turns to secular philosophical virtue theory outside of medicine. The four classical Greek virtues are justice, temperance, courage, and wisdom. These are the dispositions that Plato found praiseworthy. Homeric Greece included some of the most controversial virtues such as "cunning" and "hatred of enemies." At one point a virtue for women is considered to be "obedience to husbands." By contrast, one sixteenth-century Japanese code cited the virtues of kindness and devotion. Again the lists seem open-ended. After a few offensive concepts are dropped, the remainder often seem to be praiseworthy, but not necessarily essential to a list of virtues.

RELIGIOUS VIRTUES   By contrast, early Christianity, as exemplified in the Apostle Paul in I Corinthians, lists faith, hope, and love (*agape* or charity). Roman Catholics tend to affirm both the Greek and Christian virtues, thus having a full list of seven, while Protestants, being more prone to see tension between the Greeks and the Christians, often limit their list to the three Pauline virtues. In addition to the Biblical Christian virtues, other major religions also put forward virtue lists. The Islamic Medical Association of the U.S.A. and Canada lists in its "Oath of a Muslim Physician" the virtues of honesty, modesty, mercy, fortitude, wisdom, and understanding. The ancient Hindu Caraka Samhita lists care, attention, humility, and constant reflection. The famous Confucian virtues are humaneness, compassion, and filial piety. Filial piety is important in ancient Chinese medical ethics. It has been seen as implying that Chinese physicians are ideally like family members treating patients as brothers rather than the more distant "professional" relation that is the norm in Western culture. By contrast, there is no standard list of virtues in Judaism. It is a religion of the law with much more focus on norms of right conduct. Nevertheless, virtues such as *Gemilut Hasadim* (loving kindness) and *Tzedek* (loyalty or obedience) are often cited. Compassion, benevolence, self-respect, faithfulness, and humility are sometimes mentioned.

CARE AS A VIRTUE   The appearance of **care** on the Hindu list calls for further comment. Care is also emerging on other lists. Nurses, in particular, have recently placed emphasis on something they call *care* as have feminist bioethicists (Carse, 1991; Edwards, 2009; Gilligan, 1982; Grypdonck, 2009; Jecker and Reich, 2004; Noddings, 1984; Veatch, 1998). Figuring out exactly what *care* means is a difficult task. A common thread in all of this literature, however, is the need of health care professionals, especially physicians, to return to an ethic with a more caring attitude. Sometimes *care* is seen as overlapping with the virtues of concern, compassion, and patient-centeredness. This suggests that at least part of what care theorists have in mind is promotion of care as a virtue. They might then be suggesting both that medical ethics needs to shift away from an ethic of morally right action to return to a virtue ethic and that, among the virtues one might choose, *care* deserves special consideration as either a virtue or a cluster of virtues for health professionals.

One is left with a sense of relative disorganization in virtue theory. Various writers within these traditions might pick somewhat different lists. Sometimes it is not even clear whether a concept such as *care* refers to a particular virtue, a package of virtues, or some other element of ethics. Some items, however, are clearly controversial: the condescension of Percival (which was also copied by the AMA in its original code of 1847), hatred of enemies, and subservience. Others are not controversial, but nevertheless might be perceived as optional—as acceptable, but not essential.

PROBLEMS WITH THE VIRTUES

In addition to the difficulty in identifying exactly which virtues should be on one's list, virtue theory poses other problems. Two worth reflecting on are what can be called the **wrong virtue problem** and the **naked virtue problem**.

The Wrong Virtue Problem

The first problem, once one realizes how varied and sometimes controversial the virtue lists can be, is deciding whether one has chosen the right virtues for one's list. Especially if the return to virtues is considered important because it is believed that promoting virtue is a reliable way of increasing the probability of morally right conduct, it will be essential that when a list of virtues is developed one not select the wrong ones. Choosing the wrong virtues will encourage the wrong corresponding behavior. For example, if one has concluded that respect for persons involves a cluster of ethical principles that should take precedence over beneficence, then touting the virtue of benevolence risks promoting the wrong behavior. It would encourage acting to benefit the patient even if respecting their autonomy is morally more important. If one is not enthusiastic about teaching "cunning," then it will not do to include that disposition on one's virtue list. The *wrong virtue problem* is concerned with selecting the right traits of character for one's list, and, as we have seen, selecting the list may be harder than it may appear.

The Naked Virtue Problem

A second problem with virtue theory is determining why the virtues are important in the first place. Two possibilities are suggested. For some, virtuous disposition may simply be intrinsically valued—even if it had no effect on behavior. For those holding this position, virtue is its own end. It is not necessary to add that virtue might promote morally right conduct.

For others, however, virtue is not so much intrinsically valuable as it is instrumentally valued. It is often thought to be a reliable way—perhaps the most reliable way—to promote morally right conduct. Insofar as there is a correspondence between virtues and principles, one might expect that promoting the disposition to act in a certain way would be good way to increase the chance that the action would, in fact, occur. Promoting the virtue of benevolence—willing the good—according to this view is a good way to encourage beneficence—doing the good. From this second perspective, virtues are important instrumentally as a way of encouraging morally right behavior. Provided one has chosen the right virtue to promote, such promotion might increase the odds of morally right behavior.

But this raises an interesting empirical question: Is, in fact, promoting virtue—the naked disposition to incline one's will in a particular direction—the best way to encourage the corresponding behavior? One might think so, but this so-called *naked virtue problem* needs to be examined. There are other ways of encouraging morally right behavior—by the use of enforcement strategies, by creating role models, and by rewarding right behavior and discouraging behavior that is wrong. Whether simply touting a particular virtue works as a strategy is a question that would require empirical evidence to answer. While it might seem plausible that promoting a disposition toward a certain kind of conduct would be the best way to encourage it, that may not always be the case. In the worst case, leading people to think of themselves as being virtuous could generate the kind of moral self-confidence that leads people to act without more careful reflection, consultation, and controls. Some health professionals have been known to belittle consultation with committees on matters of ethics, feeling that they are morally devoted to their patients and therefore capable of doing what is right without the benefit of more institutionalized consultation in moral decision making. It is even possible in some cases that promoting virtue could lower the chance of the morally right conduct (when compared with carefully worked out standards for peer review, cautious reflection, and expectation of mechanisms for enforcing proper standards).

CONCLUSION

There has been a resurgence of interest in virtue theory in health care ethics. Some people are promoting it as an alternative to other approaches discussed in this volume: casuistry, which starts from the individual case; metaethics, which starts from the most abstract questions and deduces a systematic ethical theory by working down the levels of moral discourse; and various approaches to normative ethics that focus on the principles of right action rather than the traits of good character.

There was a moment when some people seemed to imply that the controversies between action theorists and virtue theorists posed an either/or choice—that one had to pick between an ethic of principles and one of virtues. It was as if one could not be interested in both the principles of right action and the traits of good character. Now there is generally more recognition that the two approaches are in no way incompatible. For some settings it may be more important to work out the morally correct action relying on principles in doing so. For other occasions, we may be more interested in good character than in right conduct. There is no reason, however, why the two ethical questions should conflict. In fact, given the possible correspondence between notions of right action and notions of good character, we might gain by working out both components of normative ethics simultaneously. That seems to have led to greater cooperation among the advocates of different theoretical approaches in biomedical ethics. So, just as we now recognize the need to work up and down the different levels of moral discourse, so, likewise, we will work on both virtues and principles of right action in producing a more complete understanding of biomedical ethics.

Key Concepts

Beneficence   The principle that holds that actions are morally right insofar as they produce as much or more benefit than alternative actions.

Benevolence   The virtue involving a persistent disposition to will the good.

Care   The virtue involving a persistent disposition to be concerned about others, related to but sometimes distinguished from the virtues of benevolence, love, compassion, faithfulness, humaneness, and tenderness. Care is also sometimes used as a synonym for a cluster of virtues or even for virtue theory itself. It is also sometimes considered an "orientation" to others, one that focuses on the relationship between persons.

Naked Virtue Problem   The problem in health care ethics of concentrating on promotion of virtue as a means to increasing the probability that persons will engage in morally right conduct without also instituting methods for explicating, facilitating, and monitoring the conduct through the use of codifications of moral rules, ethics consultation, and collegial monitoring of behavior.

Virtue   A persistent disposition or trait of good character in persons.

Wrong Virtue Problem   The problem that arises in virtue theory from promoting virtue without adequate attention to which virtue is being promoted.

Bibliography

Amundsen, Darrel W., and Gary B. Ferngren. "Virtue and Medicine from Early Christianity Through the Sixteenth Century." In *Virtue and Medicine*, ed. Earl E. Shelp. Dordrecht: Reidel, 1985, pp. 23–61.

Campbell, Alastair. "A Virtue-Ethics Approach." In *Case Analysis in Clinical Ethics*, ed. Richard Ashcroft, Anneke Lucassen, Michael Parker, Marian Verkerk, and Guy Widderhoven. New York: Cambridge University Press; 2005, pp. 45–56.

Carse, Alisa L. "The 'Voice of Care': Implications for Bioethical Education." *Journal of Medicine and Philosophy* 16, No. 1 (February 1991): 5–28.

de Raeve, Louise. "Virtue Ethics." In *Essentials of Teaching and Learning in Nursing Ethics: Perspectives and Methods*, ed. Anne J. Davis, Verena Tschudin, and Louise de Raeve. New York: Churchill Livingstone Elsevier, 2006, pp. 97–108.

Drane, James F. *Becoming a Good Doctor: The Place of Virtue and Character in Medical Ethics.* Kansas City, MO: Sheed & Ward, 1988.

Edwards, Steven D. "Three Versions of an Ethics of Care." *Nursing Philosophy* 10, No. 4 (October 2009): 231–240.

Ferngren, Gary B., and Darrel W. Amundsen. "Virtue and Health/Medicine in Pre-Christian Antiquity." In *Virtues and Medicine*, ed. Earl E. Shelp. Dordrecht: Reidel, 1985, pp. 3–22.

Gilligan, Carol. *In a Different Voice: Psychological Theory and Women's Development.* Cambridge, MA: Harvard University Press, 1982.

Grypdonck, Maria. "Ethics of Care, Asymmetry, Recognition and Pity in Nursing Care." *Nursing Ethics* 15, No. 2 (March 2009): 274–275.

Hauerwas, Stanley M. *Vision and Virtue.* Notre Dame, IN: University of Notre Dame Press, 1981.

Hauerwas, Stanley M. "Virtue and Character." In *Encyclopedia of Bioethics,* 3rd ed. Ed. Stephen G. Post. New York: Macmillan Reference USA: Thomson/Gale; 2004, pp. 2550–2556.

Jecker, Nancy S., and Warren Thomas Reich. "Care: III. Contemporary Ethics of Care." In *Encyclopedia of Bioethics*, 3rd ed. Ed. Stephen G. Post. New York: Macmillan Reference USA: Thomson/Gale; 2004, pp. 367–374.

Lebacqz, Karen, "Patients' Responsibilites: II. Virtues of Patients." In *Encyclopedia of Bioethics*, 3rd ed. Ed. Stephen G. Post. New York: Macmillan Reference USA: Thomson/Gale; 2004: 1992–1994.

MacIntyre, Alasdair. *After Virtue*. Notre Dame, IN: University of Notre Dame Press, 1981.

McCullough, Laurence B. "Virtue, Etiquette, and Anglo-American Medical Ethics in the Eighteenth and Nineteenth Centuries." In *Virtue and Medicine: Exploration in the Character of Medicine*, ed. Earl E. Shelp. Dordrecht: Reidel, 1985, pp. 81–92.

Noddings, Nel. *Caring: A Feminine Approach to Ethics and Moral Education*. Berkeley, CA: University of California Press, 1984.

Oakley, Justin. "Virtue Theory." In *Principles of Health Care Ethics*, 2nd ed. Ed. Richard E. Ashcroft, Angus Dawson, Heather Draper, and John R. McMillan. Chichester, West Sussex, UK; Hoboken, NJ: John Wiley and Sons, 2007, pp. 87–91.

Oakley, Justin. "A Virtue Ethics Approach." In *A Companion to Bioethics*, 2nd ed. Ed. Helga Kuhse and Peter Singer. Chichester, UK; Malden, MA: Wiley-Blackwell, 2009, pp 91–104.

Pellegrino, Edmund D. "Character Formation and the Making of Good Physicians." In *Lost Virtue: Professional Character Development in Medical Education*, ed. Kenny, Nuala and Wayne Shelton. Amsterdam; Oxford: Elsevier, 2006, pp. 1–15.

Pellegrino, Edmund D. "Professing Medicine, Virtue Based Ethics, and the Retrieval of Professionalism." In *Working Virtue: Virtue Ethics and Contemporary Moral Problems*, ed. Rebecca L. Walker and Philip J. Ivanhoe. Oxford: Clarendon, 2007, pp. 61–85.

Pellegrino, Edmund. D., and David C. Thomasma. *The Virtues in Medical Practice*. New York: Oxford University Press, 1993.

Shelp, Earl E., ed. *Virtues and Medicine*. Dordrecht, Holland: Reidel, 1985.

Veatch, Robert M. "The Place of Care in Ethical Theory." *The Journal of Medicine and Philosophy: The Chaos of Care and Care Theory* 23, No. 2 (1998): 210–224.

Veatch, Robert M. "Character Formation in Professional Education: a Word of Caution." In *Lost Virtue: Professional Character Development in Medical Education*, ed. Nuala Kenny and Wayne Shelton. Amsterdam; Oxford: Elsevier, 2006, pp. 29–45.

Walker, Rebecca L., and Philip J. Ivanhoe, eds. *Working Virtue: Virtue Ethics and Contemporary Moral Problems*. Oxford: Clarendon Press/New York: Oxford University Press, 2007

APPENDIX

HIPPOCRATIC OATH

I swear by Apollo Physician and Hygeia and Panacea and all the gods and goddesses, making them my witnesses, that I fulfill according to my ability and judgment this oath and this covenant:

To hold him who has taught me this art as equal to my parents and to live my life in partnership with him, and if he is in need of money to give him a share of mine, and to regard his offspring as equal to my brothers in male lineage and to teach them this art if they desire to learn it without fee and covenant; to give a share of precepts and oral instruction and all the other learning to my sons and to the sons of him who has instructed me and to pupils who have signed the covenant and have taken an oath according to the medical law, but to no one else.

I will apply dietetic measures for the benefit of the sick according to my ability and judgment; I will keep them from harm and injustice.

I will never give a deadly drug to anybody if asked for it, nor will I make a suggestion to this effect. Similarly I will not give to a woman an abortive remedy. In purity and holiness I will guard my life and my art.

I will not use the knife, not even on sufferers from stone, but will withdraw in favor of such men as are engaged in work.

Whatever houses I may visit, I will come for the benefit of the sick, remaining free of all intentional injustice, of all mischief and in particular of sexual relations with both female and male persons, be they free or slaves.

What I may see or hear in the course of the treatment or even outside of the treatment in regard to the life of men, which on no account one must spread abroad, I will keep to myself holding such things shameful to be spoken about.

If I fulfill this oath and do not violate it, may it be granted to me to enjoy life and art, being honored with fame among all men for all time to come; if I transgress it and swear falsely, may the opposite of all this be my lot.

PRINCIPLES OF MEDICAL ETHICS (2001) OF THE AMERICAN MEDICAL ASSOCIATION

Preamble

The medical profession has long subscribed to a body of ethical statements developed primarily for the benefit of the patient. As a member of this profession, a physician must recognize responsibility to patients first and foremost, as well as to society, to other health professionals, and to self. The following Principles adopted by the American Medical Association are not laws, but standards of conduct which define the essentials of honorable behavior for the physician.

Principles of Medical Ethics

I. A physician shall be dedicated to providing competent medical care, with compassion and respect for human dignity and rights.

II. A physician shall uphold the standards of professionalism, be honest in all professional interactions, and strive to report physicians deficient in character or competence, or engaging in fraud or deception, to appropriate entities.

III. A physician shall respect the law and also recognize a responsibility to seek changes in those requirements which are contrary to the best interests of the patient.

IV. A physician shall respect the rights of patients, colleagues, and other health professionals, and shall safeguard patient confidences and privacy within the constraints of the law.

V. A physician shall continue to study, apply, and advance scientific knowledge, maintain a commitment to medical education, make relevant information available to patients, colleagues, and the public, obtain consultation, and use the talents of other health professionals when indicated.

VI. A physician shall, in the provision of appropriate patient care, except in emergencies, be free to choose whom to serve, with whom to associate, and the environment in which to provide medical care.

VII. A physician shall recognize a responsibility to participate in activities contributing to the improvement of the community and the betterment of public health.

VIII. A physician shall, while caring for a patient, regard responsibility to the patient as paramount.

IX. A physician shall support access to medical care for all people.

Adopted by the AMA's House of Delegates June 17, 2001.

UNIVERSAL DECLARATION ON BIOETHICS AND HUMAN RIGHTS (2005)

The General Conference ... proclaims the principles that follow and adopts the present Declaration.

General provisions

Article 1 – Scope

1. This Declaration addresses ethical issues related to medicine, life sciences and associated technologies as applied to human beings, taking into account their social, legal and environmental dimensions.
2. This Declaration is addressed to States. As appropriate and relevant, it also provides guidance to decisions or practices of individuals, groups, communities, institutions and corporations, public and private.

Article 2 – Aims

The aims of this Declaration are:

(a) to provide a universal framework of principles and procedures to guide States in the formulation of their legislation, policies or other instruments in the field of bioethics;

(b) to guide the actions of individuals, groups, communities, institutions and corporations, public and private;

(c) to promote respect for human dignity and protect human rights, by ensuring respect for the life of human beings, and fundamental freedoms, consistent with international human rights law;

(d) to recognize the importance of freedom of scientific research and the benefits derived from scientific and technological developments, while stressing the need for such research and developments to occur within the framework of ethical principles set out in this Declaration and to respect human dignity, human rights and fundamental freedoms;

(e) to foster multidisciplinary and pluralistic dialogue about bioethical issues between all stakeholders and within society as a whole;

(f) to promote equitable access to medical, scientific and technological developments as well as the greatest possible flow and the rapid sharing of knowledge concerning those developments and the sharing of benefits, with particular attention to the needs of developing countries;

(g) to safeguard and promote the interests of the present and future generations;

(h) to underline the importance of biodiversity and its conservation as a common concern of humankind.

Principles

Within the scope of this Declaration, in decisions or practices taken or carried out by those to whom it is addressed, the following principles are to be respected.

Article 3 – Human dignity and human rights

1. Human dignity, human rights and fundamental freedoms are to be fully respected.

2. The interests and welfare of the individual should have priority over the sole interest of science or society.

Article 4 – Benefit and harm

In applying and advancing scientific knowledge, medical practice and associated technologies, direct and indirect benefits to patients, research participants and other affected individuals should be maximized and any possible harm to such individuals should be minimized.

Article 5 – Autonomy and individual responsibility

The autonomy of persons to make decisions, while taking responsibility for those decisions and respecting the autonomy of others, is to be respected. For persons who are not capable of exercising autonomy, special measures are to be taken to protect their rights and interests.

Article 6 – Consent

1. Any preventive, diagnostic and therapeutic medical intervention is only to be carried out with the prior, free and informed consent of the person concerned, based on adequate information. The consent should, where appropriate, be express and may be withdrawn by the person concerned at any time and for any reason without disadvantage or prejudice.

2. Scientific research should only be carried out with the prior, free, express and informed consent of the person concerned. The information should be adequate, provided in a comprehensible form and should include modalities for withdrawal of consent. Consent may be withdrawn by the person concerned at any time and for any reason without any disadvantage or prejudice. Exceptions to this principle should be made only in accordance with ethical and legal standards adopted by States, consistent with the principles and provisions set out in this Declaration, in particular in Article 27, and international human rights law.

3. In appropriate cases of research carried out on a group of persons or a community, additional agreement of the legal representatives of the group or community concerned may be sought. In no case should a collective community agreement or the consent of a community leader or other authority substitute for an individual's informed consent.

Article 7 – Persons without the capacity to consent

In accordance with domestic law, special protection is to be given to persons who do not have the capacity to consent:

(a) authorization for research and medical practice should be obtained in accordance with the best interest of the person concerned and in accordance with domestic law. However, the person concerned should be involved to the greatest extent possible in the decision-making process of consent, as well as that of withdrawing consent;

(b) research should only be carried out for his or her direct health benefit, subject to the authorization and the protective conditions prescribed by law, and if there is no research alternative of comparable effectiveness with research participants able to consent. Research which does not have potential direct health benefit should only be undertaken by way of exception, with the utmost restraint, exposing the person only to a minimal risk and minimal burden and, if the research is expected to contribute to the health benefit of other persons in the same category, subject to the conditions prescribed by law and compatible with the protection of the individual's human rights. Refusal of such persons to take part in research should be respected.

Article 8 – Respect for human vulnerability and personal integrity
In applying and advancing scientific knowledge, medical practice and associated technologies, human vulnerability should be taken into account. Individuals and groups of special vulnerability should be protected and the personal integrity of such individuals respected.

Article 9 – Privacy and confidentiality
The privacy of the persons concerned and the confidentiality of their personal information should be respected. To the greatest extent possible, such information should not be used or disclosed for purposes other than those for which it was collected or consented to, consistent with international law, in particular international human rights law.

Article 10 – Equality, justice and equity
The fundamental equality of all human beings in dignity and rights is to be respected so that they are treated justly and equitably.

Article 11 – Non-discrimination and non-stigmatization
No individual or group should be discriminated against or stigmatized on any grounds, in violation of human dignity, human rights and fundamental freedoms.

Article 12 – Respect for cultural diversity and pluralism
The importance of cultural diversity and pluralism should be given due regard. However, such considerations are not to be invoked to infringe upon human dignity, human rights and fundamental freedoms, nor upon the principles set out in this Declaration, nor to limit their scope.

Article 13 – Solidarity and cooperation
Solidarity among human beings and international cooperation towards that end are to be encouraged.

Article 14 – Social responsibility and health
1. The promotion of health and social development for their people is a central purpose of governments that all sectors of society share.

2. Taking into account that the enjoyment of the highest attainable standard of health is one of the fundamental rights of every human being without distinction of race, religion, political belief, economic or social condition, progress in science and technology should advance:

(a) access to quality health care and essential medicines, especially for the health of women and children, because health is essential to life itself and must be considered to be a social and human good;

(b) access to adequate nutrition and water;

(c) improvement of living conditions and the environment;

(d) elimination of the marginalization and the exclusion of persons on the basis of any grounds;

(e) reduction of poverty and illiteracy.

Article 15 – Sharing of benefits

1. Benefits resulting from any scientific research and its applications should be shared with society as a whole and within the international community, in particular with developing countries. In giving effect to this principle, benefits may take any of the following forms:

(a) special and sustainable assistance to, and acknowledgement of, the persons and groups that have taken part in the research;

(b) access to quality health care;

(c) provision of new diagnostic and therapeutic modalities or products stemming from research;

(d) support for health services;

(e) access to scientific and technological knowledge;

(f) capacity-building facilities for research purposes;

(g) other forms of benefit consistent with the principles set out in this Declaration.

2. Benefits should not constitute improper inducements to participate in research.

Article 16 – Protecting future generations

The impact of life sciences on future generations, including on their genetic constitution, should be given due regard.

Article 17 – Protection of the environment, the biosphere and biodiversity

Due regard is to be given to the interconnection between human beings and other forms of life, to the importance of appropriate access and utilization of biological and genetic resources, to respect for traditional knowledge and to the role of human beings in the protection of the environment, the biosphere and biodiversity.

Application of the principles

Article 18 – Decision-making and addressing bioethical issues

1. Professionalism, honesty, integrity and transparency in decision-making should be promoted, in particular declarations of all conflicts of interest

and appropriate sharing of knowledge. Every endeavour should be made to use the best available scientific knowledge and methodology in addressing and periodically reviewing bioethical issues.

2. Persons and professionals concerned and society as a whole should be engaged in dialogue on a regular basis.

3. Opportunities for informed pluralistic public debate, seeking the expression of all relevant opinions, should be promoted.

Article 19 – Ethics committees

Independent, multidisciplinary and pluralist ethics committees should be established, promoted and supported at the appropriate level in order to:

(a) assess the relevant ethical, legal, scientific and social issues related to research projects involving human beings;

(b) provide advice on ethical problems in clinical settings;

(c) assess scientific and technological developments, formulate recommendations and contribute to the preparation of guidelines on issues within the scope of this Declaration;

(d) foster debate, education and public awareness of, and engagement in, bioethics.

Article 20 – Risk assessment and management

Appropriate assessment and adequate management of risk related to medicine, life sciences and associated technologies should be promoted.

Article 21 – Transnational practices

1. States, public and private institutions, and professionals associated with transnational activities should endeavour to ensure that any activity within the scope of this Declaration, undertaken, funded or otherwise pursued in whole or in part in different States, is consistent with the principles set out in this Declaration.

2. When research is undertaken or otherwise pursued in one or more States (the host State(s)) and funded by a source in another State, such research should be the object of an appropriate level of ethical review in the host State(s) and the State in which the funder is located. This review should be based on ethical and legal standards that are consistent with the principles set out in this Declaration.

3. Transnational health research should be responsive to the needs of host countries, and the importance of research contributing to the alleviation of urgent global health problems should be recognized.

4. When negotiating a research agreement, terms for collaboration and agreement on the benefits of research should be established with equal participation by those party to the negotiation.

5. States should take appropriate measures, both at the national and international levels, to combat bioterrorism and illicit traffic in organs, tissues, samples, genetic resources and genetic-related materials.

Promotion of the Declaration

Article 22 – Role of States

1. States should take all appropriate measures, whether of a legislative, administrative or other character, to give effect to the principles set out in this Declaration in accordance with international human rights law. Such measures should be supported by action in the spheres of education, training and public information.
2. States should encourage the establishment of independent, multidisciplinary and pluralist ethics committees, as set out in Article 19.

Article 23 – Bioethi cs education, training and information

1. In order to promote the principles set out in this Declaration and to achieve a better understanding of the ethical implications of scientific and technological developments, in particular for young people, States should endeavour to foster bioethics education and training at all levels as well as to encourage information and knowledge dissemination programmes about bioethics.
2. States should encourage the participation of international and regional intergovernmental organizations and international, regional and national nongovernmental organizations in this endeavour.

Article 24 – International cooperation

1. States should foster international dissemination of scientific information and encourage the free flow and sharing of scientific and technological knowledge.
2. Within the framework of international cooperation, States should promote cultural and scientific cooperation and enter into bilateral and multilateral agreements enabling developing countries to build up their capacity to participate in generating and sharing scientific knowledge, the related know-how and the benefits thereof.
3. States should respect and promote solidarity between and among States, as well as individuals, families, groups and communities, with special regard for those rendered vulnerable by disease or disability or other personal, societal or environmental conditions and those with the most limited resources.

Article 25 – Follow-up action by UNESCO

1. UNESCO shall promote and disseminate the principles set out in this Declaration. In doing so, UNESCO should seek the help and assistance of the Intergovernmental Bioethics Committee (IGBC) and the International Bioethics Committee (IBC).
2. UNESCO shall reaffirm its commitment to dealing with bioethics and to promoting collaboration between IGBC and IBC.

Final provisions

Article 26 – Interrelation and complementarity of the principles

This Declaration is to be understood as a whole and the principles are to be understood as complementary and interrelated. Each principle is to be considered in the context of the other principles, as appropriate and relevant in the circumstances.

Article 27 – Limitations on the application of the principles

If the application of the principles of this Declaration is to be limited, it should be by law, including laws in the interests of public safety, for the investigation, detection and prosecution of criminal offences, for the protection of public health or for the protection of the rights and freedoms of others. Any such law needs to be consistent with international human rights law.

Article 28 – Denial of acts contrary to human rights, fundamental freedoms and human dignity

Nothing in this Declaration may be interpreted as implying for any State, group or person any claim to engage in any activity or to perform any act contrary to human rights, fundamental freedoms and human dignity.

INDEX